4/97

NEB

Murder in the Tropics

THE FLORIDA CHRONICLES

VOLUME 2

Murder in the Tropics

THE FLORIDA CHRONICLES
VOLUME 2

Pineapple Press, Inc.
Sarasota, Florida

Dedicated to Margery and Leo

Inquiries should be addressed to:
Pineapple Press, Inc.
P.O. Box 3899
Sarasota, Florida 34230

LIBRARY OF CONGRESS
CATALOGING IN PUBLICATION DATA

McIver, Stuart B.
        Murder in the Tropics / by Stuart B. McIver.
                p.   cm. — (The Florida chronicles ; v. 2)
        Includes bibliographical references and index.
        ISBN 1-56164-079-4 (hb : alk. paper)
            1. Murder—Florida—Case studies.   I. Title.   II. Series.
HV6533.F6M33   1995
364.1'523'09759—dc20
                                                    95-30649
                                                    CIP

First Edition
10 9 8 7 6 5 4 3 2 1

CONTENTS

ACKNOWLEDGMENTS

As always, there are many people to be thanked for their role in helping any author write a book. I am particularly grateful to Elizabeth Alexander, Dennis Bailey, Sallie Bingham, Heidi Boehringer, Sam Boldrick, Jo Bowman, Loren "Totch" Brown, Dorian Cirrone, Ruby Collier, Carol Cope, Judge Gerald Cope, George Crolius, Chief Lonnie Curl, Wesley Davis, Count Alfred de Marigny, Rodney Dillon, Susan Clark Duncan, Hampton Dunn, Dianne Ell, Brenda Elliott, Niki Fotopoulos, Paul George, Michael Gora, Sue Gillis, Nancy Greenberg, Tom Hambright, Leland Hawes, Christian Henz, the Highlands County Historical Society, Dan Hobby, Dawn Hugh, David Jellison, Daniel Keyes, Eliot Kleinberg, Howard Kleinberg, Joe Knetsch, Judge James R. Knott, Joan Lankford, Lynn Laurenti, Helen Landers, Mary Linehan, Chauncey Mabe, Lynn McClelland, Charles Nugent, the Osceola County Historical Society, Lynda Patten, Wingate Payne, Carla Pittman, Robert Pollard, Dr. William Rea, Melvin Richard, Gloria Rothstein, Lucille Shulklapper, Marguerite Stewart Skipper, Becky Smith, Dr. William Straight, Joyce Sweeney, Charlton Tebeau, Audrey Vickers, Noreen Wald, Carol Wanamaker, William Webster, Edward Werder, Patsy West, Larry Wiggins, Lindsey Williams, Gordon Winslow and Nick Wynne.

INTRODUCTION

'Neath Swaying Palms

The rustling palms weave a spell of their own, calming, soothing, seductive. Trade winds blow gently, tempering the heat of the tropical sun and ruffling the blue waters that seem to lie everywhere: ocean, gulf, bays, sounds, rivers, canals and lakes. Florida, it would seem, has found the perfect formula to set at ease a troubled or even an untroubled mind.

But the formula's evil twin creates a restlessness, born of envy and jealousy, fueled by the temptations of conspicuous wealth, the lure of illicit love, the chance for a big score. It brings on an irritability compounded by overcrowding, honking horns, blaring boomboxes, shrieking burglar alarms, media overkill and, sometimes, the sound of gunfire. Too much money, not enough money.

Welcome to the land of the lotus eaters, a paradise not quite in the tropics but nonetheless captured by the hedonism of tropical lands.

Out of the mix of conflicts has come a pattern of crime that has given Florida's murders a flavor of their own, a weirdness that is boldly challenging California. In selecting the stories for this book, I have tracked a widely varied cast of characters that includes killers, victims and lawmen. I have met Seminoles, daredevil aviators, a surfer, bikers, sideshow freaks, Ku Klux Klansmen, vigilantes, ghosts, rumrunners, modern pirates, devout Shakers, serial killers male and female, bookies, hit men, a great American president and a not-so-great English king.

The world of the bizarre is not concentrated in Miami, as some might think. It reaches down through the Keys, on up the Atlantic coast, across to the Ten Thousand Islands, up the Gulf coast to Tampa Bay and around the Panhandle from Tallahassee to the Spanish colonial city of Pensacola. It surfaces in north Florida's Old South locales and extends on down along the ridge to a place where hit men from Boston committed a murder that shook the pillars of a God-fearing citrus and cattle town.

Let's take a quick look at a few of Florida's bizarre killings. In the Sunshine State even alligators swim into the act. Palm Beach, the winter capital of old money, was once just one more barrier island, completely deserted except for one lone settler. When the first Palm Beacher was murdered in 1873 west of Fort Pierce, his killers disposed of his body with a true Florida touch. They stuffed his body down a gator hole.

Near Ocala's horse country, a gator named Old Joe gave the FBI a clue in tracking the murderous Ma Barker gang to the shores of Lake Weir in January 1935. In the resulting gun battle the FBI eliminated Ma and her son Fred. Old Joe is a popular name among alligators. The Wakulla Springs Old Joe was himself a victim of murder. He was a big gator, over eleven feet long and weighing 650 pounds, much beloved by locals in the Wakulla Springs area, just south of Tallahassee. On August 1, 1966, he was killed by a bullet from a .32-caliber rifle. The National Audubon Society and the Edward Ball Foundation offered a five thousand dollar reward for Joe's killer. The case is still unsolved. Old Joe, however, is not forgotten, respectfully preserved in the lobby at the late Ed Ball's Wakulla Lodge.

Florida's Ku Klux Klan has observed Christmas in its own distinctive way. On Christmas Eve, 1921, the Key West Ku Klux Klan lynched Manola Cabeza by hanging him from a palm tree. Then on Christmas night, 1951, the hooded ones blew up the Brevard County home of Harry Moore, secretary of the Florida Chapter of the National Association for the Advancement of Colored People, killing Moore and his wife. Peace on earth, good will toward men.

No Florida murder, however, was more bizarre than the 1992 murder of the Lobster Boy, a sideshow freak, in the carnival town of Gibsonton. He was killed by a hit man hired by the Human Blockhead.

It is not, however, the strangeness of Florida's crimes but rather their frequency that has alarmed Floridians. Actually, some statistics show that crime has declined since the Golden Age of the Roaring Twenties, when Prohibition and a runaway real estate boom ruled a land of bootleg whiskey and fast deals.

Today's fears have been heightened to some extent by politicians who exploit the frenzy with simplistic calls for longer prison terms and heavier duty for Old Sparky, the not-really affectionate name given to the state's electric chair. The unrest has been intensified by TV stations which hype the convenient yellow-tape visuals of crime scenes, body bags on stretchers, hysterical family members and crashed getaway cars. Police cars flashing blue light beat a talking head anytime.

Ron Cochran, Broward County's sheriff, said it best: "A good short-term answer to Florida's crime problem is, 'Don't turn on your local TV news.'"

Ironically, prison terms today often run longer than those in the past. For example, the killers of the first Palm Beacher received eight-year terms for a particularly vicious crime.

The strangest jail term in the annals of Florida justice came in 1867, during the Reconstruction turmoil following the Civil War. At Micanopy, one

James Denton shot and killed Alec Johnson, a black who Denton said was insolent. When civil authorities refused to arrest the killer, United States troops, who were occupying Florida, apprehended him. A mob, however, promptly set Denton free. Next, the military commander seized prominent Micanopy citizens and held them hostage for a short while. A year after the murder, Denton was finally hauled into the Circuit Court of Eastern Florida, Judge B. A. Putnam presiding. Denton was convicted of manslaughter and ordered to pay court costs of $225. Judge Putnam also sentenced him to jail. The length of his term: one minute, sixty seconds.

The speed of trials was much swifter in earlier times. You could be tried, sentenced and executed in the time it takes to pick an O. J. Simpson jury. On February 15, 1933, less than three weeks before Franklin Delano Roosevelt was scheduled to take the oath as president of the United States, Guiseppe Zangara, an unemployed bricklayer, fired five shots at the president-elect. The shots missed FDR, but four other people were wounded. One, Anton Cermak, mayor of Chicago, died. Thirty-three days after the shooting, Zangara was electrocuted.

Whatever happens today probably has a parallel in the past. In July 1993, twenty-year-old Bobby Kent was beaten by a baseball bat and stabbed to death by a gang of his former so-called friends in Weston, in western Broward County. He was a bully, they said, and they were afraid of him. Seven young people were convicted of the murder.

In 1910, Edgar Watson, of Chatham Bend in the Ten Thousand Islands, so terrified his neighbors on nearby Chokoloskee Island that they united to shoot Mr. Watson to death. He, too, was a bully and they, too, were afraid of him. No one was even indicted.

In March 1985, in the wealthy Broward County enclave of Sea Ranch Lakes, Roswell Gilbert fired two shots into the head of his wife, Emily, who was disoriented by Alzheimer's disease and wracked with pain from a bone disease. Arrogant and unrepentant in court, he was convicted and sentenced to twenty-five years in prison.

In 1911, a mercy killing occurred in St. Cloud, in Osceola County. A young woman dying of tuberculosis was befriended by the town's Shaker religious community and lovingly cared for for several years. Eventually, her pain became unendurable and two prominent Shakers acceded to her request and ended her suffering with a powerful dose of chloroform. The state attorney wanted an indictment. The grand jury flatly refused to indict. The town perceived the mercy killers as people who acted out of kindness.

Could it be that today's viewer of television and violent movies and reader of mysteries and true crime considers murder just another source of public entertainment? In February 1994, T. M. Shine, a writer for the Fort Lauderdale Sun-Sentinel, constructed a Valentine's Day "South Florida Gangster Guide," in celebration of Chicago's Valentine Day Massacre. The story provided a self-guided, drive-by tour past the south Florida houses of such mob luminaries as Al Capone, Meyer Lansky and Johnny Rosselli. The guide did not encourage a drive-by shooting.

The little town of Oklawaha, short on Seminole and Civil War battle sites, holds an annual reenactment of the Ma Barker/FBI shootout. The Oklawaha Shootout (Ma Barker Meets Defeat) is the cornerstone of an annual January festival, which also includes arts, crafts and good Florida barbecue.

Murder is a mean, ugly part of life, but this seems to increase rather than lessen people's interest in the ultimate breakdown in human relations. Ours is a violent society and people still tune their sets to crime news and police dramas. And, fortunately for authors, they still read mysteries and stories of the crime that surrounds them.

MURDER IN PARADISE

The Gold Coast and Tampa Bay: To many, these are magic words that mean paradise by the sea. That's why more people live in these two areas than anywhere else in Florida. More people means more motives for mayhem.

CHAPTER 1

"Tigertail, Him on Long Sleep"

---

*Who killed the chief, star of popular
Miami tourist attraction?*

Miami's moon shone down on the little Indian village nestled beneath stately royal palms on the south bank of the Miami River. Some twenty Miccosukees from the families of Jack Tigertail, Charlie Billie and John Osceola slept in chickees at Coppinger's Tropical Gardens, a popular attraction that exhibited the Indian "way of life" to the tourists who by 1922 were beginning to flock to Miami each winter.

Assistant manager Phil James, a swimming instructor from Kansas City, slept in a small building on the property. A sharp sound broke through his sleep. Could it have been gunfire? Half-awake, he heard someone at the door, calling his name. James dressed quickly. Just outside, in the darkness, stood Charlie Billie.

"Tigertail, him on long sleep."

James had trouble figuring out what Billie was trying to tell him. Finally, he learned that Jack Tigertail, the head man at the village, lay on the dock at the attraction's alligator farm. He asked Billie to show him.

"No, you go," said the Indian and gave the manager a shove.

James found Tigertail on the dock. He had been shot. The manager knelt down to check for any signs of life. There were none.

James left immediately for the jail in nearby Miami. At 1:10 A.M. on March 8, 1922, he notified M.H. Rolfe, who served the county both as jailer and as a deputy sheriff. Rolfe, a friend of Tigertail's, sent deputies to the scene to launch the search for the killer of Miami's most popular Indian, the man the white community called "chief."

The quest would lead into the folkways of Florida's unconquered Indians, into the strange world of the illegal plume bird trade, into the nighttime forays of Prohibition's dangerous rumrunners. Fanned up by the city's biggest

1

newspaper, the case would become a cause celebre. And in the end, the search would leave the murder unsolved.

* * *

At the time of his death, Jack Tigertail was fifty years, three months and seven days old. He had been born in the Big Cypress Swamp, where the Indians hid out after the Third Seminole War ended in 1858.

Drainage of the Everglades in the early 1900s devastated the Indians' world. Canals destroyed traditional canoe trails to familiar camps and hunting grounds. Income from the sale of otter and wildcat pelts, gator hides and egret plumes at trading posts at Miami and Fort Lauderdale plunged.

In 1914, Henry Coppinger, born in Cork, Ireland, opened Coppinger's Tropical Gardens, Alligator Farm and Seminole Indian Village on the south bank of the Miami River at 19th Avenue.

The Irishman offered tourists lush tropical foliage, a menagerie of gators, crocodiles and monkeys, tropical fruit drinks and a village where several Indian families went about their lives as well as they could with intruders from the Anglo world walking into their homes. A curio shop sold "authentic" Indian souvenirs — many of them from Mexico. In time, the Indians at the camp produced more and more arts and crafts for sale. To the Indians, a tour of duty at Tropical Gardens meant a decent living at a time when traditional sources of income were literally drying up.

In 1918, Jack Tigertail, who had been living in an Everglades camp twenty-five miles west of Homestead, moved his family into Tropical Gardens for the winter tourist season. A large, handsome Indian, he communicated easily with his own people and as the tribe's business agent with the white world that surrounded them.

The star of a tourist attraction, he was, in fact, a celebrity Indian, so popular that in 1921 he was picked as the symbol of Hialeah, a new city developed on the Miami River Canal by aviation pioneer Glenn Curtiss and rancher James Bright. A photograph of the chief, arm extended, was transformed into an outsized figure pointing the way to Hialeah, a Seminole/Creek work meaning "pretty prairie." Developers also used his picture in real estate ads.

Tigertail once accompanied the Miami Advertising Club to an advertising convention in Atlanta to help publicize Miami. A close friend of his, L. S. Clopton, who had been given the Indian name of *It-ta-tor-ne-ke* by the Seminoles with whom he had dealt for two decades, rendered to Tigertail a glowing tribute: "Jack was true blue to his friends from the soles of his large naked feet to the top of his enormous bushy head. He was a man and a gentleman."

* * *

Rolfe and his deputies had only a short wait before the case's first big break. Tigertail's cousin, Charlie Billie, a man of few words earlier in the day, came to jail, ready to talk.

"White Man Charlie come to landing in skiff. He had whiskey and we all drank. White man tried to buy plumes. Chief Tigertail, he say, 'White man too cheap.' White man grab gun. Charlie Billie leave and go behind bush and wait. White man open gun two times. 'Bang!' Chief him fall. White man sculled boat away. I go to Jack Tigertail. He say, 'Me going on long sleep. White man in boat just here, he shoot me.'"

An examination of Tigertail's fatal wound revealed that he had been shot in the back by a rifle. The bullet entered just above the left hip, traveled upward and emerged from his upper left chest.

Rolfe immediately went up the river from the scene of the crime. Upstream a short way on the opposite side of the river, he found the skiff Billie had described. Lying in the bottom of the boat were a whiskey bottle and a .30-caliber steel-nosed Winchester cartridge.

The skiff was tied up next to a cabin cruiser. Rolfe went aboard and found a man packing his clothes into a tomato crate. The man was White Man Charlie — Charlie Veber.

Veber was taken immediately to jail. Charlie Billie identified him emphatically, "Me sure, sure."

The accused, thirty-five, was a former game warden noted for his marksmanship. He was also a gator hunter, a trapper, a plume hunter, a trader with the Indians — and a player in Prohibition's major growth industry, rumrunning. Within forty-eight hours of the murder, a coroner's jury had indicted Charlie Veber. He engaged the law firm of G.A. Worley & Sons to defend him.

* * *

The Roaring Twenties roared loudly in Miami. Winter tourists flocking to the Magic City drank in its sunshine — and its moonshine. Regular runs by Miami smugglers to the Bahamas and Havana kept the natives and visitors well-lubricated despite the U.S. Coast Guard.

Just up the river from the automobiles and the beat of the Jazz Age, all was quiet at the Indian village at Tropical Gardens. For many hours not a word was spoken, not even by the children. Fires were started in the village, using green wood to create clouds of smoke to keep the troubled spirit of the murdered man from returning to the camp.

Tigertail's widow moved to another chickee. There she removed her beads and let her hair, usually worn up, drop down around her shoulders. Wearing a black and blue dress, she would remain in total silence for four days and not remarry, or pin her hair back up, for at least three years.

Burying the chief presented a problem. By custom, he could not be buried at the place of his death, Tropical Gardens. The tribe denied James Bright permission to bury him with a monument in Hialeah, the town for which he stood as symbol.

The Indians, however, accepted the request of an admiring white community that Tigertail become the first Indian ever buried in the Miami City Cemetery.

Arrayed in his finest garments, Jack Tigertail was laid to rest in an Indian ceremony, almost totally surrounded by Miami's whites. Only one Indian, Charlie Billie, was present and he carefully avoided looking at Tigertail as he was buried with his rifle, cooking utensils, an old flashlight, pieces of leather, knives, beads and other items.

Billie, reporting back to the village after the burial, said simply: "Him all right."

As the city awaited the trial, *The Miami Herald* launched a drive to raise money for Tigertail's widow and six children. Pictures of the chief, his widow and a daughter were prominently featured to support the drive. Hialeah founder Glenn Curtiss gave one hundred dollars, while four members of the Coppinger family pitched in twenty-five dollars. Jailer Rolfe gave two dollars.

The strangest contribution came from the Coconut Grove Audubon Society, strange because Billie had testified that Tigertail was killed over a dispute about bird plumes. The Audubon Society had been formed to stamp out the illegal trade in plumes, used then to decorate women's hats.

The fund was managed by Henry Coppinger Jr.; Judge Frank Stoneman, father of author Marjory Stoneman Douglas; and Charlie Billie.

Meanwhile, Billie, one of the few Indians at the camp who could speak, read and write English, had taken over leadership of the village. His genes were impressive. His father was Billy Fewell. Legend had it that Fewell, sometimes known as Key West Billy, had paddled his canoe from the mainland to Key West.

After a death, the Indians traditionally moved away from the death scene's evil spirits to a new camp. But Billie assured the senior Coppinger that the families would continue living at Tropical Gardens. Said the new chief: "My people here satisfied. We no go back to Glades because Chief Tigertail go on long sleep. White man him punish man who take Seminole's life. Seminole say it is well. Him all right."

A giant Jack Tigertail in replica points the way to boomtime Hialeah. (Historical Association of Southern Florida)

One day before the trial was to open, a bizarre alligator hunt gave the state a break. A number of small alligators, due to be shipped north, had escaped from a sack at Tropical Gardens. Young Jack Coppinger crawled under a hibiscus bush looking for baby gators, then called out, "There's a gun in here."

Jack handed the badly rusted rifle out to Phil James. He discovered an empty shell in the barrel. Could it have been the missing murder weapon?

* * *

The morning of March 23, little more than two weeks after the murder, the trial of Charles Veber began at the Miami courthouse, Judge H. Pierre Branning presiding. The courtroom was packed as the state presented evidence about the chief's fatal wound and testimony from Henry Coppinger Jr. placing Veber at the Gardens early in the evening.

On the second day, the court skidded into a maze of convoluted testimony. Although Charlie Billie could speak English, the state chose to use an interpreter for him. The reason? His inconsistent accounts of the murder convinced the prosecutor that he did not always understand the questions. William King was picked to interpret for Billie.

The problem was that testimony was needed from another Indian, young Cory Osceola. The court was told he spoke a dialect different from Billie's, although both knew Miccosukee. Cory needed the translation services of Jimmie Gopher. The law thought kindly of Gopher since a tip from him led to the arrest of John Ashley, head of South Florida's most notorious gang, for the murder of Desoto Tiger in 1911.

To interrogate Cory, attorneys spoke in English to King, who translated the question into a dialect that Gopher could understand. Gopher then translated the question into language that young Cory could follow. Cory answered in his dialect to Gopher, who then started the message back through the pipeline.

At times, questions and answers brought on long exchanges, only to have the end product emerge as a simple "Yes," often followed by laughter in the courtroom.

Osceola's testimony, mercifully brief, revealed that he had sold a .30-.30 caliber Winchester to Veber a week before the murder. Cory had bought the rifle two years earlier from Bert Lasher, who ran a smaller version of Tropical Gardens on the New River in Fort Lauderdale. Lasher, like Veber, dealt in illegal plumes. He would later be convicted of plume law violations on a tip from Ivy Stranahan, wife of Frank Stranahan, who operated a trading post on the river.

Cory, however, looked at the gun, then told the court that the rifle found in the hibiscus bushes was not the one he had sold to Veber.

Billie, the key witness, presented other problems. In court he spoke only in a whisper. The judge had jurors circle their chairs around him to listen, a meaningless move since he was whispering in a language foreign to them.

He told the court that Veber arrived at the dock at eleven o'clock at night with a bottle of whiskey, which they shared. He then asked Tigertail for feathers. The defendant, Billie said, offered eight dollars for the white plumes, then lowered his bid to five dollars. Tigertail replied, "They were good feathers, worth eleven dollars."

Billie said: "I told Jack Tigertail I would give sixteen dollars for the feathers. Veber told me to shut up. I shut up and went to the camp."

Lying down, back at the camp, he heard a shot. When he went back to the dock, he saw Veber leaving in a skiff, he said.

After Billie's testimony, defense attorney Worley asked the judge to instruct the jury to return a verdict of not guilty. He contended Veber was charged with killing a man named Tigertail, which was not the victim's real name. Worley, ever quick to pounce on a technicality, said it was actually "an unpronounceable Indian name."

The court said no. Tigertail's "unpronounceable name" was in fact Hotelkaemarta. Charlie Billie's Indian name was Howalkaleehojo, or Wild Cat's Foot.

Billie's testimony continued well into the next day, followed by questioning of Phil James, Henry Coppinger Jr. and his mother, Mrs. Marie Coppinger. She told of being awakened by a shot, followed by the sound of someone crashing through shrubbery and knocking flowerpots to the ground. Then to the east she saw two bright lights, like those of an automobile, flash on the royal poinciana trees at the Gardens before disappearing into the darkness.

Veber took the stand on Monday, March 27. He admitted visiting the alligator farm in the afternoon of March 8 but denied he had returned later to buy egret plumes from Tigertail. He also insisted he had paddled the skiff back to the larger boat, where he had been sleeping, he said, at the time the murder occurred. He said he had loaned the smaller skiff to three men, one of whom was named Alderman. (Could he have been Veber's fellow rumrunner Horace Alderman, who was hanged in Fort Lauderdale five years later for the murder of three lawmen?)

The defendant admitted buying the rifle from Cory Osceola, but said he had given it to a friend who in turn had loaned it to a man who was going to Bimini, a major port in the booze trade. Both men involved backed up Veber's claim.

In final arguments to the jury, the younger Worley led off for the defense. He charged that the state had not proved whether the chief was shot from land or water or with what gun. He contended that Billie was drunk the night of the murder. He challenged the veracity of the interpreters, then flung a new thought at the jury:

"The finger that pulled the trigger and killed Jack Tigertail was not that of a white man but of an Indian."

The senior partner of Worley & Son began his defense in late morning and rambled on insultingly about the history, religion and superstitions of the Indians. "The state is relying altogether on public sentiment and not on the facts in the evidence," said Worley.

The following morning, prosecutor John Gramling gave a strong summation of the state's basic case, contending simply that the murder grew out of a quarrel over egret plumes, then turned ugly as the men continued to pass the bottle around.

In late morning, the jury began its deliberations. At 8:15 P.M., some eight hours and forty-five minutes after they started weighing the evidence, the jury gave its verdict:

"We, the jury, find the defendant guilty, as charged, and recommend him to the mercy of the court."

Charlie Veber listened calmly to the verdict, which promised him life in prison.

Fortunately for him, his attorneys were listening even more closely. The next day they filed an appeal for a new trial, based on the wording of the verdict. Worley & Son contended the jury had found Veber "guilty as charged," not "guilty of murder." It was only a technicality, but it was enough to give Veber a second trial.

At Tropical Gardens, the Indians left it to the white man's law to settle the murder of Tigertail. What could they do, confronted with such a complicated, mysterious way of arriving at justice?

Some of them knew Veber hadn't killed Tigertail. But they saw no reason to intrude in someone else's process. Better to mind their own business. White man's law had not exactly been kind to them. Besides, Veber was hardly an admirable man, living out his life on the wrong side of the law.

So White Man Charlie sat in jail for another eight months while the Miccosukee circle of life moved on. Corn and vegetables were planted, fish were caught, game was killed and camps were moved to better locations in the Everglades. A new head man claimed the leadership from Charlie Billie. He was Charley Tigertail, Jack's brother, an enterprising Indian who ran a successful trading post in the western Everglades.

At the end of the tourist season, Tigertail's widow moved to a new camp near a sugar plantation on the Miami River Canal. The fund for the family had reached $1,654.54.

On November 20, the second trial began. Veber had spent eight months in jail but, in one sense, time had been kind to him. Miami had quieted down since that feverish "rush to judgment" in March.

Once again, the state's case rested almost totally on the testimony of Charlie Billie. This time the defense worked hard to discredit him. They built a strong case that Billie was drunk the night of the murder.

Worley Senior raised other doubts, hinting at friction between Tigertail and the Indians living at Musa Isle, a rival Indian village.

"Don't you know one of the Indians in Musa Isle camp was found in a tree with a gun ready to kill Jack Tigertail?" he asked Charlie Billie.

"There was no such thing happened," replied Billie.

The lawyer asked Cory Osceola why he sold the rifle to Veber.

Said Cory: "Because it was bad luck to keep it. . . . It would cause its owner to go crazy."

Bad luck had certainly pursued the young Miccosukee. Since the first trial, Cory had lost his right arm in a railway accident. Later, however, he would become one of his tribe's most outstanding leaders.

On Saturday, November 25, Veber took the stand for a full day of testimony. He openly admitted that he had cruised out to Gun Key the night before the murder to pick up a cargo of bootleg whiskey from Bimini. But he denied visiting Tropical Gardens at midnight to buy feathers.

In his summation for the defense, the elder Worley declared that Veber's arrest was due to "public sentiment running wild — to wild, unreasonable, brutal excitement." Charlie Billie's testimony, he said, was "a suspicion rather than evidence, and actuated by some secret motive."

The Indians, said Worley, thought Veber had done the terrible deed "because they knew Veber was supposed to possess a rifle over which the evil spirits hovered."

It took the jury just two hours and forty-five minutes to bring back a different verdict this time: "We the jury find the defendant not guilty."

Veber walked out of the courtroom with this mother and went home, a free man for the first time since early March. Four months later, he would be arrested again on a whiskey charge.

But if Veber didn't kill Tigertail, who did?

Worley declared it was probably another Indian, maybe one from Musa Isle. But he presented no evidence, just a few phrases to raise "reasonable doubt" in the minds of the jurors.

Still, with the trial over, the issue calmed down. A "no-count" white man had been put through trial twice and now the matter was settled.

In Tropical Gardens, matters were less clear. Taboos and customs had been violated. Jack Tigertail, it was suspected, had become much too friendly with the wife of another Indian. It was a matter that should have been brought before the council.

Instead, the cuckolded husband shot him. Again, a violation of the tribe's laws. But in 1922, what was a band of less than two dozen Miccosukees surrounded by the white man's city to do? Best just to let the circle of life go on.

So, who was the murderer of Jack Tigertail?

In the camps and the villages his name was whispered softly: "Charlie Billie."

CHAPTER 2

A Femme Fatale Named Chubbie

---

*Celebrity pilots and a ghostwriter formed
a deadly Miami triangle.*

Flying from London to Australia in 1927, Captain William Lancaster, English war hero, and Mrs. Jessie Keith-Miller, record-setting aviatrix, crashed near Singapore. Together in Miami five years later, they crashed again, this time as two-thirds of a deadly international triangle that brought death to its third member, Charles Haden Clarke.

A writer from New Orleans, Clarke, twenty-six, had moved in with them to ghostwrite the memoirs of the Australian-born divorcee. Like Lancaster, he wound up in love with her. He also wound up dead on April 21, 1932, shot in the head in her home. The police said Lancaster, thirty-four, did it.

It appeared to be a classic triangle, two men in love with the same woman. To complicate it further, both men wanted to marry her. Even more complicated, both already had wives.

At the apex of the triangle was a woman named Chubbie, hardly a name for a femme fatale, better understood, perhaps, from another word used to describe her — stacked. She was a petite woman, just eighty-five pounds, but the tiny package that was Chubbie had packed a lifetime of achievements into just thirty years. In aviation's pioneer days she had learned to fly, and soon blossomed into a world famous aviatrix, holder of two United States cross-country flight records.

Her personal magnetism drew both men to her. Then, in April, as one newspaper put it, "the house changed from a love nest into a house of death."

Miami had never before seen anything like the trial of Captain Lancaster, held in the blazing heat of August. To a city struggling to recover from a real-estate collapse, a killer hurricane and a nationwide depression, the story unfolded like an overheated soap opera. It had a little of everything —

a handsome, dashing defendant, a moody victim battling a malady that no one in court would mention by name, a large dose of adultery, the betrayal of friendship, a glimpse into the glamorous and sometimes seedy world of aviation, alien smuggling, even a touch of chicken stealing.

* * *

In 1927, Charles A. Lindbergh captured the admiration of the world by flying solo across the Atlantic Ocean. In those days, pioneering pilots who forged new skyways between continents and countries became instant heroes — and heroines. In London in that memorable year of 1927, Jessie Keith-Miller met Captain William Newton Lancaster, who had flown with distinction for the Royal Flying Corps.

Lancaster was planning a flight from London to Australia. Enthralled by the captain and his bold venture, she agreed to finance the flight and to fly with him to Australia, leaving England in late 1927. On the flight they fell in love. In the exotic land of Persia, as Iran was called in those days, Lancaster succumbed to the charms of the curvaceous Chubbie. He decided to leave his wife and daughter.

On the flight, not every thing went as smoothly as their lovemaking. They crashed in the Dutch East Indies. For nearly three months they had to remain in Singapore, recovering from injuries and waiting out repairs on the plane.

In February 1928, they resumed their flight to Australia, where they were officially greeted with exuberant fanfare. Lectures and personal appearances brought them money and fame, even a discussion with a Hollywood company about a film.

Part of the money Lancaster earned financed flying lessons for Chubbie with the Red Bank Flying Instructors in New Jersey. Once she had earned her pilot's license, Chubbie proceeded to set United States women's records for both east and west cross-country flights. In 1931, they settled in Miami, by this time beginning to emerge as an important international aviation center.

At a 1931 Christmas party, Bill and Chubbie met Charles Haden Clarke, a reporter who had worked for the *New Orleans Times-Picayune*. He was visiting his mother, Ida Clyde Clarke, who taught creative writing at the University of Miami.

Haden Clarke agreed to ghostwrite a book on the adventurous life of the diminutive aviatrix. To save money in those depressed days, the writer moved in with Lancaster and Keith-Miller.

Times were so tough that they resorted on occasion to stealing chickens

Captain Bill Lancaster and "Chubbie" Keith Miller before their flight from London to Australia
(National Air and Space Museum, Smithsonian Institution)

to put food on the table. No wonder Lancaster and Chubbie responded when
they learned of an opportunity to join Latin American Airways, a cargo airline to be based in Mexico.

Lancaster, knowing Chubbie's tendency to drink too much, told Clarke
to take care of her while he was away. In Los Angeles, he learned just how
good that care would be. J. F. Russell, a member of the new company who
would shortly land in jail in Key West for smuggling aliens, showed him a
letter his wife had written to him: "Was round at Chubbie's tonight. She and
Clarke got all ginned up together. Don't tell Bill, but I believe she is being
well satisfied."

Lancaster said he trusted her. Still, he became increasingly uneasy when
he noticed that the letters she had been writing him regularly stopped coming. Matters grew worse when he learned that Latin American Airways
wanted him to fly illegal aliens across the border into Nogales, Arizona, at
"one thousand dollars a Chinaman," payable in gold. Russell suggested the
possibility of smuggling dope.

The time had come, Lancaster concluded, to call off the deal and return
to Miami. Taking off in a Curtiss Robin, he flew to St. Louis, where a dis-

turbing letter awaited him. In it Clarke told him he and Chubbie had fallen in love and planned to get married.

In St. Louis, Bill Lancaster purchased a .38-caliber pistol and a box of cartridges. He loaded the gun before continuing on to Miami. He landed at the Viking Airport at the Venetian Causeway in Miami, where he was met by Chubbie and Haden Clarke. Lancaster kissed Chubbie and greeted the ghostwriter with, "Hello, old man."

That night the three of them talked about their dilemma but resolved nothing. At 12:45 A.M., Chubbie said, "Good night, chaps," and went to her bedroom. On the sleeping porch, the two men lay down on beds about three feet apart.

Chubbie lay awake, apprehensive when the voices sounded quarrelsome. After she heard them laughing, she relaxed and went to sleep.

At about 3 A.M., she awakened to a pounding on her bedroom door. Lancaster called out: "A terrible thing has happened. Haden has shot himself."

First reports in the press, where it was the lead story on page one, described the death as a suicide. Clarke had been shot in the right temple and the gun lay on the bed beside him. Two typed notes were found signed in pencil. Police found no useful fingerprints on the gun, the notes, the typewriter or the pencil. Chubbie and Lancaster informed the state's attorney's office of the triangle. Remorse at the betrayal of a friend was given as a motive for the suicide.

A newspaper account described Chubbie's courage even after several hours of questioning: "Despite the fact that her face was chalk-white and her eyes showed intense weariness, she held her head up and walked past the news reporters clustered around the antechamber with the unconcern of a tragedy queen."

The police, however, were not buying the suicide story. They kept digging. Finally, Lancaster came forward to admit he had typed and signed the two notes. He was arrested and charged with murder in the first degree.

*   *   *

When the trial began on August 2, 1932, it dominated the Miami newspapers despite an oversupply of exciting and important news. The 1932 Olympic Games were under way in Los Angeles, Franklin D. Roosevelt was challenging President Herbert Hoover for the presidency, a man named Hitler was striving to take over Germany and down in Winston-Salem, North Carolina, torch singer Libby Holman was suspected of murdering her husband, the heir to the R.J. Reynolds tobacco fortune. But in Miami people turned their eyes toward the Dade County Courthouse, where a trial the likes of which had never before been seen in south Florida was starting.

More than 150 people, mostly women, jammed into the overheated courtroom, while just as many more milled around the hallways, waiting to push their way in whenever trial-watchers fainted or sickened from an August heat that mere fans could not cool.

For his attorney, Lancaster turned to a talented Miami attorney named James M. Carson, who hailed from the cattle country around Kissimmee. Author Nixon Smiley described him: "His image in the courtroom was that of a simple, conscientious man who would have been unable to defend a guilty person. His method of questioning was simple and direct but his arguments were persuasive."

Said state's attorney N. Vernon Hawthorne at the start of the trial: "We have drama, tragedy, adventure, love, hate and financial reverses; riding one day on the crest and the next in the gutter. Behind it all is the undying love of Bill Lancaster for Chubbie, which was exploded when he received the news that his beloved had been taken by the best friend of his life."

In his opening statement, Carson contended that without the suicide notes there would have been no indictment against his client. Lancaster, he said, "lost his head and did a fool thing." The reason, said the defense attorney, was to prevent "the ghost of the dead man from coming between Lancaster and Chubbie."

The "heartthrob" of the triangle, as the press called Chubbie, testified for three and one-half hours, presenting a particularly strong case for Lancaster. She believed Clarke's death was a suicide, caused by a number of factors, among them remorse at the tangled mess he had helped create, financial worries, discouragement at many rejections as a writer, and a moody personality. "He went from heights of joy to depths of despair," she said.

Chubbie testified that one morning after a heavy bout of drinking home brew, a concoction of the Prohibition, she and Clarke awoke to find themselves together in her bed. After that his ardor increased, she said.

Keith-Miller's testimony brought out Clarke's worry about a physical condition, sometimes called a malady but never mentioned by name in court. Examined by her doctor, she was told she had not contracted venereal disease.

Earl Hudson, police emergency officer, who questioned Chubbie and Lancaster at Jackson Memorial Hospital, said that Clarke, shot around three in the morning, lived on at the hospital until nearly noon.

Hudson said Lancaster "asked if the boy had any chance of coming to long enough to say anything."

Lancaster told Hudson that the reason Clarke had killed himself "was that Haden Clarke had contracted a contagious disease and that it was preying heavily on his mind."

Of particular delight to the spectators was the reading aloud of a diary kept by Lancaster. It was filled with affectionate references to his beloved. "Chubbie is adorable, as always." "Chubbie perfect!"

On January 6, 1932, he wrote about spending an hour in jail for driving while drunk. Actually, Chubbie had been driving, but he took the wheel and the blame to spare her embarrassment. "American justice is all wet," he wrote. By April his references to Chubbie were becoming increasingly distraught, particularly after Russell showed him letters that said Clarke had taken his place in Chubbie's affections.

Russell, brought up to Miami from the Key West jail, gave the court a few laughs as he tried to evade questions about his previous alien-smuggling activities. He had served time for smuggling bales into Texas — not bales of marijuana, but bales of hay. Inside them Syrians were hiding and trying hard not to give away the game by sneezing.

Damning testimony against Lancaster came from M. G. Tancrel, president of Latin American Airways, who was also in jail, charged with impersonating a U.S. naval officer. Tancrel, who hailed from the island of Mauritius in the Indian Ocean, told the court about remarks the captain had made in Nogales: "Lancaster said, 'I'll go back and get rid of that S.O.B,' and later in El Paso: 'I've seen a lot of dead men and one more won't make any difference to me.'"

On August 8, Captain Lancaster, who spoke in a "soft, clear and heavily accented British voice," took the witness stand. Under questioning from his attorney, Carson, he told the court the story of his life. Born in Birmingham, England, he later moved with his family to London. During World War I he enlisted in the Royal Flying Corps, serving as a flier until he crashed in a snowstorm in 1918.

After the war he continued to fly, serving in a "small war" on India's northwest frontier. In 1927, he joined forces with Jessie Keith-Miller, who financed his long-planned flight from England to Australia, a flight previously performed by only one flier.

Publisher George Putnam, who married aviatrix Amelia Earhart, engaged Lancaster and another flier to make the first flight from the U.S. mainland to Bermuda. They were forced back to Hampton Roads, Virginia, when it became clear the plane's fuel capacity was too low for them to make it. Lancaster's next job called for flights around the Caribbean to demonstrate a new engine. He crashed in Trinidad and was hospitalized for three months.

Chubbie, now a pilot, had her troubles, too. At the end of November 1930, she was reported missing on an overdue flight from Cuba to Miami. Lancaster, in Pittsburgh, borrowed a plane to fly to Washington, then borrowed another plane from the Navy and flew to Miami to look for her. The word came then from Nassau that she was safe. She had been forced down on Andros Island in the Bahamas.

Lancaster's testimony, particularly appealing to the women in the courtroom, was interrupted while the defense trotted out six famous aviators to testify as character witnesses for the English flier. Among them were Keith Bon, a World War I flier and rubber merchant from Singapore who flew over from Paris to speak up for the captain; Clyde Pangborn, already famous for his round-the-world flight; and Captain Frank Upton, of Fort Pierce, a Congressional Medal of Honor holder.

As the trial neared its end, attorney Carson began to hammer hard on the theme of suicide. Witnesses appeared who had heard Clarke speak of killing himself. Others characterized him as "a drug addict, a drunkard, a man of many and indiscriminate love affairs and a never-do-well." Richard Richardson, a Coconut Grove resident who had written a play about the Russian "holy man" Rasputin, said Clarke had once told him if he ever killed himself he would do it by shooting himself over the right ear.

Dr. Albert Hamilton, a ballistics expert from Auburn, New York, declared: "What I have seen compels me to state that the shot that killed this man was self-inflicted. It was a contact shot when the gun was pressed hard against the head and the head was pushed hard against the muzzle of the pistol. . . . There is not one scintilla of evidence to support the theory of murder."

Hamilton had brought Clarke's skull to the courtroom to underscore the points he was making. Once, the skull slipped out of his hands and sailed upward into the air. The state's attorney grabbed for it and missed. Hamilton finally caught it, juggled it, then hugged it to his chest like a wide receiver. The spectators laughed.

Near the end of the testimony, Captain Lancaster displayed a letter from Captain James H. Doolittle, whom he described as "the greatest flier in the world." Doolittle had written a letter attesting to the good character of Lancaster and offering to help him in any way he could. A decade later, as Colonel Jimmy Doolittle, he would lead an incredible World War II bombing raid on Tokyo.

On August 16, the lawyers began presenting their final arguments. Said state's attorney Hawthorne: "Lancaster is guilty of violating four of the Ten Commandments: Thou shalt not kill, steal, commit adultery, bear false wit-

Jessie Maude "Chubbie" Keith-Miller (National Air and Space Museum, Smithsonian Institution)

ness, and Mr. Carson says this man's moral code shines like a star on a background of filth." He was upset that Carson had likened Lancaster to General Robert E. Lee.

Carson was in good form. "You men of the jury, compare the jailbirds of the state and the warbirds of the defense, and send back the word to old England that justice is done."

Chubbie listened without expression, then said at a brief recess, "I am interested only in freeing old Bill."

The defense attorney blasted the state because neither an autopsy nor an inquest was held. He was particularly savage in his attack on Hudson. He characterized the hapless policeman as "one of the heroes of this trial, who blindly, like a blunderbuss, went through the house and destroyed papers which are most valuable to the defendant. I am sorry for people like Earl Hudson that he can't go on emergency calls without trying to railroad somebody. He's just a dumb, thick-headed cop without the intelligence to be foxy, and who has power."

At 11:45 A.M. on August 17, the case went to the jury. Four hours and fifty-nine minutes later they returned. E. B. Leatherman, clerk of the court, read aloud the verdict: "Not guilty."

The courtroom turned into a carnival as the crowd surged forward to congratulate the captain. Bailiffs, deputies, sheriff and police were no match for the women of the Lancaster fan club. Lancaster lingered in the court shaking hands with well-wishers and thanking them for according him, "a Britisher in their midst, sympathy, kindliness and justice."

* * *

Relief was short-lived for the English-born aviator and his Australian-born "heartthrob." The day after the trial, the U.S. immigration service set in motion deportation proceedings.

Both departed Miami for England, leaving behind a city that had been thoroughly entertained by the first in what would be a long line of juicy murder trials. But was Captain Lancaster really innocent? He had learned that Clarke had stolen the love of his life. He had said he would kill his rival. He had bought a gun and loaded it before returning to Miami. Then within twenty-four hours of his return his rival was dead — of a gunshot wound.

Was he innocent or was the jury swayed by his attractive, compelling personality during a long session on the witness stand? Or was it the skill of his highly regarded attorney?

Whatever, they moved on with their lives. Captain Lancaster had eyed the record set by Amy Johnson Mollison, who had flown from London to Cape Town, 6,250 miles, in four days, six hours, forty-five minutes. On April 10, 1933, not quite a year after the death of Haden, he took off in a de Havilland one-seater. He stopped at Barcelona, Spain, then at Oran, Algeria, for fuel.

From Morocco he attempted a night flight to Gao, near Timbuktu. He knew there were no beacons to guide him and the lack of light on his instrument board would make steering a compass course all but impossible. Still, there was a record to be broken.

Jaunty as ever, he replied: "I'll manage with matches."

Chubbie never saw him again. He was reported missing somewhere in the vast Sahara. Rumors surfaced that he was on a special mission for the British Secret Service. Chubbie married Lieutenant John Pugh, of the Royal Air Force, and moved with him to Southeast Asia. They were living in Singapore when the Japanese overran the city in the early days of World War II. She followed Lancaster into oblivion.

Then in February 1962, a French camel corps patrolling the desert found the almost perfectly preserved body of Lancaster, where he had died in his plane.

As he had before, he kept a diary, this time of the last terrible days of his life, enduring without food or water a cruel sun in the day, the cold of a desert night after sundown. Did his thoughts turn again to the tragic event of April 21, 1932? Did he confess a terrible crime to prepare his soul for eternity? He did not. He made no mention of Charles Haden Clarke.

He did, however, remember the great love of his life. As he waited for his agonizingly slow death, his words to her were: "Chubbie, my darling, give up flying and settle down."

CHAPTER 3

Target FDR

---

*In Miami, an assassin sought to
kill the president-elect.*

In his inaugural address as the thirty-second president of the United States, Franklin Delano Roosevelt moved quickly to reassure a nation shaken and battered by bank failures, bankruptcies, foreclosures and unemployment. Said the new president on March 4, 1933: "The only thing we have to fear is fear itself."

Seventeen days earlier, fear itself had crackled like electricity in the balmy air at Miami's Bayfront Park. That February night, an assassin stalked Roosevelt and left a legacy of terror for the crowd gathered to greet the man they had elected, overwhelmingly, to lead them out of the Great Depression.

Happily, Guiseppe Zangara's bullets missed the president-elect. But four others were not so lucky. One, Anton Cermak, the mayor of Chicago, would die of his gunshot wound. Another victim, the wife of the president of Florida Power & Light Company, would struggle with poor health the rest of her life.

And Zangara would die in Florida's electric chair in swift, pre-Miranda justice just five weeks after he fired again and again and again at Franklin Roosevelt.

They were an unlikely trio, Roosevelt, Cermak and Zangara. The paths of these three men crossed tragically at 9:35 the night of February 15, 1933. The setting was an open-air, public park facing Biscayne Bay, near the site of today's Bayside.

The crowd, estimated by some to be as high as twenty-five thousand, was in a festive mood, abuzz with excitement at a chance to see the man who had ousted Herbert Hoover from the presidency by a huge margin.

In those days a new president did not assume office until March. The wealthy, patrician Roosevelt had taken a twelve-day fishing trip in

Bahamian and Florida waters aboard Vincent Astor's *Nourmahal*, described in the *Fort Lauderdale Daily News* by its editor, August Burghard, as "not a yacht as we understand the term. It's an ocean liner. . . . palatial."

The yacht docked at Pier One in Miami at 9:15. At nearby Bayfront Park, Roosevelt planned to say a few words to the crowd, then travel in an open car to the Florida East Coast Railway station, where he would board the *Havana Special*, bound for his home state of New York.

As a member of the Democratic Party's national executive committee, Robert H. Gore, publisher of the Fort Lauderdale newspaper, had invited a number of his party's leaders to join FDR at the park that evening, among them Mayor Cermak. They were seated on the bandshell platform. It was to be a moment of triumph for the mayor, a staunch supporter of Roosevelt in his battle to gain the Democratic nomination.

A mild-looking man with thinning hair and steel-rimmed spectacles, Cermak had gone to work at age eleven in a Chicago factory for two dollars a week. By the time he was twenty-one, he owned a forty-wagon hauling business. A man of great courage, he had been elected mayor on a reform ticket aimed at cleaning up Chicago. To do the job, he would have to battle it out with the country's crime boss, Al Capone. Balmy, relaxed Miami must have seemed a million miles away from his crime-ridden city on that triumphant evening.

Guiseppe Zangara had arrived in Miami in December 1932, hoping the warm weather would relieve an unrelenting stomachache or, as he called it, "a pain in the belly." An unemployed bricklayer who had been in the United States for about ten years, he struggled along doing odd jobs. Although an antisocial loner, he was nonetheless a hard worker, and was regarded as harmless.

But in truth, the tiny Zangara — 101 pounds on a five-foot-one frame — was consumed by a hatred of people who had wealth and power. In his native Italy, he had once bought a gun to shoot King Victor Emmanuel III, but he was unable to slip in close enough. Later, in America, he nursed vague plans to assassinate two presidents, Calvin Coolidge and Herbert Hoover. Ironically, he was a registered Republican.

The morning of February 15, Zangara arose early at his rooming house at 125 Northeast Fifth Street in Miami. He had no work for the day. A meal of hard bread, cheese and coffee did little to ease his chronic stomachache. Maybe, he thought, a walk would help.

At a newsstand he glimpsed a headline: "Miami Awaits Visit Tonight of Roosevelt."

A plan began to take shape. He was so poor, and others were so rich. He blamed this dreadful injustice on kings and presidents. Now, this evening in

Miami, he saw a chance to right a wrong. At a Miami Avenue jewelry shop, he tried to buy a double-barreled, sawed-off shotgun.

"I lika buy shotgun. How much you get?" he asked Harry Rubin. The proprietor refused to sell him a shotgun. "Then you sell me pistol, a pistol for about six dollars?"

Alarmed at the bulging eyes and the tense muscles in the man's neck, Rubin refused. Zangara walked across the street to a pawnshop run by Gordon Davis, an acquaintance of his. Davis sold him a hammerless .32-caliber, five-shot revolver and ten bullets for eight dollars.

A few minutes before 9:30, Miami motorcycle policemen came into view, leading the president-elect's parade to the cheers of well-wishers along Biscayne Boulevard. FDR rode in a four-door, green convertible seated behind Miami's mayor, R.B. Gautier. Roosevelt flashed his jaunty trademark smile and waved at the crowd. The president-elect spotted his old friend and political ally, Mayor Cermak, on the platform and waved to him.

Crippled by polio a decade earlier, Roosevelt found standing difficult. He pushed himself into a sitting position on the back of the seat and took a microphone offered by Fred Mizer, of radio station WQAM.

"Mr. Mayor, friends and enemies."

The crowd laughed at the word "enemies," just as Roosevelt had intended them to do. Only one person knew that a deadly enemy lurked just fifty feet away from the president-elect.

FDR chatted informally about fishing and joked about the ten pounds he had gained. He talked less than five minutes, then handed the mike back to Mizer, as the crowd cheered.

At that moment, Cermak arrived and leaned over to shake hands with Roosevelt. The mayor straightened up and FDR leaned forward to look at a six-foot telegram being brought to him.

A shot rang out, then a second.

"There seems to be some little excitement here," said Fred Mizer into the WQAM microphone. "Somebody's shooting firecrackers. Well, that's all, folks. Goodnight." He signed off, and in the process missed his chance to give his listeners the eyewitness account that would have earned him a place in journalistic history.

Screams followed, then shouts from policemen and Secret Service agents.

"Don't let him kill Roosevelt!" someone shouted.

Secret Service men stepped between the president-elect and the small, dark man with a gun. One yelled to the driver of the convertible, "Get the president out of here!"

Chicago Mayor Anton Cermak is led away, mortally wounded. (Historical Association of
Southern Florida)

The driver, a uniformed policeman, started the engine. Motorcycle
patrolmen raced their motors and turned on their sirens to clear the way.

FDR looked around. He saw two men holding Cermak, bleeding from a
chest wound. "Stop," Roosevelt ordered his driver. The mayor was brought
to the car. Roosevelt helped him onto the seat beside him as he collapsed.

Mrs. Joseph Gill, wife of the FPL president, had also been badly wounded. Two others had been hit, but not as seriously.

The president-elect refused to leave until all the wounded were loaded
into the open cars. Joe Gill, FPL president, rode on the running board of the
car that carried his wife, already unconscious from her wounds.

In the lead car, FDR rode with his arms around Cermak. "Don't move, Tony," he said. "It won't hurt if you don't move."

One unwelcome visitor rode with Roosevelt's motorcade. Zangara, attacked and subdued by an angry crowd, had been seized by police and strapped to the luggage rack of the second car. He, too, was bound for the hospital, for treatment of head wounds inflicted by the crowd. The motorcade took just ten minutes to reach Jackson Memorial Hospital.

Police began to piece the story together. An eyewitness account from a Mrs. W. F. Cross showed how close FDR had been to taking one of the bullets:

"When the president-elect stood up to make his speech, so many stood up in front of me I couldn't see, so I stood up on one of the benches, and this man stood up with me and the bench almost folded up. I looked around and saw he had a pistol and he began shooting toward the president-elect. I grabbed his hand which held the pistol and pushed it up in the air and called for help."

At first, Zangara refused to talk, then poured forth his story, quoted in newspapers in cleaned-up English: "I tried to kill President-elect Roosevelt because I have been in constant torment from a stomach operation. . . . I meant to shoot the president-elect while he was talking, but the people in front of me were standing and I am such a short fellow. . . . I stood on the bench and pointed the gun at Mr. Roosevelt. . . . I do not know whether or not I shot Mr. Roosevelt but I want to make it clear that I do not hate Mr. Roosevelt personally. I hate all presidents, no matter what country they come from, and I hate all officials and everybody who is rich."

The day after the shooting, Roosevelt visited the victims at the hospital. Mrs. Gill was still unconscious.

"Tony, you're looking great," he told Mayor Cermak. "You'll be up and with us anytime now."

"I hope so," the mayor replied. "I hope I'll be up for the inauguration anyhow, but I feel pretty bad now."

At 9:55 A.M., FDR boarded the train for New York. A brief appearance at the Fort Lauderdale station, planned for the night before, was canceled, even though a crowd of well-wishers had gathered.

The following morning, Zangara was arraigned on four counts of attempted murder. After a weekend in jail, he pleaded guilty on February 20. He was sentenced to eighty years in prison.

"Don't be stingy!" he told the judge. "Give me more. Give me a hundred years!"

"Perhaps you'll get more later," replied Judge E. C. Collins. The judge knew that two of the shooting victims remained in serious condition, although Mayor Cermak had shown some improvement.

On March 4, 1933, Franklin Roosevelt took the oath of office, but his friend and political ally, Anton Cermak, was not present. He had taken a turn for the worse. Two days after FDR assumed the presidency, the mayor died of multiple complications.

Three days later, Guiseppe Zangara stood before Circuit Judge U. O. Thompson and pleaded guilty to the murder of Mayor Cermak. "I try to keel president because I no like government," said Zangara. "Large peoples maka lotta thing wrong for money. Everything wrong for money. No money, no crook business . . ."

Zangara paused, then asked: "You give me 'lectric chair?"

"Yes," the judge replied.

At Raiford Prison on March 20, guards strapped Zangara into the electric chair. His last words: "Push the button. Quick!"

And it was quick. Just thirty-three days after he fired at FDR, Zangara was executed. He was clearly guilty but just as clearly deranged, a condition that would have spared him the chair in later years, or under less hysterical conditions. Both the public and the press were clamoring for Zangara's blood. A Tampa newspaper even suggested that he be boiled in oil. The only media voice calling for calm was a young student writing in the *Alligator*, the University of Florida newspaper. Heavily criticized, Mel Richard, the student, would stand his ground and go on later to do battle with the notorious S and G crime syndicate.

An autopsy finally revealed the source of Zangara's pain. It was not the wealthy capitalists at whom he raged but a much more mundane problem — a diseased gallbladder.

CHAPTER 4

Framed by a King

The count faced a phony charge of killing
the Bahamas' richest man.

The duchess stirred sleepily. Awakened by the sound of knocking, her husband, the duke of Windsor, slipped on his white silk robe, bearing the royal British coat of arms, embroidered in azure, red, silver and gold. He fumbled with the door.

As though through a fog, the former Wallis Warfield Simpson, the Belle of Baltimore, caught bits of conversation: . . . rich and powerful citizen murdered . . . bludgeoned to death . . . set on fire. A stunned David Windsor, royal governor of the Bahamas, told her who had been killed.

"Sir Harry Oakes."

For the duchess the fog lifted suddenly — but for the rest of the world the haze would never really go away. A decision her husband would soon make would guarantee that a half-century later the mists of confusion would still swirl around the brutal murder of the richest man in the islands, the richest baronet in the British Empire and probably one of the richest men in the world.

Oakes had been their friend. The Duke was scheduled to golf with him later that day. After Edward VIII, the king of England, abdicated his throne "for the woman I love," he had become the duke of Windsor, assigned to the lowly post of governor of the Bahamas. He and his wife had found the living quarters at Government House in Nassau, the Bahamian capital, far beneath their royal standards. While their dwelling was being refurbished, they had stayed at Westbourne, Oakes' rambling old twenty-room mansion on his three-thousand-acre estate west of the Cable Beach area.

And now the word had come that Sir Harry had been murdered in the very house where they had stayed; actually, as it turned out, in a bedroom where they had slept.

But the duke was less concerned about the death of a friend than the squalid secrets this murder most foul might dredge up. On July 8, 1943, a day when his native land, the United States and rest of the Free World were fighting Germany, Japan and Italy in the bloodiest war the world has ever known, the royal governor took personal charge of the investigation.

After an hour and fifty minutes of dithering, the governor placed a phone call to the Miami Police Department, one of the most corrupt in the United States. He asked to speak to Captain Edward Melchen, chief of homicide. Melchen had served as the duke's bodyguard on previous trips to the area. He had one important qualification: The duke was comfortable with him.

At the duke's request, Captain Melchen left Miami for Nassau at once, bringing with him Captain James Otto Barker, palmed off in this case as a fingerprint expert. Actually, he was a former ambulance driver and motorcycle cop who had been twice demoted for departmental infractions. He did not even bother to bring a fingerprint camera. It was going to be a most unorthodox investigation, and the duke had decided it would be run by two Miamians he could control, rather than by the Nassau police, Scotland Yard or the U.S. Federal Bureau of Investigation.

* * *

Noisy and violent, a July storm had swept across Nassau that fateful night. The Honorable Harold Christie, member of the powerful Bahamas Executive Council, had spent the night at Westbourne, sleeping in the bedroom adjoining Sir Harry's. Sometime before seven he arose, he said, and went out on the upstairs porch where he usually met his friend prior to breakfast.

Oakes wasn't there, so Christie looked into his bedroom. He saw a grisly sight. On the bed lay the body of his friend, bloody from head wounds and blackened with soot. The smell of burnt flesh filled the air. The bed and the mosquito netting were burned and the walls of the room were smeared with blood and soot.

Strangest of all, the murderer had ripped open a pillow and scattered feathers across the mutilated body. The feathers, stuck to the burnt flesh, fluttered obscenely in the Bahamian breeze. Was it some sort of ritual murder, voodoo, obeah, or some other form of native witchcraft?

Who had killed Sir Harry Oakes?

* * *

A crude, overbearing man with a violent temper, Oakes had enemies, plenty of them. "A pit bull of a man," his son-in-law, Count Alfred de Marigny, called Harry Oakes.

A native of Maine, Oakes had set out in 1898 to search for gold. After fourteen years of brutalizing hardship, he found it at Kirkland Lake in Canada. His proved to be the second richest gold mine in the world. Oakes became a citizen of Canada.

His wealth was estimated at more than $200 million, roughly two-and-a-half billion dollars today. With his vast treasures, he was able to purchase from the British Crown the right to be called "Sir" and to establish homes in a number of places, among them Barton Avenue in Palm Beach, just west of the Estée Lauder mansion. Oakes also bought property in northern Palm Beach County, including the Palm Beach Winter Club and Golf Course, which would later become the North Palm Beach Country Club.

He arrived in Palm Beach in 1934 with his wife, Eunice, and their five children. There he acquired the services of an attorney who would stay with him for the rest of his life. When he first arrived, Oakes was concerned about U.S. taxes. He sought out the most prominent law firm in Palm Beach and without an appointment demanded to speak with the senior partner. Kept waiting too long, he fumed at one of the junior partners, then concluded he liked the diplomatic way the young man handled the situation.

"Do you like working here?" he asked Walter Foskett.

"Well . . . ," Foskett was hesitant in his reply.

"Right," said Oakes. "Quit now and I'll set you up in your own office. And you can have all my business."

It was in Palm Beach that Oakes met Christie, a real-estate promoter from Nassau. The Bahamas could offer him glorious relief from the heavy taxes of Canada, Christie assured him.

Oakes asked the Bahamian to find him the best house in Nassau. In a short time he owned roughly a third of New Providence Island. His impact was immediate. He built a golf course and an airport, Oakes Field. He developed a bus line and built a waterworks for Grants Town, where many blacks lived. He gave money to many charities for underprivileged children, for unwed mothers and for public schools for black children.

He was a man used to having his own way. He bought the British Colonial Hotel, legend says, so he could fire a maitre d' who had given him a hard time. He once built a golf course near his Canadian home. After a pesky bunker caught too many of his straying golf shots, he simply brought in a bulldozer and had the bunker leveled.

Although Christie's major project was the luxury Lyford Cay development west of Nassau, he also involved himself in business ventures with Oakes. One of these was Banco Continental, a Mexican bank established to help the Nazis launder foreign currencies.

A principal in this bank was Axel Wenner-Gren, a wealthy Swedish industrialist, who owned Hog Island, now known as Paradise Island, on the northeast side of Nassau. He had invented the vacuum cleaner, and his Electrolux had sucked up a vast fortune for him. He was closely watched by the FBI as a suspected Nazi agent and eventually was blacklisted and forced out of the Bahamas.

One Bahamian resident who laundered money through the Mexican bank was the duke of Windsor. Wenner Gren's accounts indicate the high-living duke slipped two million dollars into the Nazi bank in violation of British currency regulations.

One of the joys of Sir Harry's turbulent life was his beautiful red-haired daughter, Nancy. She proved to be hard to control. Her parents tried vainly to oppose her affair with a man they considered a swinging playboy/adventurer, the handsome, dashing Count Marie Alfred Fouquereaux de Marigny.

The twice-divorced count, a native of the island of Mauritius in the Indian Ocean, was nearly twice as old as seventeen-year-old Nancy. Two days after her eighteenth birthday in May 1942, she and Count Freddie were married by a magistrate in New York City. Her parents were notified after the fact.

Sir Harry was hardly an easy man to get along with, and de Marigny never developed a friendly relationship with his father-in-law. Later that year, Nancy became pregnant, not long after a severe case of typhoid fever, which she had contracted in Mexico. Two doctors concluded she was too weak to carry a pregnancy to term. Her father, furious at the count, whom he called a "sex maniac," insisted his weakened daughter have an abortion. The operation was performed at Good Samaritan Hospital in West Palm Beach.

By March of 1943, de Marigny and Sir Harry were no longer on speaking terms.

* * *

"For Lady Oakes's sake, I hope it turns out to be murder," said the duke. "For the colony's sake, I hope it's suicide."

Hugh Quackenbush, the first doctor to examine the body, was only too happy to accommodate the duke, as others would be. He mused that the death could have been a suicide, provided the head wound had been caused by a bullet.

A check by a second doctor, however, revealed four triangle-shaped wounds in a crescent pattern above the victim's right ear. Four head wounds plus burning seemed to rule out suicide.

Sir Harry Oakes (Historical Society of Palm Beach County)

Earlier that morning, Christie had told Etienne Dupuch, publisher of the *Nassau Tribune*, "He's been shot."

But police were speaking vaguely about a "blunt instrument." No serious effort was made to find the murder weapon, and no serious autopsy was performed. Nor was the murder area sealed off. Visitors moved freely in and out of Sir Harry's bedroom, free to leave behind fingerprints, handprints and footprints.

The Miami pros did not even bother to dust for fingerprints the first day, claiming it was too humid. But why should they? It wasn't a case of rounding up the "usual suspects." In this case, it was just one suspect and a highly unusual one at that. The powers-that-were had already picked their man.

* * *

It never pays to pop off about the man in charge. Of the duke, de Marigny had said: "I sometimes feel our prince is nothing more than a pimple on the ass of the British Empire."

It was not a wise remark to make about a man who less than a decade earlier had ruled England as Edward VIII. That was before he had married the twice-divorced commoner, Wallis Warfield Spencer Simpson.

Oakes and the duke were not the only enemies the count had. He was an outsider, a "Frenchy." Though Mauritius was a British Crown colony, it had once been French, as the count's name and accent would bear out. He had quarreled with Oakes repeatedly and had once threatened to "crack Sir Harry's head." Many on the island, assuming he would benefit from Oakes's will, were convinced he was the murderer. Among these was the duke of Windsor, who once wrote that he "has insidiously bought his way with his ex-wife's money into the leadership of a quite influential, fast and depraved set of the younger generation, born of bootlegging days."

De Marigny had no notion of the trap closing in on him. The night of the murder he had hosted a dinner party at his home. While not airtight, his alibi was basically sound.

Then the police questioned him at some length. Later that day, he began to pick up rumors that he was under suspicion. He did not take these seriously enough to engage a lawyer.

The morning after the murder, a policeman brought him in again to Westbourne. He was questioned by the Miami policemen. Said Melchen: "Please come upstairs. I'd like to ask you some questions on your own."

Why upstairs? wondered de Marigny. They sat in wicker chairs at a glass-topped table. On the table stood a carafe of water and two glasses.

Melchen asked him about Christie, among other things, then said:

"Would you mind pouring me a glass of water?"

"Of course not."

"Have one yourself."

As the count poured the second glass and handed the first to Melchen, Barker appeared suddenly and asked, "Everything all right?"

Shortly after that, the meeting broke up and Melchen asked de Marigny to return around four that afternoon. When he returned, Colonel R. A. Erskine-Lindop was waiting in the hall. He took the count into a room where the Miami policemen and Eric Hallinan, the attorney general, were waiting. There was silence in the room until Hallinan, an Anglo-Irishman born in County Cork, spoke:

"Alfred de Marigny, you are under arrest for the murder of Sir Harry Oakes. Do you wish to call an attorney?"

"Yes," said the count. "I would like to call Alfred Adderly."

"I shall call him for you," said Hallinan.

At his arraignment a short time later, de Marigny told the black-gowned, white-wigged magistrate that Adderly, Nassau's best trial lawyer, would represent him.

"The magistrate cleared his throat," de Marigny later wrote. "His next words sent a chill through me. He had been advised, he said, that Adderly had been retained by the Crown to help prosecute the case against me."

Fortunately for the count, his own lawyer and friend, Godfrey Higgs, who was temporarily out of the country, would return in time to defend him in court.

The count was placed in cell number one in Nassau Jail, built 150 years earlier. On orders of Hallinan, the lights in the tiny cell were kept burning brightly at all times — the better, de Marigny later observed, to see the rats and roaches that shared his tiny, filthy space. The jailer, Captain R. M. Miller, a former officer in the Canadian Royal Mounted Police, told him:

"From the moment I heard Oakes had been murdered, I could have predicted your arrest. I believe you to be innocent. Conduct yourself not only as a man, but as an innocent man. Be dignified. Be calm. Give yourself the best chance you can. Never forget they are out to hang you."

Several flimsy threads had been woven together to fashion a case against de Marigny. For one thing, it was widely known that he had threatened Oakes in the past. Furthermore, they hadn't spoken since March 29, the count said. In addition, de Marigny had singed hairs on his arms, a condition the Crown contended could have been caused by the burning of Sir Harry's body. And finally, the Miami duo claimed they had taken a fingerprint of the count's from a screen in the victim's bedroom, proof positive that he had seen Oakes considerably later than March 29 — July 8, to be exact.

Fortunately, for the defendant, Nancy Oakes de Marigny "stood by her man" from the very beginning. To help with his defense, she hired America's most famous private detective, Raymond Schindler, at a fee of three hundred dollars a day plus expenses.

Schindler, who claimed he was the first detective to "wire" an informant to tape-record evidence, brought with him a fingerprint expert and Professor Leonard Keeler, the inventor of a new machine called the polygraph, known more popularly as the lie detector.

The Nassau police hampered Schindler all the way. A week passed before he was allowed to enter Westbourne. There he found two policemen scrubbing the walls outside Sir Harry's bedroom. Their orders, they said, were to remove all fingerprints and handprints.

"You're destroying evidence," a shocked Schindler said. "Whose prints are those?"

"They're not of the accused person, sir," one of the policemen replied. "They will only confuse the evidence."

At a magistrate's hearing, it became apparent that the fingerprint, labeled Exhibit J, would be the key piece of evidence in the Crown's case. Captain Barker testified that he had lifted the print from the screen the morning of July 10 and had sent it to the laboratory for processing at noon. The print, of course, would prove that de Marigny had been in the murder room.

The count whispered to Higgs. "The man is a liar. I never saw the screen before in my life."

Captain Melchen then told the court the defendant had been taken upstairs at Westbourne at three-thirty in the afternoon.

"He's lying," the count whispered again. "It was around eleven in the morning. I can prove it."

Clearly, if it could be proven that de Marigny was in the room prior to noon, Exhibit J would become suspect. One who knew he was there was Colonel Erskine-Lindop, police commissioner, a man the defense was confident would not lie.

But the commissioner had no chance to testify. He was suddenly transferred to Trinidad.

On Monday, October 18, 1943, hundreds of people gathered outside Nassau's old two-story courthouse, hoping for one of the courtroom's 105 seats. At ten-thirty the trial began. Presiding over the classically British proceedings was Lord Chief Justice Sir Oscar Bedford Daly, arrayed in a fur-trimmed scarlet robe and shoulder-length white wig. The attorneys were equally formal, in black robes and white wigs.

At the trial, de Marigny encountered Adderly, whom he had wanted as counsel. "At least you could have had the courtesy of sending me a refusal."

"This is the first I have heard of it," Adderly said. "Had I received such a request, professional ethics would have demanded that I see you in person."

De Marigny could feel the noose tightening around his neck.

In the courtroom, de Marigny was placed in a cage on top of a three-foot elevated stand. "Yes, a cage," he later wrote. "With the kind of bars one might see in the zoo to protect the onlookers from a dangerous creature, a cage for a wild animal. I was put on exhibition."

Reporters from the wire services and the leading newspapers of the Free World covered the event, among them Erle Stanley Gardner, creator of Perry Mason. When papers were bulging with World War II news, readers were hungry for a juicy murder trial. It had all the ingredients: a wealthy victim, a playboy/nobleman defendant married to an heiress, a touch of voodoo thrown in. And the setting, a tropical island.

The first witness was Christie. He testified he had had dinner with Sir Harry and afterwards had stayed for the night. Higgs, cross-examining him, established that his car was parked that night not in front of the main entrance to Westbourne, but rather nearer to the country club next door. The attorney introduced evidence that he had left the house that night and had been seen on George Street. Christie denied it.

Christie, sweating heavily, told of finding the body the next morning and then spun an improbable tale of trying to revive his old friend with a glass of water. The photos of Oakes, however, left no doubt that the baronet was an extremely dead man.

Powerful though he was in the islands, Christie had proven to be a very poor witness. Many wondered why had he heard nothing when a particularly violent murder had been committed in the adjoining room.

For both sides, testimony proved inconclusive until the Miami bloodhounds took the stand. By now, Higgs had produced evidence which proved de Marigny had been taken upstairs before noon.

Under questioning by Hallinan, Captain Barker revealed he had lifted between fifty and seventy prints from the Chinese screen in Sir Harry's bedroom. After he ran out of Scotch tape, he lifted the final three using a strip of gummed rubber, which he then photographed with a borrowed camera.

Godfrey Higgs rose, then bowed to the chief justice: "My lord, I reluctantly ask leave to interrupt my learned friend; but I must in all candor point out that this is the first time the defense has heard anything about lifted prints. . . . I assumed that the fingerprints referred to were photographs of prints on the screen. . . .

"This piece of rubber is not the best evidence, and I know of no case in which it has been produced in court before. The proper evidence would be to produce the print on the article on which it was found."

Higgs, who had prepared for the trial by taking a course in fingerprinting, made it clear that Barker could have photographed dusted fingerprints on the screen just as easily as lifted prints on gummed rubber.

Sir Oscar faced a pivotal ruling. If he declared the tainted print inadmissible, the Crown's elaborate frame would collapse. The chief justice agonized over the decision, then passed it on for the jury to decide.

De Marigny was stunned by the court's ruling, but his counsel was more than ready. Higgs had conducted an experiment which proved that prints lifted from the screen would still show the background scrollwork on the screen's surface. For Barker there would be no letup.

Higgs: I suggest that you and Captain Melchen deliberately planned to get the accused alone in order to get his fingerprints.

Barker: We did not.

Higgs: I suggest that Exhibit J did not come from that screen.

Barker: It did come from that screen, from the number five panel.

Higgs: May I suggest that your desire for personal gain and notoriety has caused you to sweep aside truth. I put it to you, sir, you have fabricated evidence.

As Barker ended his testimony, Melchen suddenly bolted from the courtroom. Raymond Schindler, ever alert, followed him outside. He found the Miamian leaning up against the courthouse. He was throwing up.

The trial lasted twenty-five days. It took the jury just an hour and fifteen minutes to return with its verdict at 7:10 the evening of November 14, 1943.

Nancy gave her husband a "chin up" sign. De Marigny closed his eyes and bit his lips. Foreman James Sands said:

"Not guilty."

A noisy celebration erupted on Bay Street. The crowd carried de Marigny on its shoulders to his car. The count and his family and friends assembled for a small reception. After dinner, Professor Keeler, part of the Schindler team, amused the guests with his new invention, the lie detector.

The count volunteered to take the test.

"Objection," cried out Godfrey Higgs. De Marigny overruled him.

Q. Did you kill Sir Harry Oakes?

A. No.

Q. Did you put your hand on the Chinese screen between the time of the murder and the discovery of the body?

A. No.

The needle barely flickered. For the second time that day, the accused was declared innocent.

Winning in court did not end the harassment of de Marigny. Deportation proceedings against him were promptly set in motion. Before he left, he encountered an old friend and fellow sailor, Roland Symonette, who was busy with his yacht. Near the boat, the count saw a coil of rope of a kind and quality not available since before the war.

"That's a fine grade of rope," said the count. "Where did you get it from?"

"You take it. In a way, it's really yours, Freddie. At least, it was meant for you."

"How do you work that out?"

"It was ordered to hang you by."

Count and Countess de Marigny were glad to leave the poisonous atmosphere of Nassau and head for a place where they would be welcome. They sailed to Cuba. There they could relax as house guests of an old friend, Ernest Hemingway. The count would later be the godfather of the author's actress granddaughter, Margaux Hemingway.

* * *

The trial had ended, but the mystery lingered on. If not the count, who then had killed Sir Harry Oakes? Schindler had uncovered a number of leads he wanted to follow up. The duke of Windsor said no. Who was the duke covering up for?

In *A Conspiracy of Crowns*, published nearly half a century after the murder, de Marigny wrote:

"In my mind there is no doubt whatsoever that Harold Christie should have been tried and hanged for the murder of Sir Harry Oakes. While hired hands acted for him, it was Christie who ordered the fatal act committed that turbulent night in Nassau, in the summer of 1943."

The murder weapon, he is convinced, was a small-caliber gun, not the "blunt instrument" the police talked about.

Many theories swirl around the mystery. All involve Christie. Some even implicate Meyer Lansky and organized crime's casino empire. One improbable scenario contends that a Lansky minion killed Oakes with a lever during a violent argument aboard a cabin cruiser tied up at Lyford Cay. Christie, who had brought Sir Harry to the shipboard meeting, then helped

In better days Sir Harry Oakes, left, and the duke of Windsor enjoy a polo game in Nassau. (Historical Society of Palm Beach County)

carry the victim back to Westbourne and participated in the coverup.

A rumrunner during Prohibition, Christie knew Lansky back in bootlegging days. According to this theory, Christie and the duke were in league with Lansky to open mob-run gambling casinos in the islands. Oakes agreed, then changed his mind, thus creating a touchy situation, which ended in a death so accidental that it seems at odds with the Mafia's image of professionalism.

Besides, there was no evidence that Lansky showed any interest in casinos in the Bahamas, particularly during World War II. Said Robert Lacey, a famous English author who was writing a book on Lansky: "My research shows that in 1943 he was tied up in New York and Council Bluffs, Iowa."

*   *   *

Many in Fort Lauderdale remember an artist, sitting on the banks of the New River, busily painting the scene before her easel. Her work had been exhibited around the world. One of her paintings had been bought by author Rudyard Kipling.

Hildegard Hamilton, who lived on the Tarpon River, was well tuned-in to events in the Bahamas. In 1938, she had done a painting of Government House for Sir Bede Clifford, an earlier governor of the islands. She had even done a painting of Westbourne. For the last twenty-four years, she had spent her summers in Nassau.

In 1950, the FBI first heard Christie nominated as the probable murderer. The source of the information was Mrs. Hamilton. From her well-placed contacts in the islands, she had learned a version that was making the rounds. Her recounting of the story somehow reached the ears of a seaman named Edward Majava, who was possibly working on a yacht where she was a guest.

In September 1950, in Oakland, California, Majava was arrested for drunkenness. In jail he boasted that he knew who had killed Oakes. He certainly knew enough about it to bring Augustus Robinson, the Nassau police chief, to California after the Oakland police called him. The FBI likewise was interested because it was continuing to keep an eye on the activities of the Windsors.

FBI files, recently declassified, disclose that Robinson confirmed that the story naming Christie was correct. The files do not disclose why Robinson failed to act if he knew who the murderer was.

*   *   *

"Boss man," said the voice, a phrase de Marigny had not heard since he left the islands in the 1940s. Now he was visiting Grand Bahama Island more than a decade later and the familiar words startled him. He looked around to see a middle-aged black man, his face partially hidden by a hat.

The man identified himself as Rawlings, one of Oakes's night watchmen. De Marigny asked him what happened the night of the murder.

"The devil himself came to earth that night," replied Rawlings. "There was thunder and lightning all over. . . . Then we saw Mr. Harold, acting strange."

Rawlings told how Christie's office car stopped at the front door and let two men out. The man behind the wheel of the car was Frank Christie, Harold's brother. Later, the car drove the two men out to Lyford Cay. Other reports had also told of a big cabin cruiser which docked that night at Lyford and presumably returned to south Florida after the killing.

The next day "Mr. Frank asked us both where we was the night before, and I told him the weather got so bad we left early. . . . I prayed he'd believe me." Then he gave each of the watchmen a hundred pounds and told them: "You bastards pack your clothes and be out of Nassau by the time the sun rises tomorrow. If you open your mouths about any of this, I'll cut your damned throats myself."

Rawlings moved to Grand Bahama and changed his name.

"The fire was not a diversion," wrote de Marigny, "but indeed a failed attempt to leave the body so burned, in the ruins of the house, as to conceal the nature of Oakes's death. In their haste, the killers, two professionals, botched the job."

High winds and rain put out the flames. Christie, who gave the hired assassins ample room by spending the night with his mistress, Mrs. Dulcibel Henneage, returned about 5:30 A.M. He expected to find a badly burned house and inside a body so scorched people would believe Oakes died in the fire.

Now it would be apparent to anyone that Oakes had been murdered. How could Christie possibly have slept through the sound of not one but four gunshots?

The "blunt instrument" was nominated then. It bypassed the need for calling on Mrs. Henneage, a shaky backup, for an alibi, and it explained how Christie had slept through "the crime of the century."

De Marigny believes Oakes was drugged. A black viscous fluid found in his stomach was never analyzed. No one has come up with a very plausible reason for the feathers on Sir Harry's body. Maybe Christie added them to spread confusion.

Christie had a powerful motive for killing Oakes. He was facing financial ruin. The wealthy baronet had given him money to buy two thousand sheep to be delivered for grazing on San Salvador Island. Sir Harry visited the island later and to his surprise found no sheep.

His suspicions about Christie grew even stronger when he learned his old friend had double-crossed him on a favorite project of his, an airfield he wanted to build and then contribute to Great Britain to support the war effort. Instead, Christie diverted the contract to an American company and skimmed off a fat fee for himself.

Sir Harry, says de Marigny, decided then to call in Christie's notes. That move would have meant financial ruin. It would also have given Oakes immediate ownership of the promoter's dream project, Lyford Cay.

*   *   *

"For services to the Crown," Harold Christie was knighted by the Queen of England in 1964. The postwar Bahamas real-estate boom, in which he played so important a role, brought him wealth and the opportunity to travel. While visiting France, he was invited to dinner at the Riviera home of England's famous newspaper tycoon, Lord Beaverbrook. Said Beaverbrook:

"Harold, now that you're free and clear, why don't you tell us how you murdered Harry Oakes?"

Christie just smiled.

CHAPTER 5

Lobster Boy

Murder stalked a carnival town and
left behind ruined lives.

A car driving south from Tampa on U.S. 41, the Tamiami Trail, crosses the Alafia River. To the west, chemical plants belch smoke into the gray Florida sky. Just across the bridge, the driver may glimpse a nondescript building and a sign that reads "Giant's Camp." Welcome to Gibsonton, a town where a giant indeed camped and ran a combination restaurant, trailer park and bait and tackle shop.

Al Tomaini, an eight-foot, six-inch giant of a man, once appeared in the World's Fair Freak Show. There he met his wife, Jeannie, the "World's Only Living Half Girl," just two-and-a-half feet tall. She was born with the lower half of her body missing.

The Giant and the Half Girl were at home in Gibtown, as the locals call it. Here they lived in a carnival town, surrounded by their fellow carnys — bearded ladies, sword-swallowers, dwarfs, midgets, fire-eaters, magicians, clowns, strippers and roustabouts. On scraggly lawns, circus animals grazed — dwarf ponies, a five-legged cow — and in the trees a chimp might be swinging from limb to limb.

Gibsonton is a poor, mobile-home town, bypassed by the rest of America. Not even a McDonald's or a gas station serves this town of five thousand. It is a world of its own. Some call the residents of Gibtown sideshow freaks; others tiptoe more gently through the maze of political correctness, labeling them "physically challenged." They prefer to be called "carnies." Many of them simply play the cards they were dealt. They struggle courageously to make lives for themselves out of the cruel handicaps visited upon them.

One such man was Grady Stiles Jr. The shrinking world of carnival-goers knew him as Lobster Boy. His murder in Gibsonton on November 29, 1992, and the courtroom trials that followed made an even bigger world aware of him and the unique society from which he came.

                                    *   *   *

Detective Michael Willette was asleep when the call came. He woke up quickly and soon was driving south on Interstate 75 in his white, unmarked 1988 Ford LTD patrol car, bound for the carnival town of Gibsonton. When he arrived, he called out to the uniformed sheriff's deputies: "What's going on?"

"Some carnival guy got shot."

"What's the vic's name?"

"Grady Stiles Jr."

Donning surgical gloves, Willette entered a mobile home that smelled of cigarette smoke and whiskey. In a heavy armchair, a man, with blood on his face and head, was slumped over. He was wearing only a pair of briefs. Probable cause of death, the detective noted, was gunfire.

The associate medical examiner for Hillsborough County, Dr. Robert Pfalsgraf, confirmed it: "Three gunshot wounds to the head with what appeared to be one exit wound."

In his report, Willette noted, "The subject has no legs," then observed what passed for hands as Stiles was loaded onto a stretcher. On each hand his fingers were deformed into two large claws. Willette would learn shortly that he was known professionally as Lobster Boy.

After talking with carnys who had heard gunshots, police set the time of death at around 11 P.M. A neighbor, Marco Eno, told them he had seen a young man leaving the Stiles trailer just after the shots. Willette interviewed family members: Grady Stiles III and Cathy Berry, both afflicted with their father's deformity; the victim's wife, Mary Teresa Stiles; and Glenn Newman, Teresa's son by another marriage. Willette learned little, but one observation disturbed him. He was intrigued that no one seemed sad that Grady Jr. was gone. He also noted an interesting coincidence. Mary and Glenn had both ducked out of the trailer just before the killing. It was just a little too convenient.

At 5:45 A.M., Willette secured the crime scene and headed home for what remained of the night. The next morning he reviewed the murder with his partner, Detective Rick "Fig" Figueredo. It didn't bear the earmarks of robbery. Nothing appeared to be missing. Money was found in Grady's wallet.

But something didn't feel quite right.

"Nobody's showing any emotion," said Willette as they left the sheriff's

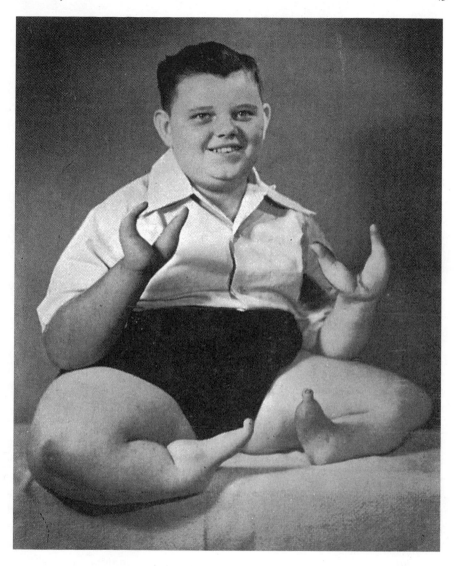

Grady Stiles Jr., the Lobster Boy (Circus World Museum, Baraboo, Wisconsin)

office in Ybor City to return to Gibsonton. "Guy gets killed in his house and his family doesn't seem to bat an eyelash."

"Coupled with the wife and stepson leaving right before the guy gets shot."

The second interview with Teresa Stiles produced more information. She told them that Grady had murdered their daughter's fiancé in Pittsburgh in 1978 and was put on probation. He had shot the boy to death, but Willette wondered how a man with claws could fire a gun. She also told them that the previous night, Grady had been watching a videotape of Ruby, a film about the man who silenced Lee Harvey Oswald with a gunshot. And she explained her and Glenn's departure as a quick visit to check on her sick granddaughter, Misty.

The detectives sized up Teresa's son as a possible weak link. Glenn Newman had a low IQ, just seventy-nine. He was billed by the sideshow as the Human Blockhead. His act consisted of driving nails up his nose without drawing blood. When the two detectives asked him to go with them to headquarters to take a lie detector test, he readily agreed.

"How'd I do?" he asked after the test.

"You lied when asked certain questions," said Willette.

"About who was responsible for killing Grady," added Fig.

In a washed-out green interrogation room, Glenn wilted, then began to cry. Without an argument, he signed a "Consent to Interview" form, giving them permission to question him without an attorney and to tape his answers. Glenn said:

"Well, this happened about a week ago. I talked to this one kid, Chris, about how my father's been abusing my mom, beating her up. He had threatened to kill her. Things like that. He'll lay in bed at night when he's drunk, say, 'I should just kill you to get it over with.' He's turned around and threatened to kill my sister. Beat her up already he has, made her jaw swell up. . . . Cathy Berry is the one that got beat up at one time. He punched her in the jaw, made her jaw swell up.

"And Mary Teresa Stiles is my mother. That's the one that he used to get drunk and lay in bed and say, 'I should just kill you. Get it over with.' He knocked her down. Choked her, beat her in the head, hit her mouth with his forehead. He killed a man in 1978."

As Glenn continued to talk, the detectives saw the basic facts of the murder emerge. His mother wanted to end Grady's abuse of her and Cathy. She gave him fifteen hundred dollars to find someone to kill Lobster Boy. The hit man Glenn found was a seventeen-year-old punk who lived just down Inglewood Drive from them. His name was Chris Wyant.

Next, the detectives drove to Gibtown to pick up Teresa Stiles. She talked almost as freely as had her son.

"Why didn't you just divorce him?" she was asked.

"I couldn't get a divorce from Grady because he threatened to kill me if I did."

"Even though you were divorced from him on a previous occasion."

"Yes, he's much worse now than he's ever been."

Shortly after midnight, they arrested Chris Wyant. Armed with more street smarts than his fellow conspirators, he refused to give a statement. No matter; Willette and Figueredo had solved the crime, less than thirty hours after the murder of Lobster Boy.

Ahead lay the trial, and a media circus it would be, given a Lobster Boy as victim and a Human Blockhead as a perpetrator.

* * *

The Lobster Boy's father, Grady Stiles Sr., had been billed as the Lobster Man. In the 1930s, carnival-goers could pay a nickel and step inside a tent to see his performance.

"Ladies and gentlemen, I am Grady Stiles, the Lobster Man," he would say. "I am a product of a genetic condition, which has run in the Stiles family since 1840. In scientific circles it is known as ectrodactyly. Ectrodactyly is a genetic condition, affecting one in ninety-thousand at birth. A baby is born with the absence of the third digit and the fusing together of the remaining fingers and toes into claws. Sometimes it affects all four limbs, sometimes two. In my case, as you can see, I have normal legs. Once the gene has latched onto a family, every child born has a fifty-fifty chance of getting the condition, which is also known as lobster claw syndrome."

One way to halt the spread of the gene is not to have children, but Grady and Edna had three. Two of them had ectrodactyly. Their youngest son, Grady Jr., was born in 1937 in Pittsburgh. Both hands were claws and both legs were stunted, ending at the knees.

The Stiles family moved to Florida, near Gibsonton, in 1944. Grady Jr. was forced to quit school and join the carnival. He was called Lobster Boy and father and son were billed as the Lobster Family. As a child, Grady's role was simply to sit in a chair and smile as spectators gawked.

Actually, young Grady liked show business and enjoyed life at Gibsonton. There he was not regarded as a freak. He could play with other children and gradually learn skills to use in later life. He learned to read, to write his own name, even to fire a revolver. In supporting himself by his arms as he crawled around, he developed enormous upper-body strength.

His claws gave him a handshake that could be excruciating. Sometimes he slapped people with a claw, knocking them to the ground, then butting them with his head.

In May 1959, Grady met Mary Teresa Herzog, newly divorced from an abusive husband, a carnival roustabout named Jerry Plummer. Teresa, born in Vermont, had been subjected repeatedly to the incestuous advances of her stepfather. At eighteen, she ran away and joined the carnival. A pretty girl with a good figure, she caught the eye of Lobster Boy and soon found herself attracted to him. He could be quite a charmer. But he was too high above her in the carnival hierarchy. She was a mere seller of tickets. He was a star.

Teresa advanced in the carnival, working first as a bally girl, one who stands in front of the tents, ballyhooing the shows inside. Next she became the Blade Box Girl, secured in a box through which swords were thrust. Later she became the Electrified Girl, placed in an electric chair and seemingly electrocuted.

Grady courted her lovingly, wining and dining her and showering her with presents. "Grady was such a charming man," she later recalled. "Everyone enjoyed being in his company."

They lived together for nine years before Grady finally married her. In the off-season she worked in a Tampa shrimp factory to augment the family income. By this time Grady was beginning to drink heavily, a pastime that too often ended in beatings for Teresa. He only hit her in the body, knowing that a battered face would diminish her value as a carny performer.

Their first child, Margaret, died of pneumonia after twenty-six days. The second, David, lived only a few days longer and died of the same disease. Their third child, Donna, was born in 1963, healthy and free of any deformity. Six years later, Cathy was born with the lobster claw syndrome.

Parenthood did not improve Grady's violent personality. As he increased his intake of Seagram's 7 and Coca-Cola, he beat his wife and children more savagely and more often, particularly Donna. Then one night he threw Teresa and the children out. Teresa turned to a family friend, Harry Glenn Newman, the Midget Man or The World's Smallest Man, just over three feet tall. He and the Stiles family moved in with Newman's mother in Ohio.

Four months later, the bad news broke. Grady had filed for divorce. Teresa was not represented since she didn't know about the hearing. In the uncontested hearing the judge granted Lobster Boy custody of the children. Terrified, the children returned to Florida to live with Grady, who had married a woman they disliked. To the new wife was born another son, Grady III. He was a lobster boy with claws and truncated legs.

Teresa married Newman and on June 8, 1974, gave birth to Harry Glenn Newman. He was a normal child and despite his midget father would grow to be more than six feet tall and weigh 240 pounds. Unfortunately, he was mentally retarded.

Meanwhile, Grady had moved his family back to Pittsburgh. At Allegheny Junior High School, Donna, fifteen, met eighteen-year-old Jack Layne and both were instantly attracted to each other. Donna began missing time from school, so one of her teachers came to her home to discuss her attendance problems.

"This teacher, she really liked my claws," Grady boasted. "So we had sex right in the house and she just kept coming back and back and back because of this. Everyone I have sex with wants to have sex with my claws. They love it when I use my claws."

Donna ran away from the battered life she was living with her father and moved in with Jack's sister. Grady demanded Donna come home, threatening to hire detectives to find her so he could turn her over to juvenile authorities. More ominously, he threatened to kill Jack. To back up the threat, he bought a .32-caliber pistol.

Donna called her father back and told him she was pregnant and wanted to get married. Actually, she was still a virgin. After she returned home, Grady agreed on a wedding date of September 28, 1978.

The day before the wedding date, Donna and Jack went out to buy her wedding dress at Zayre's Department Store. Grady went to Harry's Bar and belted down twelve whiskey doubles before returning home. When Donna and Jack came back, they noticed his wheelchair was missing. Grady asked Jack to stay and talk with him while Donna went to find it.

While she was looking, Donna heard a bang, then another. She rushed back to the house.

"When I got there, Jack comes stumbling out of the house," said Donna. "He was holding his chest in the middle."

"He shot me," Jack said and collapsed in front of her.

"It didn't seem real," she said later. "I shook Jack. He didn't move. There was blood coming out of his mouth. And I looked up, and Dad was standing on his knees looking out the window, smiling at me. . . . I said, 'Why did you do this?'"

"Because I told you I would."

"You'll die for this, you son of a bitch."

"Don't give me that shit."

"I'll see you in your grave."

When police arrived, Grady was waiting for them. "Take me. I'm ready," he said.

Jack was dead on arrival at the hospital. Grady was charged with murder in the first degree. If convicted, he could, as Donna predicted, die in the electric chair. Grady needed a good attorney and he got one, Tony DeCello.

Lobster Boy's deformity created strong sympathy for him, and DeCello decided to play heavily on this. Among the character witnesses were the Bearded Lady, a carnival midget and Paul Fishbaugh, the Fat Man whose six hundred pounds made him too large to fit into the witness chair. He had to sit in the lotus position in front of the chair.

But the best witness was Lobster Boy himself. He had been a showman since he was seven years old. Now he gave the performance of his life. A sympathetic jury found him guilty only of voluntary manslaughter.

Incarceration of the handicapped man could prove difficult. A state penitentiary official wrote Judge Tom Harper that they didn't want him in the prison system because they'd have to put a guard with him all day to take care of him. For shooting Jack Layne in cold blood, all Grady Stiles got was fifteen years' probation and no restrictions on his right to move to another state if he wished.

Grady promptly left town, thus avoiding paying DeCello his fourteen thousand dollar fee. Instead he spent the money to assemble his own sideshow, ten acts organized as one show. He would become not only a star but also an impresario.

* * *

Grady Stiles divorced his second wife, Barbara, and moved back to Gibsonton. Meanwhile, Teresa was growing bored with Newman. He had become partially disabled after a serious fall. She and her family moved back to Florida, to Okeechobee. There two important things happened, one good, one bad. Donna married Joe Miles, whose family owned a restaurant. Teresa divorced her midget husband and moved in again with Lobster Boy. In 1989, they remarried and moved back to Gibsonton.

"I still love your dad," Teresa told Donna.

In many ways, Grady appeared to have changed for the better. Kinder and more cheerful, he kept his drinking under control at first. Then he began to drink again at home and at the favorite hangout of the Gibsonton carnys, Showtown USA on Tamiami Trail. With the drinking, the physical and verbal abuse returned.

In the spring of 1992, Stiles hit the road again for his forty-seventh year in show business. It would be his last. By this time, he had integrated most of his family into the show. His daughter Cathy and her husband ran the animal oddities exhibit, which included a two-headed raccoon. Donna and Joe

Miles ran the gorilla illusion in which Donna turned into a gorilla. Glenn, the Human Blockhead, continued to drive nails up his nose. Little Grady and Teresa filled in where needed. Grady Stiles, the Lobster Boy, of course remained the star.

The 1992 tour was rancorous, filled with squabbles and fights. During this tour Teresa began to steal heavily from the cash box. She was building up a fund. In July, Teresa for the first time told Cathy, "I want him dead." Cathy agreed.

That summer, Teresa asked one of the troupe, Marco Eno, if he would kill Grady for her. Eno thought it was a joke. In the fall, Teresa asked Glenn to find someone to murder Lobster Boy for fifteen hundred dollars.

Her son contacted Chris Wyant. Chris asked his friend Dennis Cowell to drive him to the adjoining town of Riverview to meet Glenn. Just seventeen, Chris had already amassed a juvenile record. He bragged that he had killed people in drive-by shootings and he was commonly known to deal in drugs. Dennis held back from the talk between Glenn and Chris, assuming it had to do with drugs. He was wrong. The subject was killing Grady Stiles for fifteen hundred dollars, three hundred of which was paid to Chris on the spot.

The hit man then proceeded to reward Cowell for his kindness in driving him to the meeting. He bought Dennis a pair of pants, a pair of tennis shoes, a shirt and a Raiders cap. Delighted with the gifts, Dennis had no inkling that he was being set up. Next, he would be asked to drive Chris to Apollo Beach, five miles farther south on U.S. 41. There, at the home of a friend, the hit man purchased a .32-caliber Colt automatic for $150. Street-smart Chris was persuasive enough to talk Dennis into signing the paperwork for the sale.

At eleven o'clock the night of November 29, Teresa and Glenn ducked out of their mobile home, leaving a drunken Lobster Boy watching a TV screen, with Little Grady asleep in one of the bedrooms. Shortly after eleven, Chris entered the trailer. He wore jeans, black Nikes, a black and white T-shirt, a black leather jacket and a Raiders cap turned backward. Since he knew the layout, he sneaked quickly into the living room.

"Get the fuck out of my house. Don't ever come around here again," yelled Grady, who then turned back to the television. From the kitchen hallway, Chris fired into the back of Grady's head. The first shot killed Lobster Boy.

* * *

The trio — Teresa, Chris and Glenn — went on trial in the summer of 1993. Teresa, who had once played the role of a woman being electrocuted, had no reason to fear a death sentence: The state had decided not to seek the electric chair for any of those charged.

The first trial was a short one. Detective Willette, who had done a highly efficient job of solving the murder, committed a blunder on the stand. Under questioning, he stated that Glenn Newman had failed a lie detector test, a fact that was inadmissible as evidence. Judge Barbara Fleischer was forced to declare a mistrial.

The second time, the three were tried separately. Chris Wyant faced the court first, in January 1994. After two days of testimony, the jury retired to ponder the fate of the killer, charged with murder in the first degree and conspiracy to commit murder in the first degree. The case was so strong the courtroom expected a quick first-degree murder verdict. But hour after hour the jury stayed out. From the jury room came the sounds of angry screaming. After seven hours, the jury gave its verdict: guilty of conspiracy in the first degree but guilty of murder only in the second degree. One or two of the jurors had held out for reduced charges and after a shouting match the others, tired of arguing, had agreed to reduced charges. An angry Judge Fleischer called on Prosecutor Ron Hanes to prepare arguments "to go above sentencing guidelines." The judge sentenced Wyant to twenty-seven years.

On July 11, 1994, Judge M. William Graybill gaveled the start of the trial that would form the centerpiece of Lobster Boy's sensational story. Newspaper, television and radio reporters flocked to the Hillsborough County Courthouse. Teresa's attorney, silver-haired, Harvard-educated Arnold Levine, was representing her pro bono, partly in recognition of her lack of funds, partly out of sympathy for her plight and partly because Lobster Boy was going to be a media event. Levine would use the battered-spouse defense, a defense never before tried in Florida in a murder-for-hire case.

Levine would have a tough sell. The question on the minds of many was simply: Why didn't she just leave? After all, Grady had no legs. He spent most of his time in a wheelchair.

Levine told the jury Lobster Boy beat Teresa and the children with his claws and butted them with his head after he had knocked them down. Teresa's attorney had another problem. Whereas Judge Fleischer permitted the battered-wife-syndrome argument in court, Judge Graybill was not so sure he should allow it. Furthermore, there was clearly friction in the courtroom between the judge, a southerner, and the Bostonian Levine.

On the stand, Teresa was led by Levine through a recital of lifetime abuse by men — from her stepfather to her first husband to Grady. Several times she broke down and cried on the stand. No longer a pretty showgirl, Teresa, some said, looked a good ten years older than fifty-six.

When little Grady, a Lobster Boy himself, took the stand, Levine showed a silent videotape of father and son wrestling. Grady Jr. had a headlock on Grady III. The boy told the court he couldn't breathe but his father would not let up even after little Grady asked him.

A week into the trial, Judge Graybill contracted a serious respiratory illness. He was rushed to the hospital and diagnosed with pneumonia. William Fuente became the third judge to hear the case. He was soon to encounter a new piece of evidence from an unlikely source — an author named Fred Rosen, who was writing a book about the case. Levine had given Rosen a copy of the wrestling tape with sound. Silent, the tape showed an act of brutality by Grady. With audio, it became just a scene of father and son playing around.

"From that moment on, I was no longer simply an observer of this bizarre trial," Rosen wrote in his book *Lobster Boy*. "I became an active participant."

Levine brought three expert witnesses to the stand, two psychiatrists and one clinical social worker. Their testimony depicted Teresa as a passive woman of low intelligence, subjected to abuse since childhood. Completely dominated by Grady, she was afraid to run away for fear that he would find and kill her or that he might kill her children.

"It was a kill or be killed situation," said Dr. Arturo Gonzalez, a dapper, Cuban-born psychiatrist.

Since he had established a connection between Grady's drinking and his brutality, Levine pushed hard to show that Lobster Boy had been drinking the day of his death. Teresa and Little Grady had already testified that he had been drinking at Showtown USA the morning of the murder. If a drunken Lobster Boy had struck Teresa on that fateful day, it would strengthen the case that she acted only to protect herself.

Prosecutor Sandra Spoto asked Chuck Osak, owner of Showtown, if he had served Lobster Boy a drink the morning of November 29.

"No, ma'am, I did not. That was a Sunday. We're not allowed to open till one P.M."

Things got even worse for the defense. Grady drank only Seagram's 7 and the club's tapes showed no such drink was served to anyone until 6:08 that evening. At that time, Lobster Boy was home eating dinner. Next, the prosecution trotted out the state's forensic toxicologist. He testified that the level of alcohol in Grady's blood was low at the time of his death. He had not been drinking heavily on the last day of his life.

Tuesday afternoon the case went to the jury. By six o'clock they had reached no verdict, so the judge sent them home. The next morning they struggled again. At 5:11 P.M., after eleven hours of deliberation, the jury announced it had reached a verdict on the guilt or innocence of Teresa Stiles.

"On the first count, we find the defendant guilty of manslaughter with a firearm. On the second count, conspiracy to commit murder in the first degree, we find the defendant guilty."

Outside the court, Cathy said: "It's bad to say because I am a Christian. I hope that Fred Rosen, Mr. Hanes and Sandra whatever-her-name-is get the beatings and the threats my family has."

Before Glenn Newman came to trial in August, Prosecutor Ron Hanes offered him a deal. If he pled guilty to the same charges his mother had been convicted of, he would receive the same sentence. His attorney, Peter Catania, knowing he couldn't win, advised him to take the offer. Teresa advised him to fight the charges. Once again, she had talked her simple-minded son, the Human Blockhead, into a huge blunder. On August 9, 1994, it took the jury only an hour and five minutes to find him guilty of first-degree murder and conspiracy.

On August 29, less than three weeks later, Teresa Stiles was sentenced to twelve years in prison followed by five years of probation. On October 14, Glenn got the bad news. He was sentenced to life in prison.

As a show business star, Grady Stiles Jr., the Lobster Boy, was buried in Thonotosassa, Florida, at The International Independent Showmen Garden of Memorials, the graveyard of carny performers.

THE GANG'S
ALL HERE

Gangs go back a few years in Florida. They are not all alike. The Ashley Gang gave a good-ol'-boys, down-home flavor to robbery and violence. A hometown gangster ran the game bolita in Tampa's Ybor City until the Mafia decided to take it over. In the turbulent '60s, motorcycle gangs like Fort Lauderdale's Outlaws roared across the highways on their Harleys.

CHAPTER 6

The Good Ol' Ashley Boys

A lawless clan terrorized
the southeast coast of Florida.

No one knows for sure when the Ashley Gang was born, but it's fairly clear when the legend started. And it's brutally clear when it ended for them — 10:45 the night of November 1, 1924, at a bloody Dixie Highway roadblock at Sebastian, Florida.

For a decade, Florida's version of the James Boys terrorized the southeast coast and the Bahamas. Bank robberies, train robberies, moonshining, hijacking, piracy, rumrunning, an occasional murder and no less than ten jailbreaks.

They were enemies of society and at the same time rural folk heroes, good old, down-home cracker boys, wild and free as a bunch of fish hawks.

John Ashley, the tough, drawling, one-eyed leader of the gang, was a sharpshooter by the time he was eleven. He practiced by firing at an empty beer bottle, positioned with its neck toward him. He would shoot through the neck and blow out the back without touching the rest of the bottle.

John even provided an improbable love story, improbable because his gun moll was not a beautiful, shapely bimbo but rather a big, coarse backwoods woman named Laura Upthegrove, also known as "Queen of the Everglades."

In the 1890s, the Ashleys had come to Pompano from the Fort Myers area. Papa Ashley worked on Henry Flagler's new railroad, then settled into various enterprises, among them distilling what some called the best moonshine in the county.

In December 1911, John, still in his early twenties, embarked on a life of serious crime. Just before Christmas, he sold Girtman Brothers, in Miami, eighty-four otter skins for twelve hundred dollars. Those skins, it turned out, belonged to Seminoles living in the Everglades. DeSoto Tiger, the chief's oldest son, was taking them to Miami for sale. When last seen, he had been

John Ashley, wearing an eye patch, bides his time in the Florida State Penitentiary, guarded by an unidentified prison official. (Fort Lauderdale Historical Society)

sharing his canoe with Ashley. On December 20, a search party found Tiger's body floating in a slough, just off the Miami River Canal. He had been shot in the back.

Alerted to the crime, Palm Beach County sheriff George Baker made quick use of newly installed telephone wires to call Miami. An hour later, he learned that Girtman Brothers had bought a load of otter skins from a "husky young fellah whose signature on the receipt was J. Ashley."

The sheriff got a tip that Ashley was holed up in a swamp camp near Hobe Sound. He sent two deputies after the killer. They crashed noisily through the thick palmetto bushes.

Suddenly, a cracker drawl stopped them:

"Hold it right there, boys. Now put down them rifles an' put up your hands — an' then step in here. Move real easy."

They eased into a clearing and saw John and his brother Bob, brewing coffee in a tin can over a small fire.

"I'm gonna let you go," John said, "'cause I want you to deliver a message. Tell Baker I'm waitin' out here for him to come after me, an' he's not to send any more chicken-hearted deputies to do his dirty work. Now git."

Many think this was the start of the Ashley legend. In a poor, frontier land where the law was less than revered, the audacity and style of John Ashley brought chuckles of approval from struggling trappers, hunters, fishermen and dirt farmers.

More fame came to John when his picture appeared in post offices. Circulars described him as "five-ten or five-eleven, about 180 pounds, husky build. Dark eyes, dark brown hair and a ruddy complexion, usually sunburned."

Soon the Ashleys began to receive credit, or blame, for almost any new crimes. John, however, was not in a position to enjoy his new-found fame. For him the heat was on. He found it prudent to leave southeast Florida for a while.

After two years, John was tired of running. He sent word to Sheriff Baker that he would give himself up and stand trial. In a West Palm Beach courtroom packed with Ashley's friends and relatives, his trial began in the summer of 1914. He was confident no local jury would find him guilty. What he hadn't counted on was how strongly the locals felt about him. You were either a friend of John Ashley's or you were scared to death of him. Unable to impanel a jury, the state called for a change of venue. That meant moving the trial to unknown, unfriendly Miami. The Ashley contingent exploded in fury. Oblivious to the rain, the clan assembled outside the courtroom to plan their next move.

As the sheriff's son, Bob, escorted John toward the jail, Joe Ashley hand-ed his son a plate of home-cooked food. Baker took it and walked through the rain with his prisoner. At the jail door, he handed the plate to his pris-oner and said: "Here, John, hold this while I unlock the door."

The jailer turned his back for a moment, then heard the sound of the plate hitting the ground. He looked around to see John disappearing over a ten-foot chicken-wire fence.

Within an hour, a six-man posse was tracking him. He proved much too elusive, vanishing into the Everglades.

Hiding out in the Glades, John became a bitter man, hounded again by posses. At this time, the Ashleys emerged as a gang, consisting at first of John as leader; his father, Joe; and three tough, mean brothers, Ed, Frank and Bob. Brother Bill was the "straight" Ashley. The only time he ever served was for the relatively genteel crime of moonshining.

A newcomer from Chicago, the vicious Kid Lowe, showed the gang the benefits of his specialty — robbing banks. Their first target in February 1915 was the bank in Stuart. With a haul of only forty-five hundred dollars, it proved to be a clumsy caper, particularly in the getaway department.

"All right, which one of you can drive an automobile?" Lowe asked the bank customers. "It's either drive us out of here or get shot."

One promptly agreed to drive. As they left, four men fired after them. Lowe, in the front seat, turned and shot back at their pursuers. One of his bullets struck the rear window frame and ricocheted into John's left eye.

Three hours later, a sheriff's posse captured John Ashley, lying on a bloodstained bed of pine needles, too overwhelmed by pain to resist further. He was sent to Miami to stand trial for the murder of DeSoto Tiger.

On June 2, 1915, Bob, reputed to be the meanest of the Ashleys, appeared at the jail and blasted jailer W.C. Hendrickson away with two rifle shots. When Mrs. Hendrickson grabbed a shotgun, Bob fled. In the shootout that followed, he killed Miami policeman Bob Riblett, but not before Riblett had shot him in the abdomen. Sheriff Dan Hardie carried the dying Bob Ashley to the hospital.

"Come on, boy, you're going soon," said Hardie. "Tell us the whole story."

"Go to hell," answered Bob. He rolled over to the wall and died an hour later.

By morning, a clamor rose to bring John to trial. Ashley's lawyer felt the time had come for a deal: Drop the murder charge and John will go quietly to West Palm Beach to stand trial for the Stuart bank robbery. The state accepted and with little fuss he was found guilty and sentenced to seventeen years in the state penitentiary at Raiford. There he was fitted with a glass eye.

Sixteen months later, he walked away from a road gang. In 1921, he was arrested again for transporting a load of moonshine. Back he went to Raiford.

During a Sunday visit from his father, he learned that brothers Frank and Ed were running bootleg whiskey from West End on Grand Bahama Island. The gang had also raided government warehouses on Bimini, stealing whiskey and cash, then had branched out to highjack loads from other rumrunners.

On a later visit, his father gave him a stunning piece of news. Frank and Ed had failed to return from a run to West End. Were they lost during a storm, or wiped out by rumrunners they had robbed? Bo Stokes and his gang were suspected. Soon, they vanished, too.

Three of the five Ashley brothers had now been killed, but the gang lost none of its toughness. In May 1922, the gang hit the Stuart bank again, this time netting $8,113.14. One of the new gang members was Hanford Mobley, a seventeen-year-old who idolized his Uncle John.

By now, Bob Baker had replaced his father as sheriff. He was determined to break up the gang. Through the improved telephone system, he alerted police all over the state and promptly captured three of the bank robbers, including young Mobley.

Three of the gang, including John, escaped from Raiford. The gang now had its leader back. They headed for new camps in the swamps southwest of Stuart, near Gomez, where the Ashley family had lived for several years.

John sent for Laura Upthegrove. He had first met her near Gomez, just across the Intracoastal Waterway at Peck's Lake, a mangrove wilderness where he had set up a camp while running booze from Bimini. Laura's half-brother, Joe Tracy, was a member of the gang.

What did John see in this Amazon, who swaggered and snarled her way through life with a .38 revolver strapped to her hip? Maybe he was just plain hard up after his time in prison. What Laura lacked in physical appeal she made up for in other useful skills, such as the ability to size up a bank and an alertness to possible traps. Unfortunately, she was also a heavy drinker of moonshine and given at times to wild, irrational rages.

John led the gang on a daring train robbery. Five masked men boarded the Florida East Coast train near Fort Pierce, lifting the passengers' wallets. A gallant John walked through, waving two thirty-eights and calling out: "You ladies keep your pocketbooks. We're just robbin' the menfolks."

Pressure was building on every sheriff's office from Sebastian to Miami.

South Florida was glorying in a land boom and wild frontier gangs were hardly good for business. And Sheriff Bob Baker, hampered now by the loss of a leg due to a gunshot wound, was even more determined to get the Ashleys.

In January 1924, Baker got a tip that the gang was hiding out in a swamp just west of Stuart. The night of January 9, Baker closed in on the gang with seven heavily armed men. Pestered by mosquitoes, the men waited for daylight.

At dawn, the sheriff and three men crawled closer to the camp. Ashley's mongrel dog, Old Bob, spotted them and woke up the gang. Deputy Fred Baker, no relation to the sheriff, fired at John and missed. Heavy gunfire exploded from both sectors.

Then came a pause in the shooting. Deputy Baker pushed aside a palmetto frond for a better look. A rifle sounded and the deputy dropped dead, a bullet through his head.

Furious at the killing of his deputy, the sheriff ordered a five-minute fusillade, then signaled for his men to storm the camp. They found it a disaster area, its tents torn to shreds by bullets and buckshot.

John and most of his gang were gone. The sheriff found three casualties: the dog, Old Bob; John's father, Joe Ashley, dead of a bullet wound through the head; and a screaming Laura. She shrieked obscenities at the deputies. She had reason to be upset. She had been shot in the rear end with shotgun pellets.

The gunfire drew a crowd. Searching the camp, they soon found plenty of Old Ashley moonshine whiskey. Boiling with anger at the shooting of Deputy Baker, the drunken mob drove Ma Ashley out of her home and burned it to the ground. Next, they burned down the Mobley home, then torched a country store whose owner sometimes helped Old Joe make moonshine.

John had been shot in the hip during the raid, but he was still a dangerous man. Several posses sighted him, but hesitated to rush him. Once, he suddenly appeared on a path, dropped to one knee, aimed his rifle at an approaching posse and waited. As soon as they realized who he was, the searchers backed away.

In March, Ashley left the state. By August, he was homesick. In late summer, he appeared again at Gomez. By September 12, the gang was ready for what would prove to be their last bank job.

In West Palm Beach, Joe Tracy engaged a taxi driven by a young black, Wesley Powell. Near Deerfield, three men with guns — John Ashley, Shorty Lynn and Clarence Middleton — suddenly stepped in front of the cab. They

The Ashley Gang (Sun-Sentinel)

tied Powell to a tree; then John gave him a strange, taunting message:

"We're aiming to rob the bank at Pompano, boy, an' Ah want you to take a good look so you kin tell Bob Baker exactly what we look like." He paused to drop a rifle bullet in Powell's pocket, then continued: "You give that to sheriff Bob and tell him I got another one just like it waiting for him — if he's man enough to come and get it."

They reached the Pompano bank just before closing time. Shorty Lynn and Clarence Middleton aimed their pistols at cashier C. H. Cates and teller T. H. Myers.

Still limping from his hip wound, John supervised the scooping up of five thousand dollars in cash and eighteen thousand dollars in securities. Then, with Tracy at the wheel of the getaway cab, Ashley called back: "This time we got it all, goddamn it."

They abandoned the cab near the Hillsboro Canal and vanished. Apparently, they had a powerboat waiting to take them up the canal all the way to Lake Okeechobee. Too many posses had made their old Everglades camps too dangerous. At the lake, they hid out in an abandoned two-story building. Two World War I machine guns were positioned in the upstairs windows.

Laura joined them there, as did Hanford Mobley, who came home to help his uncle after he read about the swamp ambush in a San Francisco newspaper.

Busy with his re-election campaign, Sheriff Baker finally got the break he had been seeking. On November 1, 1924, an informant told Deputy Elmer Padgett the gang would be passing through Fort Pierce, driving north on Dixie Highway that evening.

Padgett and two other deputies drove to Fort Pierce to meet with J.R. Merritt, the St. Lucie County sheriff. Merritt was a caricature of a sheriff, a heavy-set, tobacco-chewing man who wore two pistols and a pair of handcuffs on his gunbelt and a wide-brimmed Stetson on his head. Some considered him worse than the Ashleys.

Merritt decided the Dixie Highway bridge over Sebastian Creek, twenty miles north of Fort Pierce, was the place to stop them. The sheriff and five deputies, three from Palm Beach County, set up the roadblock on a Saturday evening.

Why was Sheriff Bob Baker not with them? Officially, the claim was the pressure of the upcoming election. Others thought that in reality the sheriff at the moment of confrontation was simply scared to death of Ashley.

Padgett was not terrified. Friends for years, he and John Ashley had turned against each other. Each man had sworn to kill the other on sight.

Late that Saturday afternoon, a black T-model Ford touring car drove into a gas station. John Rhea, pumping gas, recognized John in the back seat. Next, Ashley went to a haberdashery store and bought a pair of khaki pants. The owner knew the outlaw's size from memory. John then limped to a barber shop for the trim that would last him the rest of his life.

A half hour later, the gang turned up at Church's pool hall. The other customers left immediately. The Ashley gang shot pool for two hours. Debonair as always, they left generous tips, then drove off toward Sebastian and a date with a deadly roadblock.

At Sebastian, the sheriff had stretched a chain across the bridge and had hung a red lantern on it. At 8 P.M., a telephone message told them Ashley had left Fort Pierce. Swatting mosquitoes, the lawmen waited and waited at the roadblock.

At 10:45, the black touring car finally appeared. It drove up to the chain and stopped.

Stepping out of the darkness, four lawmen armed with sawed-off shotguns surrounded the car. Merritt called out: "All right, Ashley, don't move, don't reach for your guns and don't say a word. Just get out with your hands held high — and quick."

Chief Deputy Wiggins flung open the front door and pulled the teenage Mobley into the road. The deputies opened the other doors. John Ashley climbed out, followed by Lynn and Middleton.

They stood there in the glare of the car's headlights, each covered by a shotgun. Merritt told his men to search the gang while he went back for handcuffs.

"How about a cigarette?" asked Ashley. A deputy shook his head.

Merritt reached his car, opened it, grabbed the cuffs — then slammed the door.

Suddenly, a deafening blast of gunfire shattered the silence. John Ashley and his gang lay dead in the mud. The gang's Ford became its hearse as the bodies were taken to Will Fee's combination funeral parlor and hardware store in Fort Pierce.

"We've got the Ashleys here," shouted Deputy Wiggins.

"Dead or alive?" asked a cautious undertaker from an upstairs window.

"Dead as hell."

By noon, the survivors of the Ashley clan — Ma Ashley, brother Bill, a couple of Mobleys and the Queen of the Everglades — had all arrived at the funeral parlor. Laura was denied admittance. "The bodies have been stripped and you're not John's wife," she was told. She started screaming: "I've seen John Ashley naked as a jaybird, you bastard, so it don't make much difference now." The undertaker let her in.

Ma Ashley wanted a Christian burial for her son. Since none of the clan stood well with the church, she wired Major John Bourterse of the Salvation Army in Miami, asking him to conduct the service.

On Tuesday, a day when the nation was electing Calvin Coolidge president and re-electing Bob Baker sheriff, John Ashley was laid to rest in a simple grave on the family's Gomez property. Armed policemen stood guard as Major Bourterse sent him on his way.

Sheriff Baker had boasted that someday he would wear John's glass eye on his watch chain. Padgett had scooped the eye out at Sebastian and had given it to Baker.

Laura's threat to Baker was a chilling one: "If you don't put that eye back again, I'll crawl through hell on my hands and knees to kill you."

The eye was returned in time for burial. Or so the legend goes.

So much about the Ashleys is shrouded in confusion, conflicting stories and tall tales. Some say they left the car so meekly because they were drunk on moonshine. But that leaves the question: How did they really die?

The sheriff said the outlaws reached for their six-shooters, an interesting claim since it assumes they had not been searched as he ordered. Three different deputies claimed credit for killing Ashley.

The most intriguing story asserts they were handcuffed, then shot. A passing motorist said he saw the four of them in handcuffs, then read in the Sunday paper that they had all been shot. Other observers said they saw the marks of handcuffs on the wrists of the dead men.

When the inquest was held, one day after the burial, a young attorney, Alto Adams, who would later become the chief justice of the Florida Supreme Court, represented the Ashley family. In light of these rumors, he asked that "the bodies be exhumed by court order so that they can be examined again." The judge conducting the inquest denied the request.

The short years that remained were not good to Laura. She was in and out of jail, charged with drunkenness, gambling and bootlegging. One night during a violent argument with a drunk she had shortchanged, she went into a frenzy, then drank a bottle of Lysol and fell to the floor, writhing in agony.

The man summoned Laura's mother. "Hadn't we ought to get a doctor?" he asked.

Laura's mother answered sadly: "No, let her die. She's better off this way."

CHAPTER 7

Death of an Elder Statesman

*Dapper Charlie Wall was king of the
Tampa underworld for thirty years.*

Lois, a secretary at Tampa police headquarters, answered the phone.

"Do you all have any reports of a prominent Tampan being murdered?" asked the *Tampa Tribune* police reporter. He was checking a rumor that a locally famous gambling overlord had been murdered.

"Who do you mean, like Charlie Wall?"

The reporter was stunned.

"Only kidding," said Lois. "It was just the first name that popped into my mind."

But why not Charlie Wall? Three times in the past, rival gangsters had tried to wipe out the elder statesman of the Tampa underworld.

He even testified about a 1938 attempt on his life before the U.S. Senate Special Committee to Investigate Crime in Interstate Commerce, chaired by Tennessee Senator Estes Kefauver, famed for his coonskin hat. Wall survived the attack, although buckshot from a shotgun peppered him, or as he told the senators, "kind of, as they say, glimpsed me."

Within five minutes, word came in to the police station. No more "glimpsing" for Charlie. This try, the fourth, had succeeded.

On April 20, 1955, his wife, Audrey, had returned to their Ybor City home from a week's visit with her sister in nearby Clermont. She had found her husband's battered, blood-soaked body lying on the floor of his bedroom. He was wearing a white nightshirt, drenched in so much blood it wasn't even clear what the precise cause of death had been.

The coroner's autopsy report spelled it out. Multiple blows to the head, probably with a blackjack, nine deep cuts around the left temple and a gash in his throat, five-and-a-half inches long and "very deep." The cuts had killed him.

His pockets were empty except for small change, even though he was known to carry large amounts of cash on his person.

On his night table lay his fully loaded .44-caliber revolver. On another table only a few feet from the bloody body lay a book he had apparently been reading — *Crime in America*, by Senator Kefauver. The book contained the "glimpsing" story.

* * *

State Attorney James M. "Red" McEwen, the Tampa police and the Hillsborough County Sheriff's Office faced what is always one of the toughest mysteries to solve — a gangland killing. Nobody wants to talk.

For over half a century, Wall had been a major player on the Florida crime scene. He had a lot of enemies, and two of them were Santo Trafficante, the Elder and the Younger, each destined to carry the mantle of Gulf Coast Godfather. The Mafia wanted no Anglos on its turf, even if the Anglo was seventy-five and living in semiretirement.

Charlie Wall was more, however, than just a gambling overlord. He was actually an establishment gangster. A descendant of a prominent Florida family, he was also related to other prominent Tampa clans, among them the Lykeses, cattle barons and shipping magnates; and the McKays, pioneer shippers, financiers and newspaper publishers. Among the pallbearers at his funeral at St. Mary's Episcopal Church were a Lykes and a McKay. A large crowd gathered to pay its respects, a bizarre blending of Tampa lowlifes and Tampa respectables. Drawing on his connections in both those worlds, Wall had became the virtual political boss of Tampa, called by one crusading editor "the most wicked city in the United States."

Right from the start, police faced a formidable puzzle. How did the killer or killers get into Wall's home? There was no sign of a forced entry. His eight-room bungalow on 17th Avenue was protected at the side and rear yard by a six-foot-high brown board fence and in the front by a brick fence topped with iron spikes. His garage was connected to the house by a closed tunnel with reinforced sides. A large Doberman pinscher roamed the back yard.

The conclusion from a police report: "Apparently he either was friendly with the killer or the assailant surprised him while he was preparing for bed."

The night he was killed, Monday, April 18, Charlie Wall had gone to one of his favorite watering holes, the Turf Bar and Lounge, then to Nick Scaglione's new Dream Bar. Scaglione, himself a reputed member of the Tampa gambling fraternity, told police Wall had been drinking too much. He drove him home that night and waited, he said, until the old man entered his home a little before 8 P.M.

Joe Diez telephoned Wall a little after eight. Charlie said nothing about anyone being in the house with him. Diez, recently arrested on a moonshine charge, had been his bodyguard/driver on one of the previous attempts to kill him. Diez said Wall was "quite high."

Police checked out Audrey Wall to see if she might have been involved in any way in her husband's violent death. They cleared her early in the probe. Charlie did not leave behind a vast fortune. His estate was valued at just $7,261.15. Audrey was the gambler's second wife. His first had divorced him in 1928, charging cruelty. He was, she said, guilty of "a constant abuse and staying out at night and things of that kind."

A baffled Red McEwen summed it up: "It looks like the killer had more on his mind than just killing him. I am sure that he wanted to let it be known that the killer didn't like him."

* * *

Charlie Wall was born in 1880 into one of Tampa's pioneer families. His father was the distinguished doctor John P. Wall, who had directed the Confederate hospitals in Richmond during the Civil War. He later gained international recognition for his pioneering yellow fever studies.

In 1885, when Tampa was a city of just three thousand, Dr. Wall was named to head the newly formed Board of Trade. One of the board's major achievements was to bring Florida's cigar industry from Key West to Tampa.

Thus was born the picturesque Cuban community known as Ybor City. It would prove to be a significant location in the career path Charlie would follow.

When Charlie was thirteen, his mother died. Two years later, his father, speaking at a medical conference in Gainesville, died suddenly. Charlie was left in the care of a stepmother whom he despised. Her answer to disciplinary problems was the whip. The young orphan responded by sleeping under the house and hanging out in pool halls. Next, Charlie got a job in a gambling casino, where he quickly demonstrated an unusual talent for calculating the odds.

Meanwhile, life at home became intolerable. At seventeen, he shot his stepmother with a .22-caliber rifle. He was sent to a juvenile detention home.

His uncle by marriage, Dr. Howell T. Lykes, the wealthy founder of what would eventually become one of Florida's biggest business empires, stepped in then and tried to rescue him from a dreadful home life. He sent him to the Bingham School in North Carolina. Charlie didn't last long. He was promptly caught in a whorehouse. The headmaster called him a "corruptive influence" and expelled him.

Back in Tampa, the excitement of the illegal world of gambling called to him again. He became a courier, then a bookie. As he learned the game, he saw a huge opportunity. Ybor City, center of Tampa's thriving cigar industry, was populated mostly by Cubans who loved a gambling game called bolita, a Spanish word meaning "little ball."

By 1900, bolita had become the single largest illegal money-making enterprise in Tampa's corrupt history. Each night, crowds of mostly Cuban gamblers and curious spectators gathered at one of the lavishly decorated sporting parlors to watch the throwing of the "little ball." One hundred ivory balls with bold black numbers were displayed on a large table, then packed in a velvet sack which was tightly tied. The bag was thrown from person to person until a designated catcher grabbed it and isolated one ball in his fist. The game's operator then tied a string around the isolated ball. When he cut the sack just above the string, the winning ball dropped into his hand.

Players picked their numbers from "dream books," which related dreams to lucky numbers. With a nickel investment, a bolita devotee could win four dollars, a payoff of eighty to one. The house and the sellers shared a twenty percent margin of profit.

In the wide-open world of Tampa at the turn of the century, few cared that the game was against the law. What concerned the city's power structure was the export of the game's profits to Cuba.

Charlie Wall was the answer, a brilliant, unscrupulous man with his feet planted firmly in both worlds. He knew gambling and he came from the right people. It didn't matter that he was the black sheep of his family. What mattered was that the Anglos, not the Cubans, control bolita in Tampa.

The bolita king chose to live in his new kingdom, building his home in Ybor City. It was an exotic enclave, spiced with the aromas of tobacco, *café con leche* and Cuban cooking from such Tampa institutions as the Columbia Restaurant.

Charlie represented his domain with style. He was an impressive figure, standing six-foot-two, always dressed impeccably in fashionable straw hats and expensive white linen suits which earned him the name "the White Shadow." He was soft-spoken and polite, a smoothie. He was also deadly. Six people who challenged his leadership were murdered.

Dr. Ferdie Pacheco, TV's "Fight Doctor," famed for his commentaries on boxing, who grew up in Ybor City, wrote about him in his memoir, *Ybor City Chronicles*: "For years I had heard stories about the legendary Charlie Wall, who lived in my neighborhood when I was a child living in my grand-

father's house on Columbus Drive. Occasionally, I would see him driving
his big Cadillac, and he would always wave back at us sitting on the stoop.
Sometimes a small man drove him. Everyone knew that was his bodyguard,
who was named Baby. Charlie never sat in the back seat but always next to
Baby in the front seat. In the coffeehouses, the life of Charlie Wall was told
and retold many times."

Wall knew how to play the game. Bribery bought police protection, and
ballot-box stuffing controlled elections. Philanthropic acts softened possible criticism. He donated large sums of money to churches. During the cig-
arworkers strike of 1910, he provided food for nine hundred cigarmakers
and their families. They survived to buy many a bolita number.

In the Roaring Twenties, Tampa's Italian gangsters made big money from
illegal booze. With the clout that money brings, they began seeking new
fields for expansion. Charlie Wall was in the way.

On June 9, 1930, assailants in a car speeding by Wall's home fired at him
as he was standing in front of his garage. He was hit in the left shoulder.
Still, he was quick enough to fire off three shots at his attackers.

His injury was slight, but the king had been challenged. The attack signaled the start of a long and bloody war between the strictly local mobsters
and the new breed of out-of-town Mafia gangsters, patient and loaded with
money far beyond Charlie Wall's hometown resources.

In 1931, Wall, who had never spent a day behind bars, was arrested on a
narcotics charge and sentenced to two years in jail. The conviction was
overturned, but his arrest was one more proof that he was no longer invul-
nerable.

Gangland killings followed. Then in 1938, Wall's partner, Tito Rubio,
was gunned down in front of Charlie's newest Ybor City gambling house,
El Dorado. A year later, a panel truck pulled in front of Wall's car only a
block from his house. Charlie ducked under the dashboard and stepped on
the accelerator. He got away, but not before one of the six loads of buckshot
fired at him nicked him in his right shoulder.

By that time, Charlie Wall saw that the time had come to cut his losses.
He loosened his grip on Tampa gambling and affiliated with operations on
the east coast of Florida: the Royal Palm Club and the 86 Club in Miami,
The Farm in Hallandale and the S and G Syndicate on Miami Beach.

Wall's political base was tottering, too. In the 1943 elections, a reform
candidate, Curtis Hixon, was elected mayor, soundly defeating Charlie's
heavily favored candidate. Salvatore "Red" Italiano, a power in the Italian
syndicate, delivered a sizable bloc of votes plus fifty thousand dollars in
cash to the Hixon campaign. Soon after the election, raids began on Wall's
gambling houses.

He kept his home on 17th Avenue, however, and continued to operate in Tampa — but on a diminished scale. In 1944, when he was visiting his hometown, a Buick pulled up in front of his car. Shooters broke the Buick's rear window and aimed straight at Charlie. His bodyguard, Baby, threw the car in reverse and backed up at high speed, maneuvering desperately and adroitly through heavy Nebraska Avenue traffic. The talk of Tampa bars and coffeehouses, Baby's feat achieved the status of legend.

That same year, Charlie was hospitalized with gunshot wounds to his body. An unidentified assailant had fired a shotgun blast at him in front of his home.

Sixty-five years old now, Charlie Wall continued to lower his profile. By the time the Kefauver Crime Committee reached Tampa in 1951, Charlie Wall was presenting himself more as a consultant to the industry than an active player. In *Crime in America*, Senator Kefauver described him: "One of the purely local racketeers whom the committee interrogated was Charles M. Wall, a nonchalant, almost whimsical seventy-one-year-old gambler." Senator Lester Hunt, from Wyoming, called him "the elder statesman of the Tampa underworld."

Santo Trafficante Sr., Tampa's Mafia Godfather, and Santo Jr., the heir apparent, declined to testify, invoking their Fifth Amendment rights against self-incrimination. Another Trafficante man the committee really wanted to interview was nowhere to be found. Red Italiano, Italian-born ex-convict, had left town. The hearings did, however, establish a comfortable working relationship between Italiano and the Hillsborough County sheriff, Hugh Culbreath, known in Cuban bolita circles as Cabeza de Melon — Melon Head.

By the 1950s, Charlie's star had dropped low in the sky, almost totally eclipsed by the rise of the Santo Trafficante crime family. They were powerful not only along the Gulf coast as far west as Alabama but also in Cuba. In Havana, they owned all or part of five casinos and hotels.

In January 1953, Santo Trafficante Jr. was walking alone to his car. From a passing car, two shotgun blasts were fired at the future head of the family. Pellets struck his arm, but his wounds were slight. But apparently they were not forgotten.

Santo Trafficante the Elder died of cancer in August 1954. His son, thirty-nine, took over the leadership of a powerful Mafia family. In less than a year, Charlie Wall, seventy-five, was dead. After his assassination, two major bolita bankers for the Trafficantes boarded a train for New York and never returned to Tampa. They were Fano Ferraro and Red Italiano, wrote the "mob lawyer," Frank Ragano, years later.

Once, in 1938, Charlie Wall told a Tampa grand jury, "On the principle that the devil takes care of his own, I think I will be all right." By 1955 the devil had acquired newer, younger and more powerful friends.

CHAPTER 8

Susie Cream Cheese

---

*Susan Bacon's fling with Outlaw motor
bikers ended in death.*

Pretty, blonde Susan Bacon opened the wrong door. She should have stayed in her own affluent, safe, orderly domain. Susan moved easily within the world of rising young businessmen, stockbrokers and investment bankers, people on the way up, like Wayne Huizenga, the man who would one day bring major league baseball to Florida. Among her friends were the mayor of Fort Lauderdale and the sheriff of Broward County. Her people were life's winners.

A British subject, she had been educated in Jamaica, Switzerland and London. She spoke three languages, but one she couldn't grasp was the lingo of the motorcycle gangs. Worse yet, she didn't know their code. Maybe she didn't even care. They lived in a rough, dirty world on the other side of a door she dared to open.

All over America, motorcycle gangs began to spring up after World War II. Defiantly, they named themselves Hell's Angels, Pagans, Sons of Satan, Coffin Snatchers, Warlocks and Iron Horsemen. The biggest, most powerful and most dangerous gang was the Outlaws. At one time, its Broward chapter alone boasted almost two hundred members. The Outlaws knew only too well the code of the world around them. They simply didn't like it. The biker gangs called themselves "one-percenters," at odds with ninety-nine percent of society and proud of it.

Susan Bacon had little inkling of how brutal their world really was. She did not know or care that an "old lady," as the Outlaws called the women they used, never sassed a member, never said "no" to their sexual advances, and never, never slapped a biker in the presence of his fellow gang members. She did not even know what tribal taboos she had broken and most certainly did not know the terrible penalty she would pay as a December sun cast its first light over the Everglades.

*   *   *

About three o'clock in the afternoon of December 28, 1970, three young men, not gang members, were riding motorcycles in Markham Park, a new county recreation area in the Glades, far west of the settled areas of Broward County. They stopped suddenly when they saw a young blonde lying on her back on coral rock. Drenched in blood, she had been dead for several hours.

The autopsy revealed that one bullet from a shotgun had blasted away much of her right shoulder. The other, from a pistol, penetrated her heart and killed her. She had not been sexually assaulted. The alcohol level in her blood indicated she was intoxicated at the time of her death. A sheriff's detective squad headed by Sergeant Carl Carruthers found few clues at the crime scene. One that caught their eye was a small, torn piece of yesterday's *Fort Lauderdale News* lying beside her body. Somehow it seemed out of place.

Who was she? She was well-dressed in a black turtleneck blouse that zipped up the back, a gray miniskirt, pantyhose and black shoes. Fingerprints brought the answer. She had no record, but she had undergone a fingerprint check when she applied for a job as a waitress at the Moonraker, a ritzy restaurant on Fort Lauderdale's Intracoastal Waterway.

The young woman was identified as Susan Gail Bacon, thirty-one, the daughter of Mr. and Mrs. S. Charles Bacon, who lived in the posh Harbor Beach area. Her father, a former Shell Oil executive, was president of Plantation Builders. Among the family's friends were Edmund Burry, the mayor, and Ed Stack, the sheriff who would be in charge of the investigation. Now the pressure to solve the murder accelerated.

"You usually know within the first forty-eight hours whether or not you're going to solve a murder," said Sergeant Edward Werder.

Within those forty-eight hours, the sheriff's five-man homicide team assembled information to trace her last hours. Her purse was found on Florida's Turnpike, near Pompano Beach. Her green Mustang was located on the Ocean National Bank parking lot on Fort Lauderdale Beach. Susan had spent her last night bar-hopping on the beach, from the Parrot Lounge to the Button to the Sandbox Bar. At the Sandbox, she had been shooting pool with Outlaws. Then nothing more until the discovery of her body the following day.

One other piece of information tied her to the Outlaws. Shortly before

Christmas, she had been beaten by someone at the Crossroads, a country and western music bar at State Road 84 and U.S. 441. The Crossroads was an occasional hangout of the bikers.

A telephone tip broke the case open. At a parking lot in a northeast Fort Lauderdale warehouse district, the detectives found an abandoned white two-door 1965 Chevrolet Impala with an Ohio license plate. Inside the car they found a newspaper with a piece torn out of it. It matched exactly the paper found beside Susan's body.

Ohio police gave them a quick answer on the car's owner. Rudolph Lunsford, of Brookville, Ohio, had reported the car missing after a trip to Fort Lauderdale. Sergeant Werder was on the next plane to Ohio. Not far from Dayton, Brookville had a police force of only five men, apparently enough for the little town of roughly four thousand. Very little violent crime surfaced in Brookville in those days. "Last year we had a robbery, but we think it was a false report," the chief told Werder.

Lunsford told Werder he and a friend, Larry "Shotgun" Shockey, twenty-one, had gone to Fort Lauderdale for the Christmas holidays. From Lunsford, Werder gleaned small scraps of information, just enough to help loosen up Shockey, who came in to talk to the sergeant the night of January 9, 1971.

Shockey told the sergeant he and Lunsford belonged to an Ohio motorcycle gang, the Legions of Hell. The name was ferocious; the members were not. When they went to Florida, they sought out the Outlaws. They soon found themselves playing with the big boys. A newspaper reporter called Shockey "a big country boy who got in over his head with people who were too tough for him to handle."

The shy, soft-spoken Shockey admitted he and Lunsford had gone to the Sandbox, even admitted he knew a young blonde the Outlaws called "Susie Cream Cheese." He dropped a few names: Sleazy, Striker T., Mediator, Sly Willie, Grubby, Roadrunner and Blue, the Outlaws' enforcer. Werder kept him talking into a tape recorder most of the night.

"It's only right," said Shockey. "I must live with my conscience."

By 4 A.M., the sergeant had the story line of what had happened that terrible night in the Everglades. But what he had was still a far cry from a case that would hold up in court. First, he needed a typed copy of the confession to convince a judge to extradite Shockey and Lunsford to Florida. The Brookville police force was too small to afford a secretary. The chief found a woman who agreed to spend her Sunday typing the interview, an exhausting twelve-hour process.

Next, Werder needed positive identifications. The sheriff's office sent pictures of the Outlaws by airline to Dayton. A courier went to the airport and brought back photos for Shockey. He identified Susie; Grubby, who was Ed Summers; and Blue, whose name was James Starrett.

The day Shockey and Lunsford arrived in Fort Lauderdale, sheriff's officers arrested Starrett and Summers near the county courthouse. Werder figured they were on the way to talk to the two Ohioans, partly to shut them up and partly to learn how much they had already given away to the police. One thing was sure, said Werder. Starrett, as tough as they come, gave away nothing.

* * *

To understand what happened the night of December 27-28, police delved deeply into the background of Susan Bacon. She was born in Bogota, Colombia, the daughter of an English Shell Oil executive. British by birth and choice, she spoke with an English accent and was proud to be a subject of the Queen. After her family moved to Fort Lauderdale, she made good use of her linguistic skills at the Goodbody and Co. brokerage firm. At Goodbody she made friends among the city's most influential and prominent citizens.

She dated stockbrokers and businessmen before developing a more serious relationship with a rising young executive, the president and founder of Southern Sanitation, Inc. His name was Wayne Huizenga. After the affair broke up, Susan went into what some called a deep depression. She moved to Jacksonville, where she worked for a brokerage firm. Then she suffered what in those days was discreetly called "a nervous breakdown." She came back then to Fort Lauderdale in June 1970 and lived with her parents in their beachside apartment.

For a while, she moved restlessly from job to job, working briefly as a waitress at the Moonraker (now Yesterdays), as a secretary at Le Club International and later at a brokerage firm in Pompano Beach. Then she settled in with a compatible job as a rental agent for Pershing Automobile Leasing. She worked the Port Everglades area, where her linguistic skills could be employed in talking with new arrivals from cruise ships. Sometime just before Christmas, she began to make occasional visits to the Sandbox, a small Fort Lauderdale Beach bar.

"Susan Bacon?" said one of the barmaids. "Sure, I remember her. She used to come in here in the middle of the day, order a beer and sit there reading a book. She always had a book with her — big, thick novels. That's why I remember her. She was the only person I've ever seen who brought a book to read in a bar."

If she'd stayed with her novels, the story of her life surely would have had a happier ending. But the Sandbox was where she opened the door to the world of the Outlaws.

Susan Bacon spent Christmas Eve at a party she had helped organize for 150 children from the Migrant Mission in Pompano Beach. Four days later, on the last Sunday of her life, she was back in Pompano, but this time she was playing with the big boys, boys much too big for her.

On the last bar-hopping night of her life, she started out with stockbroker friends, then moved on to a different kind of "drinking buddy." At the Sandbox, her fourth stop that night, she shot pool with an Outlaw called Striker T. He persistently and unsuccessfully tried to make out with her. When the bar closed, Susan went with the Outlaws and their "old ladies" to the home of their leader, "Big Jim" Nolan, in Pompano Beach.

Susie Cream Cheese, as they called her, sat on the floor with several of the Outlaws, drinking Ripple wine. Next to her was the persistent Striker. Another pass from the motorcyclist from Columbus, Ohio, and Susan committed an unforgivable act. In front of his fellow cyclists, she slapped Striker T.

"Blue jumped down and put his finger in her face and said, 'You don't slap one of my brothers,'" Lunsford testified at the trial. "And she reached up and slapped him in the face. He got real mad, almost crazy, and slapped her around a couple of times."

Blue the Enforcer kicked her in the face with his heavy cowboy boots, then held a gun to her head.

"Somebody said, 'Don't kill her here,' and he more or less walked around and cooled down," Lunsford said.

Grubby Summers brought Susan a wet towel for her bleeding mouth. Then he and Lunsford, on orders from Blue, drove to a nearby service station to buy gas for Lunsford's car.

Next, a drunken Susie Cream Cheese was forced into a bedroom and stripped naked. The gang gathered around for what it hoped would be a good show. A nude biker named Sleazy mounted her. But nothing happened. He was too drunk. The gang roared with laughter at an inept show by two failed performers, Susie and Sleazy.

Later, after Lunsford returned with the car, Blue shook her awake, so she could get dressed to leave. He told her he had "some alligator friends she'd like to meet."

Susan Bacon recovered her composure enough to dress herself, put on her pantyhose neatly and take her purse. She went with Starrett and Shockey to the car. Shockey was worried when he overheard Blue tell local

Outlaws he was going to take one of the Brookville newcomers along with him when he took Susie home. "I heard Blue say he didn't trust us," said Shockey. "I figured he was going to either drop Susie off somewhere along the way or kill her. I figured he'd kill whichever one of us he took with him, too."

Blue, who was carrying a pistol, drove and Shockey sat beside him. In the back seat, Susan Bacon went to sleep. Blue drove south on the turnpike to the State Road 84 exit, then turned west for another ten miles. It was just turning daylight when they reached Markham Park. Blue told Susan to get out of the car and sit down on the ground.

"Well, the girl went and sat down," Shockey said in his statement to Werder. "Blue got the shotgun out of the trunk. The safety wouldn't work so I hit it with a screwdriver and got back in the car and I heard two shots fired."

He also said Susan pleaded with Blue not to shoot her. She promised not to tell police about the beating. "And then he shot her," said Shockey.

As they drove back to Pompano on the turnpike, Starrett had Shockey throw her purse out the window. He also said he was hungry and was going to get some breakfast.

Blue Starrett told a different story. His first impression of Susie Cream Cheese, he said, was one of aloofness. "And," he added, "she was pretty arrogant." When he made sexual advances, "she slapped me. I said she shouldn't do that." He admitted slapping her and kicking her, though he claimed he was aiming his booted foot at her shoulder.

At Markham Park, he said he saw "Shockey hitting her with a coke bottle. Shockey came back to the car, reached in and got a screwdriver. A few seconds later I heard a shotgun blast, then another blast."

Shockey, who had cooperated with the court, pleaded guilty to murder in the third degree, a charge applied at that time to a death occurring in connection with the commission of a felony. His sentence was thirteen years.

Prosecutor Warner Olds sought a first-degree murder conviction for Starrett, the cold, blue-eyed enforcer. For ten hours the jury deliberated, then brought back a verdict that stunned the court. The verdict on Starrett was the same as Shockey's — guilty, but only in the third degree. Circuit Court Judge Stewart La Motte sentenced Starrett to the maximum, twenty years at hard labor.

"I get the feeling — I'm just guessing — that the jurors weren't sure which of the two fired the weapons. They apparently felt they had to compromise."

Some observers felt, too, that another factor in casting doubt on Starrett's role was Shockey's nickname — Shotgun. An ironic twist was that the two men convicted of the crime shared the same birthday, September 21.

"Who knows what happened?" said Susan's sister, Diana. "Who can tell? We all take chances, we all go to bars. All I can say is it was just a bizarre twist of fate."

PEACE ON EARTH

The Ku Klux Klan has plenty of white sheets. One thing it lacks in Florida is the Christmas spirit.

CHAPTER 9

Christmas Eve, Key West

A murderous holiday left the island with a supply
of curses — one voodoo, one phony.

Peace on earth, good will toward men — the spirit of Christmas. But not in Key West in 1921.

The holiday season exploded into a tropical wave of violence, culminating in a grisly murder. Many participated, yet no one could say which one was the killer. No one was ever charged. For the record, the crime just sits there as an unsolved murder and another Key West legend.

The legend lives on partly through a rich supply of curses — one a voodoo curse on the killers and another a phony, wordy curse on the city itself.

Merry Christmas, everybody.

* * *

Because his family came from the Canary Islands, off the coast of Spain, Manolo Cabeza was known around Key West as Isleno, the islander. After serving with distinction in World War I, a decorated Cabeza returned to Key West, where he owned and ran the Red Rooster, described variously as a bar, a coffee shop and a sporting club. It was located on Thomas Street, near a Key West waterfront that knew no shortage of action after the sun went down.

In Prohibition days, rumrunning from Havana pumped money into the Key West economy and plenty of forbidden booze into the bars, whorehouses and illegal gambling dens along the waterfront. It was a lawless world, but Cabeza, powerful and muscular, was well able to take care of himself and any unruly patrons at the Red Rooster. One old Key Wester, Perucho Sanchez, called him "one tough, mean *hombre.*"

Among the ladies of the evening who covered the waterfront was Angela, a beautiful mulatto, called a "high yellow" in those days. Black hair and black eyes complemented a complexion described as "silky smooth, *café au lait* skin."

The handsome Cabeza took her off the streets and brought her into his apartment as his common-law wife. They lived together in a second-floor flat on Petronia Street, not far from today's Ernest Hemingway House and Museum.

The Key West of the 1920s was a tolerant, live-and-let-live town. Still, it was a long way south of the Mason-Dixon Line and there were still a few taboos lurking in the tropical shadows. One of them was miscegenation. A white man could slyly pleasure himself with a Negro woman. He could not, however, live openly with her without raising eyebrows and, in Isleno's case, the horsewhips of bigots.

"Isleno began living with a brown — a mulatto girl," recalled a friend, cigarmaker Norberto Diaz. "They lived in a room right in back of the coffee shop. People talked about his living with a brown but nobody didn't really think much about it. I think a man's got a right to live with any kind of woman he wants to. If he wants to live with a brown, that ain't nobody's business but his own."

The Ku Klux Klan was less tolerant.

The night of December 23, 1921, five automobiles loaded with hooded men pulled up in front of Cabeza's home. He fought back at his attackers, ripping the masks off two of the men. He recognized them both.

Cabeza, powerful though he was, was no match for the Klan's numbers. They beat him with baseball bats, then pinned his arms and bound him with rope from a commercial fishing boat.

The Klansmen took him to the outskirts of the city. There they stripped and whipped the proud Spaniard, then tarred and feathered him. When the police investigated, he told them the men ordered him to leave town because he was "living with a Negro woman." He told them, too, that he hadn't recognized any of his assailants. Revenge was not a job he was going to leave to the police. He told friends he knew two of the men. Cabeza would handle the payback his way.

That night, as Cabeza lay in bed in agony from a burst kidney, Angela reached far back into her Afro-Cubano heritage. She called up the gods of voodoo. There in the candlelight she made her sacrifice of chickens, mixed blood and bones. She screamed her curse on the Klansmen of Key West, "violent death to all who had harmed my husband."

The next day, Christmas Eve, Cabeza, racked with terrible pain, set out

CHAPTER 10

Christmas Day, Mims

*A bomb sends terrible greetings to a
Florida civil rights leader.*

Could the peace and good will of the Christmas season at least slow down the bigotry and violence that had swept Florida the last half of 1951? Harry Moore hoped so when he called his far-flung family together for a holiday reunion and a celebration of the twenty-fifth wedding anniversary of Harry and Harriet Moore.

To his modest wood-frame home, nestled in an orange grove near the Brevard County town of Mims, they came. Harriet had driven up from Lake Park, where she taught school. Their daughter Annie had traveled from Ocala. Harry's seventy-one-year-old mother, Rosa, the family matriarch, had come down from Jacksonville. Harriet's brother, Master Sergeant George Sims, on furlough from service in Korea, came by for dinner. Only Evangeline had not arrived due to travel delays from her home in Washington.

And, of course, Harry Tyson Moore, relentless fighter for the civil rights of Florida's blacks, was there. His job as state director of the National Association for the Advancement of Colored People (NAACP) had kept him constantly in motion around the state. That is, until the November meeting of the state chapter, when he was removed from his post. Now he had time to spend at his Mims cottage while waiting to see what, if any, would be his next assignment. After all, the NAACP still owed him a year's salary.

Harry seemed relaxed. They had agreed to wait until Evangeline arrived before opening their Christmas presents. Tired from the day's festivities, they all turned in early. At 10:10, Harriet extinguished the last light. Ten minutes later, an explosion shattered the peaceful mood of Christmas night.

A neighbor, George Sharpe, heard the explosion, then saw a car come racing from the direction of the Moores' house. He figured kids "got hold of

on his mission of vengeance. He sought first a baggage handler at the railroad terminal on Trumbo Point. The man was lucky. He had Christmas Eve off.

Next, he went after William Decker, a box maker who worked at a cigar factory. Armed with an Army-issue Colt revolver in his belt, Cabeza hailed a cab and cruised around the city. As they drove past the Becker home, he fired wildly into the house. He then ordered the cab driver to cruise slowly past the home of a police officer.

"I do not see his car. Drive on," he ordered. They headed north on Duval Street.

Meanwhile, Decker had finished his Christmas shopping and was heading home in his Ford when Cabeza spotted him driving south on Duval.

"Turn around fast," Cabeza shouted at the cab driver.

A quick U-turn brought him alongside Decker. Cabeza leaned out the cab window and shouted, "Decker, this is how a man kills a man."

The Islander shot the Klansman through the jaw. He slumped over the wheel of his car, dead on the spot. The Ford lurched onto the sidewalk and ran into an electric pole near the Cuban Club. In the back seat of Decker's auto was a turkey dressed for the Decker family's Christmas dinner.

The crowd around the Cuban Club scattered and the cab driver sped away to Petronia Street. Cabeza leaped from the taxi and as darkness gathered ran to the cupola of the Solano building at Petronia and Whitehead Streets.

Soon a band of armed men, many of them members of the KKK, appeared on Whitehead Street and began shooting at Cabeza. He fired back. No one was hit.

Sheriff Roland Curry called the Naval Station, which sent six Marines to help arrest the Islander. The sheriff called to him and promised to protect him at the county jail if he would surrender.

"Only if McGinnis comes for me," he shouted. A. H. McGinnis, a deputy who had been a federal marshal, was the only lawman Cabeza trusted. He certainly didn't trust Curry, thought by some be a racist.

The deputy, summoned from home, went to the cupola, accompanied by the Marine guard, and led Cabeza down the stairs. A large, mostly pro-Cabeza crowd cheered and whistled as the Islander was taken to the county jail.

For a while, the Marines continued to guard the prisoner from any KKK attacks. At 1 A.M., Sheriff Curry gave the Marines a Christmas present. He told them he had "the situation under control" and let them leave.

Soon five cars with their lights out drove up to the jail. Fifteen hooded men left the cars and entered the building. By now, Sheriff Curry had gone home. The Klansmen walked unhampered into the jail and straight to Cabeza's cell. It was unlocked. Terrified, an old drunk in the next cell hid under a blanket in a dark corner.

Hooded men poured into the Islander's cell and beat him senseless with lead-weighted blackjacks. Next, they dragged him feet first out of the jail and tied him to the bumper of a car. His body bounced behind the auto as they drove out near East Martello Tower. There they hanged him from a palm tree. He was probably already dead, but just to make sure, the hooded men fired shotguns and pistols at the hanging man.

His bloody, bludgeoned body hanging from a tree was the Klan's Christmas present to Key West. KK — for Kris Kringle — had been muscled aside by KKK.

No one was ever charged in the case. The grand jury announced that Cabeza's actions had led to the lynching. After all, his "living with a Negro woman" was an affront to society.

"He had a very bad reputation," said the grand jury report. "His name was a terror to officers of the law . . . and to the citizens in general. . . . We are of the opinion that the lynching of Cabeza was not done by an organized society but by individuals unknown to us."

Angela, however, may have had the last word. Within a few years, Sheriff Curry drowned while fishing near the Dog Rocks. In the 1930s, when a bankrupt Key West became the poorest municipality in the country, Norberto Diaz, attributing still another curse to Cabeza, told author Stetson Kennedy:

"Every time I pass in front of the Cuban Club, I think of Isleno. The other day, I was down to the beach and seen the palm tree where he was hung. It's funny but that was the first coconut palm to die from the disease that's killing most of the palm trees on the island. I believe Isleno's *brujo* (ghost) is killing the palm trees, too. People say the whole island's cursed and that's why there is so much bad luck and people do not have enough to eat.

"Isleno's curse has already killed five of the Ku Klux Klan who beat and hung him. He knew who they were and called their names and cursed them for horrible deaths in revenge. He shot the Klan leader himself, one man was blowed up by dynamite when he was working on the bridges, another got caught in the Matecumbe hurricane, one was ground to pieces under his boat when it went on a reef and another went fishing and never came back. Isleno's curse killed them all. It's killing another with tuberculosis now."

* * *

Some forty years later, legend had it that a particularly flowery curse had been placed by Isleno's father, who had brought the family over from the Canary Islands. F.E.B., a columnist for the *Key West Citizen*, wrote that a copy of the curse was given to her one night in the shadows of a doorway to the Cuban Club. In her column she quoted from the curse:

"O God, let this beautiful island falsely prosper with good things, fair weather, smugness and freedom to play and to love. But, then, Almighty God, always rip from this island the sweetness. . . . As the cruel equator's sun burns the pink skin of the northern visitor, please, God, blight each business undertaking, slay the men who go off to wars, make friendships to perish, and houses to blaze containing the prissy possessions of those who are not wise enough to know that one cannot possess. . . .

"Make happy island laughs turn into groans. . . . Let every pillow be wet with the loss of a loved one. May a vicious disease strike and destroy while the cool island zephyrs sigh over the lonely and damned island people."

A fake curse, wrote Earl Adams, another columnist for the paper. Adams, a member of Ernest Hemingway's inner circle, had covered the story and knew Cabeza's father, a semiliterate man, who had never had a day's schooling. He would have been incapable, Adams said, of composing so eloquent a curse in a language that was not his own. Adams did, however, quote what the father said when he knelt at his son's grave. He prayed that "those responsible for my son's death may die a thousand times more painful death."

Merry Christmas.

Harry Tyson Moore's home after Christmas bombing, 1951 (Florida State Archives)

some dynamite and picked a quiet spot to set off a Christmas cracker."

From his home nearby George Sims heard it, too. He and his brother Arnold rushed over to their sister's home. What they saw was a horrifying sight. The front half of the house was destroyed.

Harry Moore, still on his mattress, had been hurled through the ceiling. He lay in the front yard, bleeding from the mouth. Sergeant Sims tried to lift him.

"He didn't feel like there was an unbroken bone in his body," said Sims.

Harriet was injured badly. Annie and Rosa, who had been sleeping at the rear of the house, were unhurt. The Sims brothers set about immediately trying to summon an ambulance. None was willing to transport blacks. The two brothers lifted Harry and Harriet into their car and drove thirty-two miles to a hospital in Sanford. Harry died soon after they arrived. Doctors gave Harriet a fifty-fifty chance.

On New Year's Day, 1952, Harry Moore, forty-six, was buried in a cemetery between Mims and Titusville. Six hundred mourners attended the funeral of the man who had fought for the rights of black people for nearly two decades. Harriet Moore left her hospital bed to view his body at the funeral home. It was too much for her.

"I don't much care if I live or die," she sobbed. "My husband is dead, my home is wrecked. We did what we could. Now, others must carry on." Two days later a blood clot in her brain ended her life.

*   *   *

Born in Houston, Florida, a small community near Live Oak, Harry Moore attended Bethune-Cookman College in Daytona Beach. Nicknamed "Doc," due to his proficiency in math and science, he became a teacher. To supplement his income he sold insurance for Atlanta Life. He became principal at a black elementary school at Mims.

Moore was incensed at the disproportionately low pay black teachers received under the prevailing policy of "separate but equal" education. He crusaded zealously for equal pay for black teachers. In 1934, he organized a Brevard County Chapter of the NAACP. He became active in the Florida State Teachers Association. He pushed, too, for increased black voter registration and in 1945 formed the Florida Progressive Voters League. A year later, Harry and Harriet were fired from their teaching jobs. Harry was just too active in the NAACP and the PVL.

At this time, Moore was named executive director of the state NAACP, a full-time, paid position. As blacks began to assert their rights, a severe backlash set in. Miami was gripped by a terrorist bombing campaign. Five synagogues, one Catholic church and many black apartment houses in Carver Village had been dynamited. Two blacks had been murdered by white gangs elsewhere in the state.

In 1951, in Groveland, Lake County, four young black men were accused of raping a seventeen-year-old white housewife. One defendant was gunned down by a white mob. Another, a sixteen-year-old black, was given a life sentence because of his age. The other two, convicted by an all-white jury, were sentenced to death. Harry Moore raised money for an appeal and the Supreme Court agreed, ordering new trials for the men on Death Row.

Willis McCall, the Lake County sheriff notorious for his rough treatment of blacks, was given the task of escorting them back to the county jail in Tavares. On the way back, he shot one to death and severely wounded the other. McCall claimed he did it in self-defense and two investigating panels backed him up.

But not Harry Moore. Moore called the verdict a whitewash and loudly demanded McCall's indictment. That demand, one writer has concluded, may well have been Moore's death warrant.

*   *   *

H. T. Williams, the Brevard County sheriff, concluded he was ill-equipped to launch a full-scale investigation. He called the Federal Bureau of Investigation for backup. Brevard County officials hoped the blast was connected to the wave of dynamite bombings in the Miami area. It was always better to blame a crime on outsiders, particularly from sinful Dade County. Samples from the house dashed that hope. Dynamite had not been used to kill Harry Moore. The bomb appeared to be TNT or some other explosive.

Walter White, executive secretary of the national NAACP, flew in from New York. He wasted no time in declaring that the bomb had been planted by someone with knowledge of both the house's interior layout and of Moore's movements.

"It looks clear," he said to a church group, "that this originated right here in Brevard County. At least three persons in recent weeks have expressed alarm over the growth of Negro voting strength in Florida and made statements that too many Negroes were getting funny ideas like Harry Moore."

Whoever did the deed, the NAACP suspected early on that the Christmas night bombings traced back to Moore's involvement with the Groveland case and with Sheriff Willis McCall. The sheriff, who would be elected to seven terms in Lake County, was an outspoken advocate of white supremacy, and had said, "I don't think there's any question about it that the white race is a superior race to the black race. I believe that's a proven fact. In their native country, they're still eating each other. We don't do that."

At that time, J. Edgar Hoover was director of the FBI. He was not noted for zeal in trying to solve civil rights cases. In fact, government documents released years later revealed that the FBI labeled the NAACP "a definite suspect" in the case. Their motive, the FBI hinted, might have been propaganda and fund-raising.

No one was ever charged with the killing of Harry and Harriett Moore, and for most people the case was soon forgotten, just one more unsolved murder. Then in 1978, a boozy Raymond Henry Jr., of Fort Pierce, contacted an NAACP official and offered to tell him what had happened that terrible night in 1951.

Home on furlough from the Marines in December 1951, Henry said he was approached in Fort Pierce by a rookie cop who asked if he had any experience with explosives.

"That nigger has to be got rid of," the cop said. "He's a threat to law enforcement and the white race."

Henry said the Ku Klux Klan promised to pay him two thousand dollars to build a bomb to kill Harry Moore. Henry agreed. Christmas Day was picked as the date for the hit. They had learned that Moore would be spending Christmas at his home, conveniently located in an isolated area.

On Christmas afternoon, Klan members drove from Fort Pierce to Mims, a distance of about eighty miles. With them was a black man named "Cowboy." He had been bribed to participate in the plot. Near sundown, Cowboy knocked on Moore's door and asked for directions in locating relatives. Moore, alone at the time, agreed to drive the man.

As soon as Moore left, Klansmen emerged from the citrus grove. Quickly, they slipped into the house and attached the bomb to the bedsprings. They ran a detonator wire from the bomb out to their hiding place in the grove. There they waited until the right moment. Ten minutes after the lights went out, the Klansmen detonated the bomb.

The Klan members headed for a Fort Pierce bar to celebrate the bombing. Drinks at the bar were paid for by the man who had financed the hit on Moore and his wife. His name, Raymond said, was Willis McCall.

Skeptical, the NAACP official asked Raymond why he had waited twenty-seven years to come forward with his story. "Money," he said. The Klan had never paid him the promised two thousand dollars. Furthermore, he was suffering from terminal cancer and wanted to ease a troubled conscience in his final days.

Local detectives and FBI agents looked into Henry's story. Their conclusion: The story was probably fabricated.

Sheriff McCall called the story "some of the bullshit you reporters make up."

In 1991, the Florida Department of Law Enforcement launched another investigation, but little new information was developed. The one positive result, however, was to bring to light Moore's civil rights record. The first civil rights leader to be murdered for his cause, he had long ago been eclipsed by those who came later, leaders like Dr. Martin Luther King Jr. and Supreme Court Justice Thurgood Marshall. Now Brevard County has given him his due, honoring him by naming a county office building after him.

FRONTIER MAYHEM

In many ways, Florida was the last frontier. On its cattle lands, there was a range war just after the Civil War. As late as 1910, a spectacular shootout in the Ten Thousand Islands wiped out a colorful but deadly outlaw.

CHAPTER 11

Range War

A sheriff's murder kicked off Florida's
Barber-Mizell range war.

It happened sometime during the nineties — the 1890s. The Census of 1890 concluded the Old West was no longer frontier. When fences began to pinch in the wide open spaces, the day of the most legendary of all Western heroes, the cowboy, was past.

Or was it?

Meanwhile, back at the ranch in the Old East, a frontier land was still in business. It was called Florida, probably just too poor to build the fences that separate frontier from civilization. True, the state had no mountains, no canyons, no purple sage, no tumbleweed, no Chisholm Trail, no Wyatt Earp, no Butch Cassidy. But Florida had cattle. Where dogies roam, can cowboys be far behind?

Frederic Remington, mightiest of all the Old West painters, hit the trail to Florida to see for himself the cowboy of the East. In 1895, he arrived in Arcadia, the capital of the cattle lands west of Lake Okeechobee. His assignment was to write and illustrate a story about "cracker cowboys" for *Harper's Weekly.*

He didn't like what he found. He airily dismissed Florida's flat, sandy prairies as "truly not a country for a high-spirited race or moral giants." He didn't like the cows, either, "scrawny creatures not fit for a pointer dog to mess on." The cowhunters, as Florida cowboys were called, fared no better: ". . . wild-looking individuals, whose hanging hair and drooping hats and generally bedraggled appearance would remind you at once of the Spanish moss which hangs so . . . helplessly on the limbs of the oaks out in the swamps."

Remington should have dug a little deeper. He would have found roundups, cattle drives, rustling, gunslingers and occasionally hostile Indians. He would even have found a range war to rival New Mexico's Lincoln County War, which gave the world the illustrious Billy the Kid. Central Florida, particularly the prairies around Orlando and Kissimmee, was already a lawless frontier, even before the Barber-Mizell range war claimed at least nine lives during just three bloody months in 1870.

The foul deed that launched the war occurred on February 21. David Mizell, sheriff of Orange County, was heading south from Orlando into enemy territory, the vast Barber ranges, controlled by a large and lawless clan which had been feuding with the Mizells for years. The sheriff's unpleasant duty was to follow up on a complaint against the Barber cattle operation. Accompanying him were his brother, Morgan, and his twelve-year-old son, William.

As they rode across Bull Creek, a single shot rang out, followed by an Indian war whoop. The sheriff fell from his saddle. His brother and son dragged the dying man to dry ground. Mizell died praying for his enemies, said William, and even asked that no one seek revenge against his killers.

No chance of that request being granted. Central Florida, in the years just after the Civil War, was not a forgiving, turn-the-other-cheek piece of America. Contributing heavily to the meanness of that hot, flat, sandy, desolate cattleland was Moses E. Barber and his extended family.

As far back as the 1830s, Moses Barber was rustling cattle from the Seminoles of north Florida. Between 1850 and the start of the Civil War in 1861, his cattle operations ranged from the Carolinas to the marshes of the St. Johns River east of Orlando. On this vast range he maintained several homes and several wives, each spaced discreetly a two-day cattle drive apart. He was quite friendly, too, with Brevard County cattle baroness Jane Green, a rancher of such stature she even had a swamp named after her.

The Mizell ranching clan was headed by two brothers, David and John R., the latter known with respect as a "two-gun man." The two feuding families were united briefly in the Confederate cause, but after the war their trails separated forever.

Despite their deep roots in the South, the Mizells cozied up to the Republican party which governed the state during the postwar Reconstruction years. The Barbers remained unreconstructed Confederates, bristling under military occupation. They were angry, too, at the new Orange County government's practice of bypassing elections by appointing public officials who then imposed heavy taxes on cattle herds.

Those were lawless, troubled days. Cattle rustling was widespread. Cattlemen carried firearms not just on the range but also on the streets and into the buildings of the little frontier town of Orlando.

In 1868, David W. Mizell was appointed sheriff of Orange County and his brother, John R., judge of county civil and criminal courts. Now, for the first time, the feuding Barbers and Mizells were on opposite sides of the law.

The first clash was not long in coming. Sheriff Mizell drove off a number of Moses Barber's cattle to compensate for the patriarch's nonpayment of county taxes. Moses issued a chilling threat to the sheriff:

"Stay off Barber lands or you will leave feet first."

The fall term of the Circuit Court of Orange County was scheduled to open in Orlando on Monday, October 26, 1868. Over the weekend, someone burned the log courthouse to the ground. A temporary courthouse was established in the hotel next door. Court was not a happy occasion. Armed cattlemen and cowboys stood around the new courtroom and glared at the officers of the court. No one was willing to testify against any cattlemen.

Before the day ended, Old Man Moses's son, Moses B.F. Barber, was charged with arson, adultery, forcibly confining and imprisoning another against his will and threatening injury to the person and property of another. On the third day of court, both of the Moses Barbers were charged with confining and imprisoning one George Bass against his will.

The following May, the senior Moses was found guilty of polygamy, and on the same day was tried along with Moses B.F. in the George Bass case. George, testifying against Moses, explained how the Barber "imprisoning" caper worked. He was driving cattle in south Orange County when Barber and two others detained him for a half hour. Moses told him: "George, we have three propositions to make. Leave the county in thirty days or take one hundred lashes or have your neck broke."

Moses told a kinder and gentler story, claiming in the process that Bass had been rustling his cattle. The jury believed George. Moses was sentenced to the state penitentiary for a year. Sheriff Mizell testified against Barber.

The elder Moses was not the first in the family to be sent to the state pen. For some time, the Barbers claimed that the Mizells had not enforced the law when it was Barber cattle that was stolen. They even charged the Mizells with rustling Barber cattle. Jack Barber said he found a prize heifer of his in a Mizell herd. He took it back, but the sheriff caught him and Jack was given a prison sentence.

To protect his son from "foul play," Moses accompanied him and the sheriff for part of the trip. While they were on a St. Johns River steamboat on the way to Palatka, Jack asked the sheriff for his chewing tobacco. Mizell shoved it into his mouth so hard it cut the prisoner's lip.

"This day, Dave Mizell," snarled Moses, "you've started on the road to hell."

Hell wasn't long in coming, but Sheriff Dave would not be its only guest.

When word reached Judge Mizell of his brother's murder, he immediately dismissed the war whoop as a ruse. Moses Barber had threatened Sheriff Mizell if he ever again set foot on Barber lands, and Moses and his boys were going to pay for that threat. The judge and Jack Evans, the newly appointed sheriff replacing David Mizell, formed a posse and went to work.

Their first target was Needham "Needs" Yates, a Barber employee suspected of being the shooter. The posse tracked him until they found him in scrub land northwest of Kissimmee, near the Disney World of later years. They stood Yates on a pine stump and riddled him with bullets and buckshot. To commemorate the event, the scrub where he was killed was named Needs Scrub.

Next, the posse went after Old Moses, home now from prison. At a creek about ten miles south of Orlando, Judge Mizell almost caught Moses and another Barber riding with him. But the posse's horses bogged down in the marshes of a stream and Moses got away. Again, as a tribute to the momentous event, the stream was named Boggy Creek.

Young Moses was not as lucky as his father. He was captured at Lake Conway. The posse took him out in the lake, tied a plowshare around his neck and dropped him into the water. The terrified Barber tried to swim. When they saw he was going to make it to shore in spite of the plowshare, posse members opened fire and killed him. His brother, Isaac, was captured and taken to the home of Sheriff Evans. There he was killed, reportedly while trying to "escape."

How many people were killed probably will never be known, partly because the shootings took place in more than one county. The number usually given was "at least nine." All the gunshot victims on the official Orange County list, with the exception of the sheriff, have an "X" before their names. At the bottom of the list is this notation: "David Mizell, Sheriff, was waylaid and murdered by Parties Unknown. All the others where Gunshot wounds are given as Cause of Death were arrested by Deputy Sheriff upon suspicion of being instrumental in the death of Mizell and shot while attempting to escape."

The noisy gunfire from Orlando did not go unnoticed. A Tampa newspaper, the *Florida Peninsular*, began to question so many "escape" shootings. The paper condemned Sheriff Evans as a "tool of the Radicals," as the Republicans were called then. He was, the paper said, a familiar figure in Tampa until he "had to leave here with a load of buckshot in his back for his general rascality."

Shootout on Florida cattle range as depicted by Frederic Remington (Florida State Archives)

The partisan *Peninsular* attacked the Republican governor, Massachusetts-born Harrison Reed, for not sending in troops to stop the warfare before any more people were killed. "Old Moses Barber was waylaid and murdered on the 10th (of April) . . ." a later *Peninsular* story reported.

Not so. Old Moses and his nephew Jack, whose lip had been cut by chewing tobacco, escaped northward by boat on the St. Johns, then headed west to Wakulla County. Along the way, Moses dropped in on his wives and told them to claim his cattle in their areas for themselves. He wanted no more of the Florida cattle country. Moses Barber died in November 1870 at the age of sixty-two. Jack lived on until 1916, a respected Orange County citrus grower near Lake Conway — and Lake Barber.

Judge Mizell, who led the campaign against the Barbers, became a powerful figure in the state Republican Party, which held power until Reconstruction ended eight years later. Later, he worked his way down the east coast of Florida, settling in a farming community a little north of Fort Lauderdale. When the town was incorporated on June 6, 1908, as Pompano, he was elected its first mayor.

The artist Remington never had the pleasure of dodging the bullets of the Barbers and Mizells, but he did eventually meet the most famous of all the Mizells, Morgan Bonapart Mizell, better known as "Bone." He was the son of the same Morgan Mizell who was riding with the sheriff the day he was ambushed.

Remington had saddled himself with a romanticized image of the cow-boy as the great American hero. In Bone Mizell, the most famous of all Florida cowhunters, he found a drunk and a practical joker who spoke with a lisp. Bone covered his embarrassment with a quick, sharp wit that delight-ed his many admirers. Bone sometimes lit his pipe with dollar bills and was known on occasion to ride into a saloon and down his first drink of the day while still seated on his horse.

Bone was range foreman for cattle baron Ziba King's outfit along the Peace River. An expert horseman and a crack shot with rifle or six-shooter, he won the respect of his peers through his highly developed skills in run-ning roundups and cattle drives and attending to the workaday details of the business, identifying, branding and keeping mothers and calves together. Bone was a working cowhunter. His fame came, however, from his colorful life, tall tales and practical jokes. He didn't need to be a hero. People just liked fun-loving Bone Mizell.

Once, he married a couple using a Sears & Roebuck catalog instead of a Bible. He meant no disrespect. After all, he was illiterate, though he was known for his knowledge of the Scriptures. Bone himself never married, but he once went as far as buying a marriage license.

His most outlandish prank involved a corpse. Sometime around 1890, Bone's old friend, John Underhill, died at a cow camp in Lee County. A solitary grave became his home on the range.

A little later, a young Jewish boy from New Orleans drifted into the cat-tle country and became friendly with Bone. The boy, already in failing health and weary from years of worldwide travel, died on the range. Bone buried him next to Underhill. A few years later, the boy's parents heard about his death and sent money to an undertaker to have the body exhumed and returned to New Orleans for a proper burial in the family plot. The undertaker hired Bone to collect the body for him.

As he rode out to the unmarked graves, two thoughts kept passing through Bone's mind. The young Jewish boy, sick of traveling, had told Bone he never wanted to see another train, never wanted to go back home. On the other hand, Bone's friend, John, had always wanted to ride a train. He just never had enough money for a ticket.

"Well, sir, it didn't seem right," Bone mused. "It seemed even less right after a few drinks to sort of fortify us for the digging job. Here was a free train ride ahead, a funeral so damned fine this country had never seen the likes of it — probably with four white horses pulling the hearse."

So Bone switched corpses. John Underhill finally got his train ride.

Bone was not above a little rustling now and then. Most of the charges against him were dropped, but in 1896, in a Fort Myers court, he was convicted of rustling and sentenced to two years at hard labor in the state penitentiary.

Before his commitment, a petition for his pardon was moving ahead in Arcadia. When told that he couldn't be pardoned until he had served time, his supporters decided to give him a good send-off. They bought him new clothes and escorted him to the train station.

The prison was well-primed for its honored guest. Bone was greeted by a prison official who conducted him on a tour of the institution and then fed him dinner. The noted cowhunter praised the prison management in an after-dinner speech. That brief interlude qualified as time served. Bone was promptly pardoned and put back on the train to Arcadia.

Bone was a heavy drinker, too heavy. Near the end of his life, the Kings, for whom he had worked for so many years, sent him to dry out at a sanitarium in Hot Springs, Arkansas. But in time, he returned to his old habits.

On July 14, 1921, he took the Atlantic Coast Line Railway from Arcadia to Fort Ogden. From there, he wired the Lykes brothers, cattle kings from Tampa for whom he had worked, asking them for money. Later that day, the money arrived but Bone never saw it. He died there at the depot. The official cause of his death: "Moonshine —went to sleep and did not wake up."

Bone Mizell was immortalized by a Remington painting of "A Cracker Cowboy," a cowboy ballad with words by Ruby Leach Carson and music by Dottie and Jim Bob Tinsley, and a poem by Geraldine Kent Thraikill, which closes with these words:

In a railway station Bone heeded a mute command
To search for greener pastures on a far-away strand;
Sans adieu he boarded a train for the Promised Land
And there Bone greets old friends with jokes and welcoming hand.

CHAPTER 12

Ghosts in the Courtroom

A lawyer used a bizarre defense for killers
of the first Palm Beacher.

"You want to hang these men? Why, their ghosts will come back and haunt you for the rest of your days."

The attorney for the men charged with murder pointed a bony forefinger at the jury. It was a cynical tactic, based on the lawyer's contempt for the Ocala jury made up of four ignorant white men and eight recently freed slaves, widely believed by the white power structure to be extremely superstitious.

The lawyer spoke of staring eyes and clammy tongues, of death damp on the hands of innocent men found guilty, of the horrors of the tomb.

Would it work, the defense attorney's bold move to scare the jury out of a guilty verdict? Would they walk, the murderers of Augustus Oswald Lang, a man who would one day acquire a modest measure of fame as the first resident of a precious piece of real estate that would bear the name Palm Beach?

Born in Bavaria in 1821, Lang was working as an assistant keeper at the Jupiter Lighthouse when the Civil War broke out in April 1861. Orders came promptly from Washington to darken the Jupiter light to make navigation more difficult for Confederate blockade runners. Sympathetic to the South, the keeper refused to carry out his orders.

Lang and two men he recruited did the job for the keeper. Next, the trio walked south along the beach for some seventy miles to Key Biscayne, where they broke the lens in the Cape Florida Lighthouse.

Lang, a German who had served in the U.S. Army from 1845 to 1850, then disappeared into the tropical jungles on a barrier island on the east side of Lake Worth, partly to avoid reprisals by Confederate sympathizers in south Florida, but mostly to concentrate on his horticultural pursuits. In

Germany, he had been a gardener for the King of Saxony.

Lang built a small driftwood cabin and settled in about fifteen miles south of the Jupiter Lighthouse. It was a good place for him to work. For one thing, he had the island all to himself. Furthermore, it supported a healthy growth of tropical trees and plants, but few of the palms that would later give the island its name. The palms were planted in 1878 after a shipwreck left the island's oceanfront littered with coconuts.

The recluse remained out of sight until 1866, when a fall storm cut a new inlet in the beach ridge on the east side of the freshwater lake. Michael Sears from Biscayne Bay saw the new inlet and sailed through it in a small schooner. As he cruised south from the inlet, he saw a small house in a clearing. A white man came out of the cabin and greeted him. He said his name was Lang and asked how the war was coming along.

"War?" said Sears. "What war?"

"Why, the War between the States, of course," said Lang.

"The fighting's been over for more than a year."

The next fall, after a hurricane struck the east coast, Lang and a sailor named Charlie Moore were rumored to have found a shipwreck containing a chest and a money belt with some eight thousand dollars in gold coins.

That same year Lang, tired of his lonely existence, moved north near the settlement of Fort Pierce. A small town had grown up along the Indian River at the site of the Seminole War fort. It was a sparsely populated area of farmers, citrus growers and cattlemen. A lawless community lay to the west of town. Lang acquired a sizable piece of land on Tenmile Creek, which flows into the north fork of the St. Lucie River. He raised oranges, sugar cane, bananas and other fruit and plants and operated a ferry across the creek. In completing his turn away from the reclusive life, he married a local girl named Susan Priest.

Unluckily for Lang, his property was all too close to the domain of outlaws and fugitives. Their leader was a Florida cracker named Elias Jernigan. In that gang of lawbreakers, Lang simply did not fit. He was clearly not one of them. For one thing, there was his German accent. Furthermore, he was an educated man in a land where few could read or write. As a horticulturist, he approached farming scientifically. His fruits and vegetables were far superior to the slapdash crops grown by his neighbors. And then there was the shipwreck rumor. Was he also a rich man?

Jernigan resented his aloof neighbor so much he made an abominable deal with nineteen-year-old Tom Drawdy. Tom wanted to marry Jernigan's daughter. Jernigan gave him harsh terms: Kill Lang for me and you can have my daughter.

One day, when Susan Lang was seven months pregnant with their first child, Drawdy and Allen Padgett came to the Langs' cabin. They said they wanted orange tree cuttings to improve their groves. Lang gave them the orange slips and Susan served them lunch. After they had eaten, the men asked Augustus to carry them across Tenmile Creek in his boat.

Susan assumed he would be back shortly. Then she heard gunfire — seven shots. As darkness approached, Lang still had not returned. She walked down to the creek and saw her husband's empty boat tied up on the other side. It appeared to be smeared with blood.

Terrified, she headed immediately to Fort Capron to seek help. The distance was ten miles through the woods, and darkness closed in on her before she reached her destination. To her dismay, Susan found she could expect no immediate help from the law. The Brevard County sheriff's office was some ninety miles away in Titusville.

A group of Fort Capron men escorted Susan back home. There they found the house and the nursery trashed. Had the outlaws been looking for gold coins? Susan Lang took no chances. She returned to the home of her parents in Fort Pierce to await the birth of her baby.

Ten days would pass before the sheriff arrived with a posse of ten men. He would have to confront Drawdy and Padgett. It would mean a trip into outlaw country. Worse still, the sheriff learned that Drawdy, Padgett and the outlaw band had prepared for a siege. Armed and well-provisioned, they had assembled in one cabin and had sworn to fight to the death. The sheriff and his posse went back to Titusville.

Life went on in the land of the outlaws. Gunfight or no gunfight, there was a wedding to perform. And strangely enough, a professor from Brown University in Providence, Rhode Island, was on hand to witness the ceremony. Later he wrote an account of it for *Forest and Stream*, America's most popular outdoors magazine.

Professor John Whipple Potter Jenks, who had come to Florida to collect exhibits for the Brown University natural history museum, had engaged the services of Jernigan to transport a small sailboat via oxcart to the Kissimmee River for the princely sum of forty dollars. From the river, Jenks and his fellow explorers could sail south into Lake Okeechobee.

While waiting for the rest of his party, the professor learned about the murder contract. When the wedding day arrived, he was invited to the ceremony as an honored guest. Wrote Professor Jenks:

"As suggested by Tom, towards sundown of the day following our return I observed men, women and children gathering at the cabin, mostly on foot, but some on horseback and others in oxcarts. At length a man rode up of graver mien and with horse more richly caparisoned than any other I had seen. Soon Mr. J. brought him to my tent, and taking me aside said, 'This man is a justice of the peace, and has come sixty miles to marry Tom to my daughter tonight, but there is a hitch in the arrangement, as last week's mail has failed to bring the license sent for. . . . Now what do you advise, as the justice cannot wait two weeks for another mail, and my neighbors for ten miles around are all gathered to witness the ceremony?'

"As the malfeasance would be wholly on the part of the justice, inasmuch as should he perform his part with their consent, they would be legally married to all intent and purpose, it was finally decid-

Augustus Oswald Lang (Historical Society of Palm Beach)

ed that Mr. J. and Tom should give the justice a written obligation, with myself as witness, to send him the certificate as soon as possible, which document they both signed by making their mark, after I had assured them it was written correctly. Nothing further hindering, Tom and his bride took position on the platform connecting the two rooms of the log cabin, while the justice pronounced them, without any questioning or pledging, husband and wife.

"Tom had exchanged his teaming suit for a similar one, only more cleanly, and his bride contented herself with plain calico without ornaments of any kind, but with shoes and stockings — the first time I had seen her wear any. After the ceremony, the bride's mother and grandmother stepped up and shook hands without kissing, and were followed by her father without coat or vest, shoes or stockings, but with his shirt sleeves rolled up to his elbows, and his pants to his knees. After a long pause, I considered it my turn to shake hands with them, though, with all my knowledge of their antecedents, and at how fearful a price Tom had gained his bride, I could hardly bring my mind to congratulate them on their union. The ice broken, there was a rush for handshaking, after which Mr. J. brought out a fiddle with two strings and called for dancing."

Tom Drawdy did not have long to enjoy his honeymoon. One of his neighbors, a young man named Hendry, had witnessed both the murder and its gruesome aftermath, the disposal of Lang's body. Unable to deal with the brutal events, he lost his sanity. Still, buried within his incoherent ravings lay a tale that finally induced the law to move on the murderers.

Hendry said Drawdy and Padgett, after the murder, had weighted Lang's body down and thrown it into Tenmile Creek. They hadn't done a good job and it had resurfaced a few days later. This time they took axes and knives and cut his body into small pieces and stuffed the parts into gator holes near the creek.

Governor Marcellus Stearns bypassed the reluctant sheriff of Brevard County and pressed High Sheriff Arthur Speer, of Orange County, and High Sheriff Kit Hart, of Volusia County, into action. Supported by a sizable posse, they seized Drawdy and Padgett, placed them in irons and transported them to Ocala for trial.

Jernigan fled to the west. He boasted he would never be taken alive. He wasn't. Near Fort Thompson, just west of Lake Okeechobee, the posse tracked him down and shot him to death.

The case against Drawdy and Padgett was a strong one. Their attorney had very little to work with. When time came for final summation, he decided his best shot was to try to scare the jury. Illiterate jurors in an illiterate land, they were likely to be superstitious, he figured.

"The gentlemen of the jury have heard that spirits are very common all over the north, that some have even been heard of in St. Augustine. Supposing the jury brings in a verdict of guilty and hangs an innocent man, what could you expect but that his spirit would haunt you through life, appearing with staring eyes and clammy tongue, the death damp on his hands and the horrors of the tomb round about him?"

Just before the jury could announce its verdict, the lawyer, pointing a forefinger at the blacks, shouted out to them: "You want to hang these men? Why, their ghosts will come back and haunt you for the rest of your days!"

One account says the terrified jurors fled the courtroom. If they did, they at least lingered long enough to find the men guilty of murder. Their sentence: eight years in prison.

That same year, Drawdy's father was convicted of stealing orange trees, no mean feat. His sentence: thirteen years.

On February 23, 1874, Susan, two months short of her eighteenth birthday, gave birth to Walker Augustus Lang. She later remarried and moved to Ormond, where she lived until 1918. Walker built bridges, worked on the Florida East Coast Railway and after 1896 operated a grocery store in Fort Lauderdale. Ten years later, he placed an ad for a wife in an agricultural magazine, which led to his marriage to Nora Neal. One of their two daughters, Augusta, was named after the German-born horticulturist murdered on Tenmile Creek.

CHAPTER 13

Shootout at Chokoloskee

---

*Killing Mister Watson was a
community project.*

The islanders knew he was coming as soon as they heard his boat, each stroke of the engine signaling them across the waters south of Chokoloskee. They gathered near Smallwood's Trading Post, some armed, some just there to see what was going to happen.

Soon he came into view, steering his gasoline launch toward the landing. Smallwood's dock was no longer there. A week earlier, an October hurricane had swept it away. His launch was named the *Brave*, appropriate because he feared no man. But many feared him and with good reason.

How many people had Edgar J. Watson killed? Some of the wilder guesses put the figure at more than fifty. Too many, the islanders figured, especially after they learned that three more bodies had turned up at Chatham Bend and one of them had been a woman, big Hannah Smith. It had to stop.

Watson beached his boat on the sand and stepped ashore. He was carrying a double-barreled, 12-gauge shotgun in his left hand and a revolver inside his coat.

"I don't go looking for trouble," Watson had said many times. "But if it comes looking for me, I know how to take care of it."

Trouble too big to take care of came to Watson on October 24, 1910. Who shot first, Watson or one of the islanders? Whose bullet or bullets killed him? All that is really known is that late that October afternoon both Edgar Watson and the shootout on Chokoloskee Island passed into legend.

* * *

Along Florida's lower west coast lie the Ten Thousand Islands, a bewildering maze of mangrove keys in which a man could unwittingly get lost or could easily lose himself if he were on the run. It was wild country, the

domain of fugitives, derelicts, some harmless hermits and a few settlers trying to civilize an uncivil land, ruled, as one islander put it, by seven unwrit-
ten laws:

1. Suspect every man.
2. Ask no questions.
3. Settle your own quarrels.
4. Never steal from an islander.
5. Stick by him, even if you do not know him.
6. Shoot quick, when your secret is in danger.
7. Cover your kill.

The islands were a perfect spot for Watson, who arrived on the lower
west coast in 1892. "I killed Belle Starr," he boasted to Ted Smallwood,
who ran the trading post at Chokoloskee. Was it empty talk, or had he really killed the former Confederate spy who became an infamous outlaw in the
Indian territory west of the Mississippi? Islanders asked few questions, but
they could see for themselves the explosive anger that erupted without
warning from the otherwise genteel, well-spoken Southerner.

Not only was Watson a good farmer, he was also one of the best businessmen in the region. With his seventy-two-foot schooner *Veatlis*, he made
regular runs to Key West to deliver buttonwood for use as firewood and
charcoal. In the rich soil at Chatham Bend, his thirty-five-acre key some
twenty miles south of Chokoloskee, he raised fruits and vegetables to sell
in Key West and Fort Myers.

On his sizable sugar cane plantation, he produced his most successful
money-maker, a cane syrup called Island Pride. "It was as thick as honey, a
light amber color and had a flavor that was exquisite," recalled a Dade City
citrus grower. His mill was equipped to seal the syrup in four-sided tin con-
tainers which could then be shipped out in case lots for sale all along the
west coast. On the Chatham River, he built a warehouse beside his mill and
docks for his fleet of two schooners and a gasoline launch.

With his mill, his crops and his buttonwood business, Watson's operations were labor-intensive. He could have faced a large payroll, but
islanders kept hearing rumors that he had developed a macabre method for
keeping labor costs down. It was said he recruited workers, men and
women, from Arcadia, Punta Gorda and Tampa, usually picking drifters
without families, people who wouldn't be missed. After harvest, he handed
them not a cash payoff but a lonely grave. Many workers went to Chatham
Bend. Few came back off the island.

Watson's house, built with lumber shipped in from Tampa, was the
largest in the islands, a big, white, two-story frame dwelling with a third-

story attic. What went on inside that Gothic castle?

There were a few on Chokoloskee who liked him, among them Smallwood, who counted him one of his best customers, a man who always paid his bills. Some were pleased that he was a family man, with three small children living with him and his wife at Chatham Bend. Still, for many, a deep-seated uneasiness bordering on fear lingered.

"Any man that did his job, never said a word and never turned his back on you, better keep a good eye on him. That was one of the things I heard about him when I was a boy, growing up on Chatham Bend long after he was killed," says Loren "Totch" Brown, who still lives on Chokoloskee.

"I don't go looking for trouble," Watson always claimed. But many islanders were concluding that wherever Ed Watson went, trouble followed.

* * *

Born November 11, 1855, in Edgefield County, South Carolina, Edgar J. Watson came by his brutality naturally. His father, Lige "Ring-Eye" Watson, was a prison warden, a calling which in those days often summoned up reservoirs of cruelty. Lige's strange nickname came from a circular scar from a knife wound from one of his many fights.

At nine, the story goes, Edgar killed a black man, fearful he might tell Lige that his son had been guilty of planting peas carelessly. Within a year, Minnie Watson and her two children had fled the cruel Lige, traveling to Lake City, Florida, where she had relatives. At twenty, Edgar, a handsome six-footer with red hair and a red beard, married for the first time. He had to leave north Florida soon, however, after he killed a cousin in a drunken brawl in a tavern. On his way out of Florida with his wife and child, he is rumored to have shot and killed three more men in a tavern fight.

He next surfaced in Arkansas. There he joined an outlaw band headed by Belle and Sam Starr. Belle saw a streak of cruelty in Watson which made her uneasy. Still, she became a close friend of Watson's wife, who told Belle that Ed Watson was wanted for murder back in Florida. In a rash moment, she threatened to expose him: "I don't suppose the United States officers would trouble you, but the Florida officers might."

In February 1889, Belle set out on horseback to pay a bill at a nearby store. On the way back, she rode along a trail which brought her roughly three hundred yards from Watson's cabin. As she turned into a lane near the Canadian River, a shotgun blasted at her from twenty feet. Buckshot pellets struck her in the back and the neck, knocking her off her horse. A second blast struck her in the shoulder and the left side of her face.

Charged with the murder, Watson hired a prominent Fort Smith attorney. His lawyer made a strong case that the evidence was "all circumstantial."

Watson was released, but he wasted no time in fleeing to Oregon. There he acquired his second wife and, some stories say, another murder victim.

Somehow, he maneuvered his way back to Florida and the cattle town of Arcadia. In Arcadia, he shot and killed a rough character named Quinn Bass. Bass, the story goes, had a man on a tavern floor "whittling on him." When Watson told him to stop, Bass came at him, only to be cut down by a hail of .38-caliber bullets from a Smith & Wesson revolver.

In 1892, Watson arrived in the Ten Thousand Islands, working first in the cane fields near Half Mile Creek, on the mainland east of Chokoloskee.

At that time, Will Raymond, called by Ted Smallwood "a bad actor," owned Chatham Bend. Raymond got into trouble in Key West and was killed in a shootout with police. Watson bought Chatham Bend from Raymond's widow for $250.

Watson soon turned the rich land of Chatham Bend into a thriving enterprise, but, like his cane syrup, violence was always bubbling close to the boiling point. In Key West, he exploded into a rage when Adolphus Santini, a Corsican who was Chokoloskee's largest landowner, outbid him at a land auction. He cut Santini's throat. The Corsican, a seafaring man, survived, but Watson had to pay nine hundred dollars to settle the matter out of court.

On a visit to Tampa, a drunken Watson entered a hardware store near closing time. John T. Campbell, the store's bookkeeper and later president of the First National Bank of Bradenton, was telling a funny story about an incident at a dancing school.

Watson, overhearing the conversation, drew his revolver and fired a shot at the floor near Campbell's feet. "Well, let us see how nice you can dance." Watson spent that night in jail.

As stories about disappearing workers persisted, a deputy sheriff was sent from Key West to investigate. It was later said that Watson disarmed him, put him to work for a couple days in the cane patch, then sent him back to Key West with orders to the sheriff to leave Chatham Bend alone. If the story is true, the deputy was one of the few workers to come off the island alive.

In 1908, Watson returned briefly to Lake City, where he married for the third time. After Sam Toland refused to give Watson's bride a piano and some silver willed to her by Toland's late wife, Sam was gunned down. Watson was acquitted of murder charges, but the trial was costly for him. Captain W. H. Towles, a Fort Myers cattle king who helped him beat the rap, told him: "Now you get back to the Ten Thousand Islands as fast as you can — and stay there."

To the islanders, Lake City was far away, but Lostman's Key was in Chokoloskee's backyard. Watson bought the island only to find that a man

Edgar Watson's headquarters on Chatham Bend (Historical Association of Southern Florida)

named Tucker occupied part of it. He wrote a letter, demanding that he leave. Tucker wrote back "a sassy letter." Bad mistake. Tucker and his nephew were soon found dead.

In 1910, Halley's Comet moved ominously across the islanders' night-time sky. Some wondered if it could be a portent of doom. It was.

Ted Smallwood wrote in his reminiscences: "Some time later a man named Lesly Cox came down and I got a man to carry him down to Chatham Bend. Next day Watson came by and stayed all night on his way back home and we told him about it, and he asked if he looked like a preacher and we told him no. He said he might look like a preacher but he wasn't."

Soon Watson was joined by Herbert "Dutchy" Melbourne from Key West, "a bad actor," Smallwood called him, adding ". . . he had killed a policeman and burned a factory or two."

In March 1904, Melbourne, backed by a group of drunken friends, shot and killed Key West policeman C. T. Till. Convicted of murder, he was sentenced to hang. The Florida Supreme Court ruled that he could only be charged with manslaughter. Found guilty again, he received only a one-year sentence in the Key West jail.

In those days, prisoners could be hired out. Dutchy's services were sold to the Key West Fire Department. There he was able to organize a gang which engaged in robbery and arson. Its most spectacular achievement was burning down the Cortez Cigar Factory. For these crimes, Melbourne was sentenced to thirteen years in the state penitentiary. He escaped and worked his way down to Chatham Bend.

To Cox and Melbourne were added Frank Waller, a three-hundred-pound woman named Hannah Smith, stronger than most men, it was said, and a black fugitive named Sip Linsy.

The impression spread that Watson knew Cox from somewhere else. Had they been partners in crime in the past? Or had Cox somehow helped him win out in the Lake City murder trial? The suspicion grew that Cox might be an even rougher neighbor than Watson.

"I thought something would soon happen and it did," wrote Smallwood.

Linsy somehow escaped from Chatham Bend, fleeing terrified through the mangrove swamps until he reached Chokoloskee. What he told was a frightening, disjointed story. He said Cox had made him help kill Hannah and Waller while Watson was away. That night, when Watson returned, they killed Dutchy "and put him in the creek."

In early October, fishermen headed for the clam beds on Possum Key. Near Chatham Bend, they saw a foot sticking up out of the water. The body was a large one and they had a hard time pulling it to the surface.

What they saw horrified them. It was the body of a woman who had been cut open. Someone had jammed weights inside Hannah Smith's belly to make her sink.

Jim Cannon, a clammer, said, "Let's go to Watson's and tell him."

His son, already wiser than his father in the ways of the world, said, "No, let's go to the clam bar and tell them."

The men working at the clam bar came to the island, helped drag Hannah out and buried her, far from the Okefenokee Swamp where she was born.

* * *

On October 17, a West Indian hurricane swept across the islands. The waters rose six feet, washing away structures and docks and killing chickens and livestock. High winds laced with rain battered Chokoloskee's pioneer settlement. Smallwood's store and his stock of goods took a rain-soaked pounding.

Watson, returning from Fort Myers, came by the store and told Smallwood he was going to Chatham Bend to kill Cox. He didn't realize the shotgun shells he bought were still wet from the hurricane.

The afternoon of October 24, one week after the hurricane, the islanders heard the sound of the *Brave*, coming closer and closer to Chokoloskee.

Watson cut the motor and let his boat glide up on the beach. He stepped out then to face the posse, carrying his shotgun and wearing a black hat.

Someone called out, "What happened to Cox?" Watson said he killed him, but his body had fallen into the water and all that was left was his black hat. Watson showed the men the hat. He said the hole in the hat was made by the bullet that killed Cox.

The posse was not impressed. Then came a call to Watson to put down his gun. Quick as always, he lifted the gun to fire into the crowd. A harmless click. The shells were still damp.

A withering round of fire from the posse cut Watson down.

Inside the store, Mamie Smallwood said, "My God, they have killed Mr. Watson."

Who killed him? A better question: Who didn't? The sheriff made a half-hearted investigation, but there was no way he could learn whose bullet or bullets had killed a man most of them were glad to be rid of anyway. The islanders buried him first on Rabbit Key, but later his family had his body taken to Fort Myers to the Watson family plot.

Sip Linsy was arrested for his role in the murder of Melbourne, Waller and Hannah Smith. Linsy's account was so convincing in implicating Cox that the Key West grand jury refused to bring charges against Linsy. Furthermore, the city gave him clothes, some money and a railroad ticket back to his former home in Georgia. Convinced that Cox was still alive, the sheriff told Linsy to stay in touch in case Cox was ever caught.

Ed Watson was fifty-four when he was gunned down. His fame would spread over the years ahead, as storytellers spun yarns about his evil deeds and then embellished them. Two novels would be written about him, both, by an incredible coincidence, by authors named Matthiessen. The latest, *Killing Mr. Watson*, written by the eminent writer Peter Matthiessen, was published to wide acclaim in 1990.

Edgar Watson is, however, all but forgotten in his hometown of Edgefield, South Carolina. Edgefield proudly points to ten state governors born in the little town — from John C. Calhoun to Strom Thurmond. It does not trumpet abroad the birth there in the Savannah River Valley of the infamous Mr. Watson.

INTERLUDE:
A SOFTER CRIME

In the 1950s, a softer, gentler crime surfaced. It involved a creative use of brassieres.

CHAPTER 14

The Case of the Clinking Brassieres

*Miami snickered and the phone company squirmed
when the "bra girls" were exposed.*

From the start, it was called "the Case of the Clinking Brassieres."

It had Miamians smirking and snickering. Newspaper reporters and headline writers poured forth an endless stream of double-entrendre words and phrases. In the early 1950s, cheesecake was rampant anyway in American newspapers, which were eager for an excuse to show bare legs and plunging necklines.

And Southern Bell, the victim of the scheme, endured a battering from its stockholders, local businesses and even state regulators.

After a successful two-year run, the "bra girls," as they were called, saw their act collapse from a combination of bad breaks, bad judgment and an almost innocent view of the crime scene into which they had strayed.

Their racket began to fall apart the night of September 23, 1950. As is often the case at the end of a long, hot Miami summer, nerves were frayed and tempers were primed for explosion. Good judgment was in short supply that hot Saturday night.

Detective John Resick, of the Miami auto theft bureau, had a spat with his pretty young wife, Eleanor. He went to work and she went to the home of Rita Orr, a friend and neighbor, to spend the night.

Rita, who worked for the phone company, was upset. She had just found $150 missing from her cedar chest and even more from a stash her mother had. She insisted her sister-in-law Marie had taken it and had run off with her Marine boy friend. Eleanor advised her to call the police. At eighteen, Rita was not seasoned in the workings of the law. She made a bad mistake. She called the police.

Chief Ray Mills, from the West Miami station, arrived, listened to a confusing tale and observed a veritable silver mine: a pillow case filled with wrapped coins and several queen-sized bras. He told Rita it looked like an inside job. He said he was going back to the station and would return promptly with a fingerprint man to go over the whole house.

After he left, Rita realized just how big her blunder was. She immediately began collecting suitcases and boxes of money, most of it in rolls of quarters.

Meanwhile, Eleanor called her husband and asked him to come immediately to help out in a situation she didn't quite understand. She just knew something was wrong.

Detective Resick came quickly. Rita gave him six hundred dollars in quarters and asked him to keep them for her. He took them home and then reported in to his station house.

Rita next began moving loot to a nearby rooming house where one of her co-conspirators lived. Other women involved in the caper soon appeared, among them Rita's sister-in-law, Marie.

"What the hell did you call the police for?" Marie yelled at Rita.

Next, her wrath was directed at Eleanor Resick. "Get that six hundred dollars back here or I'll kill you."

The landlady at the rooming house, alarmed at the evening's bizarre events, telephoned still another police station.

Miami detective C. B. Newton arrived at the same time as Chief Mills, who brought with him a patrolman with an appropriate name, Carry Cash. They found the girls fighting over some two thousand dollars in coins and currency.

Then Betty Corrigan, a pretty honey-blonde, drove up on her return from a trip to St. Augustine. Bad timing. She went in to see what was happening and was promptly swept into the probe. Inside her car, police found three suitcases filled with more than five thousand dollars in coins and currency.

Where, the police wondered, was all this money coming from?

As they questioned the women, they picked up a common thread that pointed to the source. All but one of the women woked for the phone company. Could Southern Bell's phone booths be the silver fountain?

Eight women and six men, either relatives or boyfriends, were arrested and taken to police headquarters. Rita Orr's rash telephone call landed six members of her own family in jail — herself, her husband, two sisters-in-law, her father and her mother, who would be called a "a 1950 model of Ma Barker" by the prosecution, an exaggerated comparison to the gangland matriarch.

Soon the women began to break down, some in tears, some in talking jags. Apparently unaware of their right to have an attorney present, they openly revealed a beautifully simple routine for enhancing their low wages. The first police estimate of the take was roughly twenty-five thousand dollars.

Betty Corrigan was the biggest talker. She and her fellow conspirators worked in the counting room, where money was received from pay telephones. It was basically an unsupervised operation.

"It was just too easy, all that money lying around and no one even checking up on you," said Betty. "The money comes in sealed boxes. We break the seal and put it in an automatic change counter. From the counter it goes into canvas bags. But we took it out before we put it into the counter."

And where did they put it?

They simply stuffed rolls of quarters into their bras and took them to the locker room. There they met Mrs. Billie Ruth McNabb, Marie Orr's sister, who put the money in her queen-size bra and transported it out of the building. Mrs. McNabb, who was not a phone company employee, was paid five dollars a day by the bra girls.

"Sometimes we carried as many as five rolls of quarters out at one time," said Corrigan. "But we didn't do that often. It hurt."

A ten-dollar roll of forty quarters measured two and nine-sixteenth inches in length and weighed eight and one-half ounces.

As the story unfolded, police estimates rose to a dizzying and — to Southern Bell — an embarrassing level of $100,000.

The "falsy Fagans," as a writer for *The Miami Daily News* called them, had different reasons for venturing into a life of crime. Said Betty Corrigan: "My husband is a truck driver. We were saving up to buy a home."

Marie Orr said, "I was going to get married Thanksgiving Day. It would have come in handy."

Bonnie Hebert had averaged seventy-five dollars to ninety dollars a day before she quit her job with Southern Bell. "It was bad on my husband," she said. "We were spending too much money. We just got rotten through and through."

In the Hebert home, police found fifteen hundred dollars in postal savings certificates and war bonds. She and her husband had also bought a lot and a car. He was arrested for receiving stolen property one day before he was scheduled to start school at the University of Miami.

Just as the "Brassiere Brigade" saw their lives crashing around them, the case took a strange twist. Southern Bell decided not to press charges. The company's problem was that it couldn't determine the amount stolen on any given day nor could it identify the money as its own. The case, the company feared, was a weak one and a loss in court could lead to catastrophic law-suits.

Some suspected their real reason was embarrassment. They may have just wanted to get the story off the front pages.

One joker mailed in his monthly payment addressed to Southern Bra Company. It was delivered.

Stockholders in the mighty AT&T empire were bristling at the sloppy supervision of company money. Local merchants who received a percent-age of the take from phone booths in their stores were wondering how much revenue they had lost.

Wilbur King, a member of the Florida State Railroad and Public Utilities Commission, announced he wanted "a lot of information" on bookkeeping and security before considering a rate increase for Southern Bell.

A gag product, Piggy Bank Bras, equipped for carrying coins, was quick-ly produced by a Miami entrepreneur, Paul Deal.

A New York manufacturer sent Barbara Nichols, a twenty-one-year-old model, to Miami to deliver a box of Hidden Treasures bras to Southern Bell's district manager, J. M. Phillips. The bra company suggested Southern Bell make it mandatory for all coin counters to wear Hidden Treasures, claiming their product "is a built-in contour brassiere which allows no free-dom between the material and the bosom. A built-in cup which holds the bosom securely in place doesn't give the wearer room enough to even slip a thin dime into her bra."

By now, the bra girls had acquired attorneys, James Rainwater and young Harry Prebish, just three years out of the University of Miami Law School. Their first advice was to tell their new clients not to talk about the case and not to sign the confessions they had given so freely.

Rainwater next made a particularly cheeky move. Since there was no complaint from the phone company, he declared he would personally escort the six bra girls back to claim their old jobs.

They were promptly told they couldn't go back to work.

"You mean we're fired?" asked an astonished Betty Corrigan.

Next, the attorneys announced they would file a suit to recover some ten thousand dollars seized as evidence. Since the company refused to claim it, it still belongs to the girls, they reasoned.

But the battlefield was about to change. Under heavy pressure from the police and the state attorney's office, Southern Bell's Jacksonville office audited long-distance records and came up with a $646.75 shortfall on August 23, 1950, a day when Betty and Marie did the counting. The com-pany agreed on Thursday to sign the complaint.

Thirty hours after they thought they had escaped the law, the women found themselves back in court. This time some were charged with grand larceny. Some of them and the men in the case were charged with receiving stolen property.

The next day, two more people were charged, Detective John Resick and his wife, Eleanor. The six hundred dollars Resick had received from Rita had led to a charge of stealing and receiving stolen property.

Assistant State Attorney Michael Zarowny decided to push first for the prosecution of Marie Orr, Betty Corrigan and Billie Ruth McNabb. They were the only ones who had given lengthy statements to the police. The three later repudiated their confessions and refused to sign them, but the court ruled them admissible.

It took an all-male jury just eighteen minutes to return a verdict of guilty. The jurors recommended mercy and apparently Judge Ben Willard took that into account. He could have sentenced the three women to five years in jail. Instead, he gave them one-year jail sentences. But the case was far from over for them or their fellow perpetrators.

For the next six months, others were tried. Some whose roles were marginal were acquitted. Some of the cases were dropped by the state, among them the charge against Detective Resick. None of the bra girls convicted after the first trial received jail terms, just fines and suspended sentences.

Orr, Corrigan and McNabb returned $24,118 to the phone company, leaving them flat broke. Harry Prebish asked the state to pay for their appeals to the Florida Supreme Court. A newspaper account pointed out that they appeared in court in "high-neckline garb."

On July 31, 1951, they learned the bad news. The court upheld the conviction and the sentence. Prebish, who would later become one of Miami's premier defense attorneys, still had one more move to make. He asked Governor Fuller Warren and the state cabinet to pardon the girls.

"People were sympathetic toward the girls," Prebish recalled later. "A big company had a sloppy system for collecting and counting money and the girls were sorely tempted by a system that invited theft."

The pardon never came, but the sympathy vote finally worked for them. Their jail sentences were suspended and they were simply placed on probation.

"It was called the Case of the Clinking Brassieres and there was nothing quite like it," recalled Prebish. "They bought cars and things and when they were caught they didn't have any paper money, but they brought a footlocker full of quarters to the office to pay their legal expenses."

In the 1990s, the bra girls would have become national celebrities, in demand for talk shows and revealing magazine photos with and without their bras. In the 1950s, they faded out of sight as fast as they could.

DEATH IN THE
GULF STREAM

To the British islands and Scandinavia, the Gulf Stream is a
benevolent force, creating a warmer, more livable climate
and a longer growing season. To violent people, the Gulf
Stream, dark blue, deep and swift-flowing, can be used to
hide the fruits of unspeakable acts.

CHAPTER 15

Hanging a Pirate

How to execute a Gulf Stream murderer
baffled Broward County.

In January 1928, the Gulf Stream Pirate learned a piece of news that was very bad for him, but not unexpected. Already convicted of murdering two U.S. Coast Guardsmen and one U.S. Secret Service agent on the high seas, Horace Alderman was not surprised to learn that he would be "hanged by the neck until you are dead and may God have mercy on your soul."

On June 20, 1929, it was Broward County's turn for a jolting piece of information. Federal Judge Hallsted L. Ritter set the date, August 17, 1929, for the execution. For the county, the bad news was that the hanging would have to take place at the Broward County Courthouse in Fort Lauderdale and Sheriff A. W. Turner would face the squeamish task of getting the job done.

Broward's problem was this. The county had never hanged anybody before and had no idea how to go about it. How do you build a gallows? Dade County pine or possibly oak? What kind of rope do you use and how strong should it be? How do you tie a hangman's knot? About the only thing the county felt comfortable about was serving the condemned man his last good meal to send him off into eternity.

Besides, Broward just didn't want to hang a man, even as blackhearted a killer as Alderman. Schools, trash collection, law enforcement — these were the things a county government did. Hanging? No way.

But Judge Ritter said Broward had no choice. Researching his law books, the judge had discovered that a pirate who commits murder on the high seas must be hanged in the port to which he was first brought upon reentering the States. And that port was Fort Lauderdale, home of Coast Guard Base Six.

The base was located on one of Fort Lauderdale's most historic sites. In

1839, at the height of the Second Seminole War, the third Fort Lauderdale was built on government land on the barrier island east of New River Sound. In 1876, the U.S. Life Saving Service built the Fort Lauderdale House of Refuge to help shipwrecked sailors on the military reservation. But by 1929, it was serving as a Coast Guard station, kept busy during Prohibition by the flow of illegal booze smuggled into south Florida from the Bahamas and Cuba.

On August 7, 1927, *CG-249*, a seventy-five-foot Coast Guard patrol boat, set out from Fort Lauderdale, cruising toward Bimini, a favorite supply port for rumrunners. Aboard were six Coast Guardsmen and Robert Webster, a special Treasury Department agent investigating counterfeit currency being circulated by bootleggers in the Bahamas.

About one in the afternoon, the patrol boat sighted a forty-foot open-cockpit speedboat on a course much favored by rumrunners between Bimini and Miami. When the speedboat tried to outrun the Coast Guard cutter, Boatswain Sydney Sanderlin, skipper of the boat, fired a blank round from the boat's one-pound cannon.

The speedboat pilot got the point and stopped for what the Coast Guardsmen thought would be a routine search. Violence was rare in these situations. Sentences were light, so a shootout wasn't worth the risk.

James Horace Alderman was in charge of the speedboat, backed up by his first mate, Robert Weech. The search party quickly located twenty burlap-covered cases of liquor in the engine compartment. Alderman and Weech were then ordered to come aboard the cutter and be searched. No weapons were found.

Alderman asked permission to reboard his boat to pick up his personal belongings. "I'll never see them again after the boat is turned over to Customs," said Alderman.

Sanderlin went to the pilothouse to radio Fort Lauderdale. Before he could complete his call, Alderman returned, armed now with a pistol he had hidden in his boat. He shot Sanderlin in the back, then took the skipper's .45 automatic and began shooting at the rest of the crew, a pistol in each hand. After he gunned down Machinist Mate Victor Lamby, he said to the rest of the crew:

"I'm gonna burn your boat, take you out in the Gulf Stream and throw you overboard. You're shark bait."

When Alderman turned his head to call down to Weech in the engine room, the Coast Guardsmen jumped him. Hal Caudle, a seventeen-year-old Coast Guardsman from Pompano, later wrote:

"The Secret Serviceman was shot down right in front of me. Alderman raised the gun at me and I grabbed the barrel. He shot twice in my face and I don't see how he missed me. I think it was because Johnny Robinson's weight pulled me down, as he climbed over me with the ice pick. . . . As soon as I got the gun, I hit him [Alderman] in the head. . . . The skipper and the Secret Serviceman were dead and Lamby wounded, the cook wounded, and the bootlegger with ice pick holes in him and a busted head and the other with a busted head."

Lamby died the next day at the Fort Lauderdale hospital. In federal court in Miami, Alderman and Weech were charged with three murders. Weech pleaded guilty to rumrunning, testified against Alderman and was sent to prison for a year and a day.

Alderman received the death penalty. He took it calmly. "This," he said, "will not change me in any way." He was wrong. Death by hanging will change anybody's lifestyle.

* * *

Now in his late forties, the Gulf Stream Pirate, as the press dubbed him, had lived a life of unremitting crime. Born in Tampa, he had spent his youth as a fishing guide in the Ten Thousand Islands. He had guided President Teddy Roosevelt and famed western novelist Zane Grey back into the islands in search of tarpon. He became a master boatman, a master navigator and in time a master smuggler.

At a pool hall he owned in Fort Myers, he branched out to offer high-stakes gambling to rumrunners and pioneer cattlemen from the Everglades. Soon he moved into rumrunning from the Bahamas to Tampa. He made the mistake of hiring as a cook an undercover Customs agent. He and his three fellow bootleggers served year-and-a-day sentences.

After his prison term, he returned to Fort Myers. Josie Billie, a prominent Seminole medicine man, came to the pool hall with a wad of money to bet. Alderman lured him out to a secluded beach, clubbed him into unconsciousness and robbed him of five hundred dollars he had earned for a year of trapping in the swamps. Left for dead, Billie lived to testify against his assailant. Alderman served two more years in state prison.

In 1927, he was arrested on charges of smuggling aliens. Immigration authorities were told he had been contracting to bring aliens, principally Chinese, into Florida from Cuba. Sometimes, it was said, he dropped the aliens overboard after the payoff and left them to drown in the swift-flowing ocean river called the Gulf Stream. It was while he was out on bond for the alien-smuggling charge that he killed the three men aboard the Coast Guard cutter.

                                        *   *   *

Before he became sheriff in 1915, when the new county of Broward was formed, Turner had been a member of the school board in Pompano, where he owned a packinghousee, hardly the background for a hangman. As the time approached for the hanging, he struggled, too, to figure out just how to conduct the execution. The ceilings in the jail, located in a wing of the courthouse, were too low for a gallows to be built inside.

Eight days before the execution date, Judge Ritter issued another order. Aware of the difficulties with the low ceiling, he decreed that the hanging be done on the roof of the jail. A new problem arose immediately. The roof of the jail was bonded by a roofing company. A heavy gallows, plus the hangman's crew and the victim, could be more weight than the roof could stand. The bond would have to be voided. Furthermore, the thought of the hanged man dropping through the trapdoor and then bringing the whole assembly down through the roof disturbed the courthouse gang. Everybody would look bad.

By now, protests were cropping up all over Fort Lauderdale. Why did the hanging have to be on county land? Why not on federal land, either the Coast Guard base or the Indian reservation in Hollywood. The federal government, beginning to back away from its insistence that Broward do the deed, suggested that it might rent space in the jail yard to erect a gallows. The county commission, determined now to shift the hanging onto federal property, figured out a way to block even the rental approach. Permission could not be given without a quorum and for one reason or another the commission kept finding it could not seem to assemble a quorum.

Much was made of the fact that no legal execution had ever been performed in the county, a less-than-impressive claim since the county was only fourteen years old. A petition was sent to south Florida Congresswoman Ruth Bryan Owen, the daughter of William Jennings Bryan, three times the Democratic Party's candidate for president. The petition contended that Broward should not be the site for the execution since Alderman was not a resident of the county and the murder had not been committed within the county. It went on to say: "Our people are a self-respecting, home and community-loving folk, and feel that the hanging of the said Alderman within the county would create for this community a bad reputation and would result in the public generally feeling less kindly toward our county. That the unfavorable publicity which said hanging would give Broward County would result in great disparagement and irreparable damage to its citizens."

Broward County Courthouse, originally designated as the site of the Alderman hanging
(Broward County Historical Commission)

Religious protests were being made. After receiving the death penalty, Alderman was converted to Christianity through the tearful pleas of his thirteen-year-old daughter, Thelma. Before his conversion, he had been an extraordinarily vicious criminal. When told that Lamby had died, he laughed boisterously. For his first seven months in jail, the incorrigible pirate was kept in solitary confinement. Said Alderman: "I used to think heaven and hell were on this earth. It was heaven to me when I landed a load and got good price for it. When I got caught, that was hell."

In his final year in jail, Alderman, a daily reader of the Bible, converted five other prisoners. He was even being called a martyr. Alderman's change of heart, however, was not enough to impress President Herbert Hoover, an enthusiastic fisherman in Florida waters. The president declined to commute his sentence. One religious group got carried away. The Coast Guard cook, who lost an eye to Alderman's gunplay, said the group offered him a house in Palm Beach and ten thousand dollars to change his testimony. He declined.

With five days to go, Judge Ritter finally gave in to the pressure. He announced that it had been found "necessary and desirable" to change the hanging site. Alderman would be hanged at Coast Guard Base Six, the exact place where he was first brought in. Two days later, contractor J. G. Johnson erected the scaffold and gallows in the rear center portion of the seaplane hangar. He installed and checked out the trigger release device for the trap door.

The Gulf Stream Pirate seemed the calmest player in the grim game. He issued invitations to several close friends to witness his execution. "It's my personal hanging and I want to invite my friends to it."

As the time drew near, Judge Ritter banned all press coverage. He wanted no repeat of the incident at New York's Sing Sing prison when a *New York Daily Mirror* reporter strapped a small camera to his leg and photographed the electrocution of Ruth Snyder. Judges all over the country shuddered at the sensationalized coverage.

A break for the press came from an unexpected quarter. Frank McGhan thought the judge's order a high-handed affront to freedom of the press. As manager of King Undertaking Company of Miami, he was in a position to do something about it. He had won the contract to pick up Alderman's body after the execution. McGhan offered to let a *Miami Herald* reporter drive the hearse. Eddie Hay, amusement columnist, was picked. He wasn't likely to be recognized by any of the officials at the hanging.

The night before the execution, Alderman, now fifty years old, ate pork chops, French fries, bread, butter and a basket of fruit brought to him by his minister. At 4 A.M., he ate again, four strips of bacon, two poached eggs, toast and coffee. Then he was taken to a van by six deputies. Six carloads of law enforcement officials led the way from the county jail east on Las Olas Boulevard, then south on the beach road to the base at Bahia Mar.

Coast Guardsmen, some carrying submachine guns, kept newsmen from entering Base Six. One, however, slipped through: Eddie Hay, the amusement writer. He parked near the gallows, where the hangman waited. The man picked to do the deed was Bob Baker, the one-legged sheriff from Palm Beach County. His credentials were the best Sheriff Turner could find. He was, in fact, the only one in the area who knew how to tie the hangman's knot, essential if the doomed man was to be rendered unconscious quickly. Otherwise, the result would be a slow, painful — some would say cruel — death.

A wool sailor's cap did the job as a hood to cover Alderman's face. He was escorted up the nine steps to the fifteen-foot-high gallows platform. The pirate was humming, "Jesus, Here I'm Coming," as he stepped onto the trap door. Baker slipped the noose of the manila rope around his neck and pulled it tight. Finally, his legs were tied together.

U.S. Coast Guard Base Six, where the Gulf Stream Pirate was hanged in 1929
(Fort Lauderdale Historical Society)

Outside, the sun was beginning to rise over the blue waters of the Gulf Stream, a river he had crossed many times with booze and doomed aliens. Now Alderman had one more river to cross. Baker said to him, "Then, goodbye and may God have mercy on your soul."

The bolt shot back at 6:04 A.M. Alderman fell seven feet and hung there. He choked and kicked for a full twelve minutes before he was finally strangled to death. Despite his resume, Baker had not tied the knot properly. On hand was Dr. Elliot M. Hendricks, a Fort Lauderdale physician who served as quarantine officer for the base, and who had treated Alderman's ice-pick wounds when he was first brought to the base. His task now was to pronounce him dead.

It was time for newsman Eddie Hay to reenter the picture. He was jolted from his daze by a whisper from the mortician: "Come on. We take over now. Act like you know what you're doing. Help me get the stretcher out of the hearse."

Hay later wrote: "I'll never remember how we did it, but we lowered the body gently on to the stretcher, threw a blanket over it and loaded it into the hearse, closed the doors and somehow I was starting the engine. Now I know how a zombie feels or doesn't feel, automatically obeying orders. My nerves were tied into a hangman's knot."

Back at the paper, Hay quickly wrote the only eyewitness account. Then came the word. The paper was not going to run the story.

Frank B. Shutts, owner and publisher of the *Herald*, had been a classmate of Judge Ritter's at Depauw University. At the last minute, Shutts, a lawyer himself, decided he would not defy the judge's edict. He told his news editor, John Pennekamp, to pull the story.

Thousands filed by to view the body at the Alliance Tabernacle in Miami and a large crowd attended the funeral of the pirate who had killed three U.S. lawmen and probably many Chinese aliens.

It marked the end for the Gulf Stream Pirate but not for Dr. Hendricks. For weeks after the execution, he was troubled with nightmares. Said his daughter, Dr. Anne L. Hendricks: "Alderman was the only calm one at the hanging."

CHAPTER 16

Judgment Day

---

*A Palm Beach judge protected his racket
with murder — of another judge.*

"We'll have to get rid of the judge."

One judge plotting the murder of another? Unheard of. But Joe Peel was more than just a judge. And at the same time considerably less than a judge.

He was also a racketeer — protection, moonshine and the numbers game known as bolita. Now his illicit empire was threatened by another judge, stern, incorruptible Curtis E. Chillingworth, the highest-ranking legal officer in Palm Beach County.

This is why Joe Peel sat in his law office in the Harvey Building in downtown West Palm Beach and talked with a man no judge should ever associate with. The crimes for which Floyd "Lucky" Holzapfel had already served time included bookmaking and armed robbery. Nonetheless, in June of 1955, he was Joe Peel's partner.

Simple arithmetic explains why they wanted Judge Chillingworth out of the way. As a West Palm Beach municipal judge, Peel earned three thousand dollars a year, not nearly enough to pay for his Cadillac or his wife Imogene's Lincoln Continental, not even when you add in the returns from a shady law practice.

But as a player in West Palm's murky underworld, Joe took in three thousand dollars a week. Now the empire was about to crumble, and all because of a botched-up divorce case.

On June 15, 1955, Joe was scheduled to appear in Circuit Court on charges that could lead to disbarment. He had to answer claims he had lied to a client by telling her her divorce was final. She married again, had a child, then learned that Peel had never obtained her divorce. He had simply taken her money and told her everything was in order.

Ten days before his day in court, Joe and Lucky drove north to Riviera

Beach to visit another partner in crime. Big, menacing Bobby Lincoln was a power in Riviera's black community. He ran numbers and moonshine operations for the partners and also owned taxicabs and pool halls.

Joe Peel never entered Lincoln's home, preferring always to talk to him in his big, air-conditioned Cadillac. They drove over the Blue Heron Boulevard bridge across the Intracoastal Waterway to Singer Island, then continued to the undeveloped northern section of the island. Here Joe felt safe to talk.

"Bobby," said Peel, "a man is trying to ruin us and I have got to kill him."

By the time the evening's plotting was over, Judge Chillingworth and his wife Marjorie had less than ten days to live. Their murder would initiate one of the longest and most relentless manhunts in Florida history, would lead to rewards of over $100,000, would produce the state's most publicized trial, and would finally result in one of the strangest split verdicts any state has ever seen.

One murderer would turn state's evidence and go free.

One would plead guilty, cooperate with the court, then hear his death sentence pronounced.

The third, the mastermind, would receive only a life sentence, and then not serve it all.

* * *

Judge Chillingworth could point to a distinguished ancestry. His grandfather had been sheriff of Dade County and later the first mayor of West Palm Beach. His father had been the first municipal attorney for both Lantana and West Palm Beach.

In 1923, Curtis Chillingworth, just twenty-six at the time, had become the youngest judge ever to serve on Florida's Circuit Court. He had gone on to earn a reputation as one of the state's best trial judges, stiff and cold, but nonetheless a symbol of the integrity the court at its best is supposed to project. Judge James R. Knott, who succeeded him on the bench, once wrote he "was considered by many as South Florida's leading jurist, and possibly its most widely respected native son."

The night of June 14, the Chillingworths were guests of honor at a Palm Beach party commemorating the thirty-second anniverary of the judge's appointment to the bench. Among the partyers were the mayor and the town manager of Florid's ritziest enclave.

The Chillingworths left the party about nine-thirty. On a moonlit night, they drove south along the beach on Highway A1A past the mansions of Palm Beach to their oceanfront home in the exclusive community of

Judge Chillingworth (Historical Association of Southern Florida)

Manalapan. Shortly after they went to bed, a knock on the door to their seaside porch awakened them.

A man dressed like a boat captain, blue shirt and yachting cap, asked, "Are you Judge Chillingworth?"

"Yes, I am."

"Stand right where you are, Judge." Lucky Holzapfel pulled a revolver from his shirt. "Now, behave yourself, Your Honor, and we'll get along just fine. Anyone else here? Speak!"

"My wife," said the judge. "Look, we don't have much money here, but . . . "

"Shut up. Get her out here fast." Lucky cursed. Joe Peel had said she would not be home. Marjorie Chillingworth, an attractive woman in her late fifties, appeared, wearing a nightgown.

Quickly, Holzapfel and Lincoln taped the Chillingworths' hands behind their backs and then taped their mouths. As they walked across the porch, the judge worked his gag loose and whispered to Lincoln, "Boy, if you help us out of this, I'll see that you don't have to work another day of your life."

Mrs. Chillingworth loosened her gag and screamed. Lucky brought his pistol down on her head. They pushed the judge into a small boat they had beached, then dragged the dazed, bleeding woman aboard.

The engine sputtered, but finally they pushed off into the ocean's calm waters.

"What are you going to do with us?" asked the judge.

"You'll see pretty soon, Judge," answered Lucky.

The engine began to overheat, so Lucky cut it and drifted on the moon-lit sea. While Holzapfel fastened weighted cartridge belts around the Chillingworths, Lincoln got the engine started again. They cruised out to the Gulf Stream.

"This is far enough," said Holzapfel. Grinning at Mrs. Chillingworth, he pulled her away from her husband.

"Bobby, help me. Ladies first."

"Honey, remember I love you," cried out Judge Chillingworth.

"I love you, too," she answered.

Then they pitched her into the sea.

The judge lurched to his feet and plunged overboard, trying to save her. There was nothing he could do. Too weak to struggle, she sank quietly, leaving behind only a stream of bubbles.

The judge tried valiantly to swim. The killers lunged for him but he stayed out of reach. Then they started the engine again and edged up beside him. Floyd broke Judge Peel's shotgun over Chillingworth's head. Still the judge struggled.

Lucky tied an anchor around the judge's neck and threw it into the sea. As it sank, they watched his faded pink pajamas disappear into the depths of the bleak ocean.

The bodies of Curtis and Marjorie Chillingworth were never found.

*   *   *

In thirty-two years, Judge Chillingworth had never been late for court. When he failed to appear the morning of June 15, Sheriff John Kirk began an immediate investigation. He didn't like what he found at the oceanfront cottage. The Chillingworths' beds had been slept in, their cars were in the garage, but there was no trace of either of them.

Dark stains were found on the porch steps. When they they determined the stains matched Mrs. Chillingworth's blood type, police knew they were

Police search the crime scene at the beachfront home of Judge and Mrs. Chillingworth, seeking traces of the missing couple. (Historical Association of Southern Florida)

investigating a homicide, a homicide with precious few leads.

Since the murder of a judge is more than a homicide, a crime not just against a man or a woman but against a society's system of justice, the reward money was huge. It totaled $179,000. A hundred thousand dollars came from the state of Florida, twenty-five thousand from the surviving members of the Chillingworth family, ten thousand from a friend and neighbor named Harold Vanderbilt and five thousand from Governor LeRoy Collins.

State Attorney Phil O'Connell was a tough ex-prizefighter. Though he had won fifty-nine of sixty welterweight bouts, the Chillingworth murder case was shaping up as the toughest fight of his career.

How do you prosecute a homicide without bodies? He couldn't even prove a murder had been committed, much less find out who had done it. His case file grew as grand jury after grand jury sought the answer. The leads always amounted to dead ends.

Joe Peel knew O'Connell well. Anyone who aspired to a political career would have to. O'Connell was the county's political boss. And Joe had worked with O'Connell when beginning his law career.

One of four children of a respected West Palm Beach hotel owner, Joe Peel had served in the Army during World War II, then attended Stetson University Law School. At Stetson he met Imogene Clark, a beauty from Lake City, who was named "Miss Stetson." She became Mrs. Joe Peel.

When Joe started his law career, O'Connell offered him free space in his office. Wavy, black hair combined with charm and blarney marked the handsome Peel as a political "comer."

In 1953, Peel ran afoul of Curtis Chillingworth. He had committed the unforgivable deceit of representing both sides in a divorce case. Judge Chillingworth issued a severe reprimand and later said if Peel ever came before him again, he would "break" him. The venerable judge had no way of knowing how criminal a course Joe would take within the next year.

Peel had been elected a municipal judge, a position which empowered him to issue search warrants for raids on bolita and moonshine operations. Joe and Lucky, whom he had represented in a small claims court case, proceeded to develop a way of converting the low-paying judgeship into a real moneymaker.

Working with Lincoln, they developed a shrewd protection racket. They collected money from moonshiners and bolita operators in return for advance warnings of police raids. As his foray into crime widened, Peel's income rose sharply.

Whatever moral inhibitions he might have held earlier had vanished by June 15, his day in court, the day that threatened to strip him of his judgeship, the key to the protection racket. Ironically, he received only a ninety-day suspension from the practice of law, not enough to put him completely out of business.

Still, Joe was a much-changed man after the Chillingworth murders. His behavior became increasingly erratic.

He took out an insurance policy on his law partner, then tried to have Lucky kill him. In the aftermath of the botched attempt, Holzapfel was charged but acquitted, and charges were dropped against Peel and the insurance agent who sold the policy, James Yenzer.

In 1958, Peel closed his law practice and moved to Brevard County. There he and Lucky started an investment swindle.

Meanwhile, Lucky stayed busy. A man from Jacksonville was suspected of informing on moonshiners in the West Palm area. Holzapfel and Lincoln shot him, weighted his body down and dumped him a canal near Lake Okeechobee. When the body of Lew Gene Harvey surfaced, Sheriff Kirk called for help from the Florida Sheriff's Bureau.

Henry Lovern, the sharp, shrewd agent sent to work the case, came across as a slow-talking, easygoing good ol' boy. It was an act.

He made contact with Lucky's friend Yenzer, who knew about the Harvey murder. One night after a few drinks, Yenzer began to talk about the Chillingworth case.

Lovern pretended a lack of interest, but carefully checked out Yenzer's claims. He concluded then that he was onto the biggest case of his career. He persuaded Yenzer to work with him as an undercover agent. Reward money has a way of motivating snitches.

Lucky hijacked a load of guns intended for rebels trying to overthrow the Somoza government in Nicaragua. He was captured and sentenced to fifteen years. Bail Bondsman P. O. Wilbur put up Lucky's bond, only to have him escape to Rio de Janeiro.

Holzapfel was unhappy in Rio. Joe Peel was sending him very little money from their investment business.

Everybody was knifing everybody else. Still worried that Lucky could implicate him in the Chillingworth case, Peel hired Yenzer to lure Lucky back and kill him.

Meanwhile, Lovern had both Yenzer and Wilbur, understandably angry at the bail jumper, working together as undercover agents to bring Holzapfel back to the States — but not to kill him. They wanted him to talk.

In September 1960, five years after the Chillingworth murders, Lucky arrived in Melbourne to meet his two old friends in a motel room. The room was wired. Next door, Henry Lovern listened to and recorded every word Lucky uttered during a seventy-hour drinking bout. When it ended, Lovern knew the full, horrifying story of the Chillingworth murders.

Joe Peel awaited word from Yenzer that he had rubbed out Lucky, a hit for which he had already paid him eighty-three hundred dollars. The word Joe got was a good deal more ominous. The state, not the morgue, had Holzapfel.

Still, the case presented problems for the prosecutor. Since no bodies were ever found, O'Connell needed one of the three to confess to confirm that murder had actually been committed.

To save his own skin, Peel wanted to talk. O'Connell refused to give immunity to the crime's mastermind. Instead he offered it to Lincoln — for the Harvey and Chillingworth murders.

The setting for the offer was perfect: a Tallahassee prison cell. Lincoln was serving time for a moonshine conviction. In exchange for immunity for three murders, he agreed to give O'Connell the full story of the Chillingworth slayings.

Even without immunity, Holzapfel also followed with a full confession and decided to plead guilty. Despite his complete cooperation, not-so-Lucky was sentenced to the electric chair.

On March 7, 1961, Peel went on trial in the St. Lucie County Courthouse in Fort Pierce, some fifty miles north of West Palm Beach, where still powerful memories dictated a change of venue. Joe Peel faced his old mentor, Phil O'Connell. Seventeen days later, the jury found him guilty of accessory before the fact of first-degree murder, but recommended mercy. He pleaded nolo contendere (no contest) to the murder of Mrs. Chillingworth.

Joe Peel was sentenced to life in prison. Terminally ill with cancer, he was released on June 25, 1982, into the custody of the woman who would become his second wife. The niece of his former wife, Imogene, who had long since divorced him, she married Peel just after his release from prison.

Eighteen days later, he died in Jacksonville, but not before confessing his role. He had been haunted, he said, by his memory of two little Chillingworth girls who had lived just two blocks away from him while he was growing up in West Palm.

"I've often had the feeling I should sit down and talk to them," he said. "But I know that's not possible."

Unlucky Holzapfel finally saw his luck turn. His sentence was commuted to life in prison in Raiford.

Lincoln served out his time for moonshining, then went to Chicago, where he turned to religion, preaching to his flock about the wages of sin.

The wages of undercover work proved to be substantial for assorted informants who came forward to claim reward money. The biggest awards went to Yenzer, who received $55,000, and Wilbur, who was given $37,500.

Henry Lovern, who broke the case, left his job in Tallahassee and went to work for the National Intelligence Academy in Fort Lauderdale. He had received no reward money. Just an employee of the state. Just a man doing his job.

CHAPTER 17

The Sea Waif's Story

Eleven-year-old Terry Jo survived
a massacre at sea.

The tanker *Gulf Lion,* bound for Nassau, was just entering the Northwest Providence channel between Grand Bahama Island and the Biminis. Shortly after lunch, 12:35 P.M. on November 13, 1961, a crew member spotted a small boat, maybe four miles away in the swift, rough waters of the Gulf Stream. A man standing in the boat waved wildly, striving desperately to capture the ship's attention.

Gulf Lion turned back into the Gulf Stream. As the ship steamed closer, the crewman saw a dinghy with a rubber life raft tied to it. In the dinghy stood a tall, rugged, barefoot man with sun-bleached hair. Stammering badly, he gave his name as Julian Harvey, skipper of a sixty-foot sailboat, the *Bluebelle*. In the raft lay a seven-year-old girl. She was dead.

The tanker continued on toward New Providence Island. There Captain Harvey gave the Nassau police a horrifying account of the last voyage of the *Bluebelle*. Arthur Duperrault, a forty-four-year-old optometrist from Green Bay, Wisconsin, had chartered the boat at the Bahia Mar marina in Fort Lauderdale. It was to have been a week-long dream cruise in the Bahamas with his wife Jean, thirty-eight, and their three children, Brian, fourteen, Terry Jo, eleven, and Rene, seven. Harvey captained the boat and his wife, Mary Dene, thirty-eight, a former TWA stewardess, served as cook. For a family from Green Bay, *Bluebelle* seemed a particularly happy choice. The ketch was launched in 1928 from Sturgeon Bay, just thirty miles from the Duperraults' hometown.

On the fifth night between Abaco and Great Stirrup Key, the yacht was buffeted by a sudden squall, Harvey said. The storm came out of the dark November night, packing twenty-knot winds. A strong gust snapped the main mast in two. The broken portion slammed down on them, he said, "like a telephone pole," puncturing the deck and the hull. Harvey ran below to get cable cutters to free the sails. When he came back up, he found a fire in the cockpit area. At the same time, he saw the boat was taking on water.

"I realized immediately that the boat was sinking," Harvey testified, "because of the hole caused by the main mast falling. I decided to expedite the launching of the fiberglass lifeboat, blowing up the four-man emergency life raft. The passengers astern could see me doing this and they apparently made a decision among themselves to leave the boat, jump over the stern and wait for me to get the boat back to them rather than stand there facing the fire in that area."

The skipper launched the dinghy with the rubber raft tied to it and rowed clear of the sinking boat. He called out to the Duperraults and to Mary, searching in the darkness for them. Where in the stormy waters were they? He shouted but no one came. Finally, he found one of the six who had leaped overboard. Little Rene was floating face down in the water. She had drowned before he could get to her. His wife and the entire Duperrault family had died at sea.

The Nassau police were uneasy with the story. Harvey had no injuries, no ill effects of any kind other than exhaustion. Weather reports for the area mentioned no squalls. No one at the Great Stirrup Key Lighthouse observed any burning boats at sea. Furthermore, Captain Harvey did not call for a search party. The boat had sunk in the Tongue of the Ocean, where the waters were over a thousand fathoms deep. By now, Harvey reasoned, the victims of the *Bluebelle* tragedy would have been in the shark-infested waters for more than a day without any boats or flotation devices. The captain seemed too calm, too unperturbed for a man who had just lost his wife.

"Skippy" Hall, a Bahamian immigration official, took Captain Harvey to the Carlton House near the Prince George Docks. At the hotel, the skipper ate a steak with potatoes and a salad and drank a double brandy. Between eight-thirty and midnight he ordered ten more double brandies sent to his room. The night desk man who delivered the drinks reported that one of the room's twin beds was covered with "wet money that was drying out."

The next day, Harvey slipped quietly out of Nassau, flew back to Miami and checked into the Sandman Hotel on Biscayne Boulevard. In Miami, he talked at greater length with the U.S. Coast Guard, giving essentially the same story. He was still talking to them four days after his rescue when the interrogation was interrupted. The Coast Guard had good news.

At nine-thirty that morning, November 17, a watch officer aboard the Greek freighter *Captain Theo* spotted a tiny balsa life raft. On that raft was a young blonde-haired girl. She gave her name as Terry Jo Duperrault, then lapsed into unconsciousness. She wore pink corduroy slacks, a white cotton blouse and wool socks. The eleven-year-old had been sitting in the tiny float for more than eighty hours without food or water. Close to death from exposure, severe sunburn and dehydration, she was rushed by helicopter to Miami's Mercy Hospital.

"Oh, my God," said Harvey. Without warning, he left the hearing room.

Two hours later, a maid entered a room at the Sandman Motel. When she saw blood on a bedsheet, she called owner Fred Hales. In the bathroom, the owner found Captain Harvey lying on his back, covered with blood. He had slashed his left thigh and both ankles with a double-edge razor. To finish the job off, he had also severed his jugular vein.

Harvey left behind a two-page suicide note. It was addressed to Jim Boozer, an advertising executive who had been his friend since their days in Air Force flight training. The note read: "I'm going out now. I'm a nervous wreck." He also asked Boozer to take care of his fourteen-year-old son, Lance Harvey.

Julian Harvey would talk no more. To get the rest of the story, the Coast Guard could only hope the sea waif, as Terry Jo was being called, would recover to talk to them. The crew of the *Captain Theo* took up a collection to buy her a doll and some toys.

Two days went by and still Terry Jo was unable to speak. Doctors were encouraged, though. She was regaining her strength. Finally, the pretty blonde child began to tell her story from her bed at Mercy Hospital.

At nine o'clock the night of November 12, she and Rene had gone to bed. Screams and stamping noises awoke her sometime that night. Terry Jo got up and saw her mother and her brother, Brian, lying on the cabin floor not far from the galley. Blood was everywhere. She went up on deck and saw even more blood.

Captain Harvey, carrying a bucket, shouted at her, then hit her and shoved her back into the cabin. She lay in her bunk, terrified, for about fifteen minutes. Then she heard water rising about her in the cabin.

"I just laid there," she told the Coast Guard. "And then the captain came in and looked. . . . He just looked and he had something in his hand and then he went up and I heard hammering."

Now the water was up to her bunk. Wading through waist-deep water, oily with flow from the bilge, she made it to the deck. She asked an agitated Harvey if the boat was sinking. He told her it was.

". . . He said, 'Is the dinghy loose?' and I said, 'I don't know,' and he jumped in after it, I couldn't see him and I couldn't see the dinghy, so I got the little raft and got into it."

That was the last she saw of Harvey or of her family. One thing she remembered clearly. There had been no squall that night, no broken mast crashing down on the deck and no fire for them to fight.

Her tiny raft, so small she had to sit upright, floated off into the night. She was sure her father was alive. He would come and rescue her. God would take care of her, so she kept praying as she drifted in the Gulf Stream, fish nibbling at her feet through the raft's rope bottom. She waved as ships passed by and planes flew overhead. By the time the *Captain Theo* arrived, she no longer waved. Terry Jo was too weak to lift her arms.

In its official report on the tragedy, the Coast Guard wrote: "Arthur Duperrault, Jean Duperrault, Brian Duperrault and Mary (Dene) Harvey lost their lives at the hands of Julian A. Harvey prior to the sinking of the vessel. The exact nature of the circumstances whereby these lives were taken or the order in which they perished cannot be ascertained. . . . the most probable cause of the casualty was the state of mind of Julian A. Harvey at about 11:30 P.M. November 12 (1961)."

And what was the "state of mind" of Harvey that bloody night on the high seas? Most accounts conclude that the pressure that unhinged him was money. Gene Miller, a Pulitzer Prize–winning staff writer for *The Miami Herald*, wrote: "Julian Harvey aspired to the yacht club life. But he couldn't afford it."

Four months before the voyage of the *Bluebelle*, he had taken out a twenty-thousand-dollar life insurance policy on his wife with a double indemnity clause in the event of accidental death. A background check revealed that he had been married five times. His third wife and her mother had been killed when a car Harvey was driving plunged off a wooden bridge into a West Florida bayou on a rainy night. He swam away safely. The two women died. On two other occasions, boats under his command sank and Harvey collected insurance claims.

Although he had graduated from Purdue University with a degree in aeronautical engineering, Harvey cultivated the image of a dashing adventurer who lived life near the edge. As a daring pilot — apparently too daring — he twice cracked up U.S. Air Force planes before receiving a medical discharge.

Terry Jo's "state of mind" was surprisingly calm when she testified to the Coast Guard. Then the horror of what had happened caught up with her, and she developed a fear of the dark. She could not be left alone at night. Still, she proved resilient. After her recuperation, she returned to Wisconsin, not to her family home in Green Bay but to De Pere, Wisconsin, to live with an aunt and uncle. They and other relatives cared for her lovingly and shielded her from prying questions. Over the years, they helped her put the loss behind her. In time, she married and had three children.

She displayed no bitterness toward Harvey, remembering him as a likable and even-tempered skipper. "I'm not bitter and never have been," she said some two decades after the carnage. "I never saw him kill anyone and nothing was ever proven. I think about it a lot, about what might have happened. But I've never come up with any conclusions."

KILLINGS WITH AND WITHOUT MERCY

It is hard to imagine a killing with love, but one happened in Florida in 1911. It is just as hard to imagine a mother who would kill her own first-born son for insurance money.

CHAPTER 18

A Killing for Love

Shakers helped pain-ridden Sadie Marchant
"pass out of the body."

Reports reaching his Kissimmee office disturbed the sheriff. A young woman in the Shaker colony near St. Cloud had died after a long illness, but no doctor had attended her and there was no proper medical statement about the cause of her death.

Then to make matters even more confusing, rumor had it that the Shakers had assisted in her death. That, Sheriff Charles Prevatt knew full well, would be murder, the last thing you would expect of a law-abiding religious community like the Shakers.

They had come to Osceola County in 1894, and in the seventeen years that followed there had been not one report of any law, not even a minor one, broken by any member of the little group on the east side of East Lake Tohopekaliga. For the peaceful, nonviolent Shakers' first venture into law-breaking to be the taking of a human life seemed implausible.

Realizing he faced a potentially sensitive problem, the sheriff had Judge G. F. Parker accompany him on the twenty-five-mile journey to Olive Branch, the Shaker colony. It lay just a short distance past the new town of St. Cloud, which was attracting a number of retired Civil War veterans from the Grand Army of the Republic.

The colony, founded by Shakers from Watervliet, New York, had not fared well in Florida. Since the Shakers vowed a life of celibacy, their growth was dependent on converts — and conversions were just not happening in Florida. "Crackers don't make good Shakers," said Gerard Wertkin, director of the Museum of American Folk Art in New York City and an authority on the Shakers. Never bigger than twelve members, Olive Branch was down to just four people when the sheriff arrived.

Olive Branch consisted of a large chicken house, a big barn, a windmill, a sawmill and two two-story cottages, one for the brothers and one for the sisters. The colony was so small it had no meetinghouse. Services were held on the veranda of the sisters' home. The county had extended a road to Olive Branch, and the Sugar Belt Railroad had even built a station from which the Shakers could ship produce. They were much admired for their agricultural skills, especially for the production of honey, cane syrup and pineapples, which were exported to Cuba. Small as it was, the community was well-kept, beautifully landscaped with fruit trees, flowers and vines.

The sheriff was directed to Brother Egbert B. Gillette and Sister Elizabeth Sears. They told him and the judge that the young woman who had died was Sadie Marchant, thirty-five. After years of fighting tuberculosis, she had lapsed into unbearable pain. They administered chloroform to help her, as she had requested, "pass out of the body."

Arrested the next day, the two Shakers were taken to Kissimmee. Sister Sears was released on two thousand dollars bond, but Brother Gillette was committed to the county jail. A reporter for *The Kissimmee Valley Gazette* visited Gillette, who freely gave him a detailed account of the event.

"Sister Sadie L. Marchant came to our colony six years and three months ago, and at that time had only one lung. She had been suffering terribly for the past several weeks, and we all knew that the time was short when she would be called to her final reward, but a week ago Sunday, which was August 20th, the climax was reached, she being taken with a chill and diarrhea, which everyone knows is the last stage of consumption.

"Sister Sadie had always told us to let her die in peace and without pain, and asked Sister Elizabeth to let her get out of the body. She refused to eat anything more after that. Sunday night, the twentieth, she suffered terribly and towards morning begged us to kill her. I went to St. Cloud at daylight Monday morning and got some opiates to ease her, and gave her all I brought, which seemed to ease her.

"I went to St. Cloud for more, and when I gave them to her she could not keep them on her stomach. She suffered so until Tuesday noon that I went to St. Cloud and got two ounces of chloroform, which I gave to her on a cloth, and she went to sleep. I went to St. Cloud again about three o'clock and got six or eight ounces more of chloroform in a bottle, and when I returned home I found she had come out from under the influence of the first I had given her, and I gave her another dose. She passed out about ten minutes before six o'clock."

Brother Gillette, obviously shaken by Sadie's terrible suffering, continued: "Every time I gave her anything, I asked her: 'Sadie, do you want this?' and she would say, 'Yes.' She was suffering so she didn't want to live.

Before giving her the last sleeping potion, I made it a special point to tell her that if she wanted to hang on and suffer out that we would do everything we possibly could to help her. She wanted us to do as we did, and urged us to give her the chloroform. When she had become discouraged before, I had often encouraged her to hold on as long as she could so as to keep our ministry encouraged to such an extent that they would not sell our place here and move us North, as our members were so few."

Still, Brother Gillette, a deeply religious man, had his moments of self-doubt when he needed to reassure himself.

"Before God I think I did right, and my conscience is perfectly at ease. My great feeling for her caused me to commit this unwise act. . . .

"My friend, say for me to the world that in the passing away of Sister Sadie, a deeper wound was left in my heart than I ever thought could be made by any act on this earth, for I loved her as fondly as ever father loved his child, but I could not see her suffer as she was doing and not give her relief. I would have been an inhuman monster in the sight of the God of us all if I had failed to answer the cry of that innocent child, 'Give me peace. Oh, let me die without pain, and in peace!'"

*   *   *

The official name of their church was the United Society of Believers in Christ's Second Appearing. Their beliefs trace back to a seventeenth-century group of French Protestants known as Camisards. Driven from France, they moved to England, where they were associated with the Quakers. Because their intense emotions caused them to quiver during religious exercises, they became known first as Shaking Quakers, then just as Shakers.

Ann Lee, later known as Mother Ann, led a group of eight Believers to America in 1774, hoping to develop an ideal society in a land she hoped was not yet enveloped in prejudice and intolerance. Mother Ann believed that evil sprang from greed, sex and pride. Greed could be eliminated by communal ownership of all property. Celibacy, she concluded, would control the temptations of sex, and selfless humility could defeat pride. Built into their doctrine was a belief in a humanitarian pacifism that regarded all forms of violence as un-Christian. Naturally, they encountered suspicion and hostility, which tended to be softened by their kindness and honesty in dealing with people.

Near the end of the nineteenth century, utopian religious communities began to spring up in many places in the United States. In these, the Shakers produced, among other things, the fine furniture prized today by collectors. Their inventions include the circular saw. Two utopian communities were

established in Florida — the Koreshan Unity near Fort Myers and Olive
Branch. The Shaker Ministry in Watervliet, New York, founded Olive
Branch after purchasing seven thousand acres of Osceola County land for
$94,500 in 1894.

*   *   *

In Providence, Rhode Island, doctors told Sadie Marchant she had only
four months to live. Her tuberculosis had advanced beyond any real hope of
treatment. They did suggest, however, that she at least would be more comfortable at a new sanitorium established by Dr. John A. Ennis at
Narcoossee, a small Florida town on East Lake Tohopekaligo. Affiliated
with the sanitorium as its vice-president was a Shaker named Sister
Elizabeth Sears. Dr. Ennis called her "a sister truly to many an invalid in our
camp. She has never been absent from a meeting of the board; never failed
to cheer us up in our darkest hour."

When other patients went back north at the end of the winter season, a
penniless Sadie had to remain behind. Even though they knew she was
dying, Brother Gillette and Sister Sears agreed to take her into the Shaker
colony and care for her.

"Such food was prepared for her as was considered best for one in her
condition and she was frequently carried on excursions on the lake and into
the woods in the hope that the ravages of the disease might be stayed, the
Shakers even going to the expense of buying a gentle pony for her to ride,"
wrote *The Kissimmee Valley Gazette*.

Sadie Marchant lived on for six years past the four months the
Providence doctors had given her. But then, predictably, came the terminal
stage of her terrible illness. Not so predictably came the actions of the two
people who had cared for her so lovingly for so many years.

The mercy killing attracted the attention and condemnation of newspapers around the country — in Boston, Cleveland, Cincinnati and particularly in New York, where *The New York Times* said the two Shakers were
"criminals and should be treated as such." Newspapers from Jacksonville
and Tampa were harsh in their coverage of the story. The *Tampa Times*
called it "a murder of peculiar atrocity."

One nasty rumor hinted that prior to her death Sadie had been in a "del-
icate condition," a genteel way of saying that the unmarried woman was
pregnant. The gossip contended she had been intimate with one of the
Shaker brothers. Another report claimed that a chemist had examined her
body and had found her tuberculosis was not at all advanced and would
have been neither painful nor life-threatening.

There was only one way to answer the charges. Her remains would have to be disinterred. In September, Judge Parker, Sheriff Prevatt and State's Attorney John C. Jones led a coroner's jury and a physician to her grave in the Shaker colony.

Wrote the *Valley Gazette*: "Upon examination, she was found to be as pure a virgin as ever mother cradled to sleep, and further her lungs and entire system were found to be in an advanced stage of consumption."

In late September, the coroner's jury returned its verdict: "We, the coroner's jury, impaneled to consider the testimony in the case of E. B. Gillette, accused of having brought Sadie Marchant to death at Ashton by means of chloroform administered to the said Sadie Marchant, find him to be guilty of willful murder."

The coroner's jury made no mention of Sister Sears, so her case was simply continued under bond. Both she and Brother Gillette would have to wait until November 28 for the grand jury to convene. The Kissimmee newspaper, clearly emerging as a champion of the Shakers, pointed out that the coroner's jury had exceeded its mandate. Its mission was simply to determine cause of death, not the guilt or innocence of the defendant.

Dr. Ennis disapproved of the mercy killing, but still defended Brother Gillette strongly in a letter to the paper: "Knowing the man for years, understanding his high character and his love of humanity, I have come to the conclusion that the severe physical and mental strain caused by his constant labor for the material interests of the colony affected his mind to such a degree that he was incapable of deciding as to the proper procedure in the case of this poor girl. . . . The law must be kept even if dear friends suffer, but in this case the noble life of the defendant must be considered, and if found guilty, the punishment should be as light as possible."

In early October, the Osceola County Commission went on record as favoring the release of Gillette on a nominal bond or even on his word. Still, the court kept him in jail, ruling that bail should not be allowed when the charge was murder.

The mercy killing became a hot topic at a conference of governors at Spring Lake, New Jersey. Florida Governor Albert W. Gilchrist observed: "I doubt they will ever be indicted." Many governors declared they would pardon Gillette if he were convicted.

At the end of November, the grand jury began its probe into the Marchant killing. A story went out to the national press that a Shaker had been named to chair the grand jury, implying that the colony was busy rigging the jury. The Kissimmee newspaper was quick to point out that the chairman was actually the associate editor of the newspaper and in no way a Shaker. There was no real way the Shakers could have packed the jury. Only four were left in Florida, and one was in jail.

Days went by with no word from the grand jury. Then the foreman, S.J. Triplett, announced that the jury had reached a verdict. They had refused to indict the Shakers.

By law, both should have been released from custody, but State's Attorney Jones was not giving up that easily. He asked Judge William H. Price to hold Gillette over without bail and to hold the sister as an accessory to euthanasia. Judge Price agreed that Brother Gillette should be detained under seventy-five hundred dollars bond pending the next regular meeting of the grand jury. He refused to take any action against Sister Sears.

The *Valley Gazette* struck back at Jones: ". . . why should State's Attorney Jones refuse to abide by that jury's decision? Was it because his soul is overflowing with love for the laws of his state? Was it because his soul has become so calloused by a long life of connection with crime that he thinks every man is guilty who is charged with the commission of a crime? Or was it because he wanted to appear largely in the limelight as prosecutor of the most famous case in the annals of court records?"

In January 1912, the state's chief witness, William Parking Bracken, issued a public plea that charges be dropped against the Shakers: "Elder Egbert was fully aware of the fact that she was a victim of the dread disease tuberculosis when he kindly consented to accept her as a member of his family. He fully understood the nature of her disease and was aware of the fact that she had been under medical treatment without having obtained relief, and he knew that he was taking upon himself a very serious responsibility in accepting the care of such a patient, yet the kindness of his heart was such that he could not resist the inclination to assist her, and during the years that followed he always exercised toward her a large amount of fatherly respect and indulgence, and treated her as I would like to be treated if I was in the grasp of such a dreadful disease. . . . I hope . . . that when the court meets in April the case against him will be dismissed."

By now, even the state's attorney could see clearly that there was no support in the community for prosecuting the mercy killers. He dropped all charges against both of them.

The Olive Branch Colony continued to try to make a go of it, but no converts were coming along to increase their numbers. In 1924, the last of them left Florida and returned to New York State. Egbert Gillette stayed on, but not in the Shaker movement. He left the order, married Mabel Marston and continued to live in Osceola County.

CHAPTER 19

Spider Woman

Pensacola's Black Widow killed a husband,
a lover, and a son.

John Wesley Gentry II had his orders. Judi Buenoano, his business partner and live-in lover, insisted that he arrive at the Driftwood Restaurant in the old historic district of Pensacola by seven-thirty that Saturday evening in June 1983.

Judi was throwing a going-away party. One of her Fingers N Faces beauty salon employees was moving to Fort Walton Beach. Gentry's task was to greet early arrivals. That part was fine. What baffled Gentry was her insistence that he park his two-door Ford Futura on the far lot at the Driftwood. It would have been easier to park across the street in front of the restaurant or the old Hotel San Carlos.

Gentry turned into Palafox Street, a wide boulevard that led into the heart of the picturesque old Spanish section. At the corner of Palafox and Garden Streets, he saw the San Carlos, a grand hotel when it opened in 1910, now closed and boarded up for the past two years, now just a haven for the homeless. Just as Judi had insisted, he pulled off into the southwest corner of a relatively empty parking lot and parked where he was told, about thirty feet from the sidewalk.

Champagne flowed that night. At about 10:20, Judi told John that she and the girls were going out for a few drinks. He was to go home ahead of her and give her fourteen-year-old son, James, a packet of marijuana she had gotten for him.

He walked to his car at the far end of the empty unlit parking lot. As he climbed into his unlocked car, the night dial on his watch read 10:35. He started the engine, then switched on his headlights.

An explosion engulfed him. A sharp pain stabbed at the back of his neck, and his hand found it covered with blood. His shoes were blown off his feet.

He struggled out the door and tried to walk. He collapsed on the sidewalk.

*   *   *

Detective Ted Chamberlain, a former Boston policeman, studied the open trunk of the 1981 Ford Futura at the Pensacola felony garage. The bomb had exploded forward from the trunk through the back seat. The explosion blew out the front and rear windshields and the sunroof. Bob Cousson, a special agent from the Federal Bureau of Alcohol, Tobacco and Firearms, brought him up to date:

"Two sticks of dynamite in the trunk under the left back seat. It was rigged pretty good. The wires were connected to the taillights so it wouldn't go off till after dark. We thought at first it was hooked to the ignition. Since he was long-legged and short-bodied, he must have leaned forward and turned on the ignition and the lights at the same time. That might have saved his life. A two-inch piece of shrapnel went right through the headrest, shot through two layers of sheet metal, and lodged in the frame of the sunroof. If he'd been leaning back, it would have gone right through the back of his skull. The word's already out on the street that it was some kind of Mafia drug deal. Anything for a headline. . . . It was an amateur job."

Chamberlain checked with his partner, Rick Steele, who handed him a list of Gentry's personal effects. The list included four Atlanta Braves baseball tickets, a pack of Merit cigarettes and a packet of what appeared to be marijuana. "Not exactly your average drug kingpin," commented Chamberlain.

Twelve years earlier, Chamberlain had quit his job in Boston to move to the warmth of Escambia County to join his father, a retired detective. He soon found that Pensacola police saw more than their share of violent crimes, shootings, stabbings and strong-arm robberies. In 1983, Escambia County ranked fourth in the nation in assaults. Bombings, however, were so rare the police didn't even have a bomb squad. Rigged explosions were usually directed at local abortion clinics — not at automobiles.

Chamberlain had requested photographs of all other cars parked in the area. The detective studied the pictures, then asked: "Wonder why he parked in the parking lot down the street when there were plenty of empty parking places right in front of the restaurant?"

"Lucky for passersby he did," said Cousson. "Shrapnel flew for two hundred yards in all directions."

"Whose white Corvette is that parked in front of the San Carlos?" asked Chamberlain.

"Judias Buenoano, the girlfriend," replied Steele.

"Why'd she park almost two blocks away from the restaurant, where the bums hang out, instead of in the parking lot next to her boyfriend?" Chamberlain wondered.

At Gentry's Wallpaper Mill Outlet, they found dark-haired Judi Buenoano. She was wearing an off-the-shoulder Mexican peasant dress, bracelets on her arms and several rings on her fingers. Narrow dark eyes shone out above prominent and heavily rouged cheekbones.

"I've owned my own business since 1980 — Fingers N Faces," she said. "It's a beauty boutique in Town and Country Mall. I have degrees as long as my arm. I make five hundred thousand dollars a year."

"That's a lot of fingernails," said Chamberlain.

Her smile suddenly disappeared. "Unless you have any more questions you'd like to ask me . . ."

"No, ma'am, that'll be it for now."

Four days went by before the detectives could talk to Gentry in the intensive-care unit at Sacred Heart Hospital, Pensacola's newest and most modern. Gentry told them he had left the car with Judi that afternoon so her son, James, could install new speakers. Chamberlain asked who would benefit from his death.

"Judi and I have this life insurance policy together. . . . Five hundred thousand apiece."

The questioning turned next to the location of his car. "Well, Judi told me to be sure and park the car in the parking lot down from the Driftwood, on the corner of Garden and Baylen," said Gentry. "Said she didn't want the panhandlers from the San Carlos bothering us. She made a big thing out of it."

"You mean she told you not to park in front of the restaurant?"

"She was just real insistent that I park in that particular parking lot."

"Do you always do what she tells you?"

"I don't know. I guess I pretty much do."

As the two detectives walked back to their car, Chamberlain said: "You got the broad telling him where to park. You got the car left with her son working on it all afternoon. You got her telling us she makes five hundred thousand a year, and turns out she's got an insurance policy on the jerk for that amount. Doesn't it sound a little weird to you?"

* * *

The next day Detective Steele called Judi. He asked if she would come by the station and submit to a polygraph test. "All we're doing is eliminating people. It's just routine," he told her. She agreed. Twenty minutes later,

Steele received a call from a man who said, "I'm Perry Mason. I'm Judi's attorney. She's not taking the test."

Gentry gave the detectives their next big break. He told them he had checked himself into Sacred Heart in December 1982, troubled with vomiting, stomach cramps and dizzy spells. They had found nothing wrong and had released him.

"But, you know, Judi had been giving me these Vicon-C vitamins, these orange and white capsules. I noticed that every time I took them I got sick. Judi kept insisting I take two capsules a day. . . . When I got out of the hospital, she started giving them to me again, and I got sick again. So I started putting them in my pocket and I stopped gettin' sick."

Chamberlain asked him if he still had any of the capsules.

"As a matter of fact, I saved a couple, thinkin' I'd have 'em analyzed someday to see if I was allergic to 'em or something. They're still in my briefcase over at my office wrapped up in a little bag. If you want 'em, you can have 'em."

The Florida Department of Law Enforcement laboratory in Pensacola found the capsules had been tampered with. The capsules were sent to the FBI laboratory in Washington for a poison scan.

The word came back: The capsules contained paraformaldehyde, a poison with no known medical use. Continued ingestion would cause slow deterioration of internal organs, leading eventually to death. The substance would not be detected in an autopsy.

* * *

It was time to look deeper into the background of Judias Buenoano. She had been born Judias Anna Lou Welty in Quanah, Texas, not far south of the Oklahoma border, on April 4, 1943. Her father was an itinerant farm worker. Her mother, she said, was a full-blooded Mesquite Apache. In fact, Judi claimed the Apache chief Geronimo was her great-great-grandfather.

When Judi was two, her mother died of tuberculosis. Badly abused by her father and stepmother, Judi led a troubled childhood and was placed in a reformatory in Albuquerque, New Mexico. At seventeen, she moved in with dark, handsome Air Force Sergeant Art Schultz. They never married, but she took the name Schultz after a child, Michael Arthur, was born on March 30, 1960, in Roswell, New Mexico.

A year later, in Roswell, she married James E. Goodyear, another Air Force sergeant, who adopted Michael. Nine years later, the sergeant was assigned to McCoy Air Force Base in Orlando after his return from Vietnam. He died soon thereafter under mysterious circumstances. Judi collected ninety thousand dollars in life insurance.

Her next stop was Pensacola, where she moved in with Bobby Joe Morris in 1973. Four years later, Bobby Joe opened a business in Trinidad, Colorado. Later that year, Judi's house burned down. She collected forty thousand dollars in insurance money and joined Bobby in Colorado, bringing with her Michael and two additional children from her marriage with the sergeant. Six months after her arrival in Trinidad, Morris died, again under suspicious circumstances. Another fifty thousand dollars in insurance money came her way.

The year Bobby Joe died, Judi changed her surname from Goodyear to its Spanish equivalent, Buenoano. With her three children, she moved back to Pensacola and purchased a home in Gulf Breeze and a sporty MG. Two years later, her first-born son, Michael, a paraplegic, drowned accidentally in a canoe accident on East River. The insurance haul for her was $125,000. This time she bought a white Corvette.

It had started as an investigation into a botched attempt at murder. The detectives realized now they were looking at something far bigger, far more evil. They had uncovered a spider woman who cruelly trapped those closest to her in her web, then killed them for insurance money.

"A bitch does it for money, and evil does it for pleasure. This is one evil bitch," said Chamberlain. "But I'll get her. I'll get her."

Judi's claim that she was descended from Geronimo particularly annoyed him. Chamberlain's nickname was Geronimo. The detective's mother was a full-blooded Cherokee. Ironically, the great Apache chief was part of Pensacola legend. A century earlier, he had been held by the U.S. Army at Fort Pickens on Santa Rosa Island near Pensacola.

* * *

Prosecutor Russell Edgar had once put a local murderer in jail for a thousand years and a rapist in jail for 514 years. As he studied Michael's signature on his military records, he noted an odd error. The young man, somewhat retarded, could not even spell his own name correctly. He always signed his first name Michaele. Edgar reviewed the application for an insurance policy paying $100,000 for Michael's accidental death. The first name was spelled Michael. He compared the two signatures. Some one had forged the soldier's name on the policy application.

Edgar and Chamberlain stepped up the investigation. The district attorney's office in Trinidad, Colorado, found that Bobby Joe Morris's signature had been forged on two policy applications. After that, it was easy to get a court order to exhume his body from its vault at the Brewton, Alabama, cemetery. The levels of arsenic found in his remains were high enough to have killed eleven people.

Meanwhile, the Pensacola Police Department received an anonymous phone call from a woman who said she had known Buenoano in 1971 and 1972. She said Judi had told her she had used arsenic and lead to poison her husband, Jim Goodyear. Another exhumation was performed. The arsenic levels in Goodyear's remains were high enough to have killed ninety people.

*   *   *

By the time he entered school at age six, Michael was already diagnosed as a problem student. His IQ was evaluated in the dull-to-normal range. Poorly coordinated, he tended to break or lose his eyeglasses. Both eyesight and hearing were substandard. He was still wetting the bed into his late teens. By 1979, he had matured sufficiently for the U.S. Army to accept him. He attended water purification school at Fort Leonard Wood, Missouri. His training included forty hours of instruction in the handling of arsenic compounds.

Before reporting for permanent duty at Fort Benning, Georgia, Michael visited his mother in Pensacola. He was in good health when he left Missouri. By the time he reached Benning a week later, he was already suffering classic symptoms of metal-base poisoning. Within six weeks, his lower legs and arms had atrophied. He could no longer walk or use his hands. At the Army's Walter Reed Hospital in Washington, doctors found he had seven times the normal arsenic levels. He was fitted with leg braces and a prosthetic hand device which together weighed over sixty pounds.

On May 14, 1980, an article appeared in the *Pensacola News Journal,* describing an unusual accident. It was headed "Water Mishap." The story stated that a paraplegic named Michael Buenoano had drowned in the East River in neighboring Santa Rosa County. The canoe in which he had been seated overturned after it struck a submerged object. His mother was identified as Dr. Judias Buenoano, a clinical physician at the alcoholic rehabilitation center at Fort Walton Beach.

Captain Paul D. Carmichael, from Fort Rucker, Alabama, was appointed investigating officer for the Army. Michael was still officially a soldier, though awaiting a medical discharge. Judi told him her son had "weak ankles and knees" from a chemical explosion when he was at Fort Leonard Wood. In his report, Captain Carmichael had noted, "Mother very calm, no outward emotion."

The canoe was a two-seater with a center brace. Judi and James Buenoano, each wearing ski belts, occupied the seats and paddled and Michael sat in an aluminum lawn chair tied to the brace. He wore neither ski belt nor life preserver. In different interviews, Judi and James gave different stories. One version stated the canoe turned over when their fishing line became entangled in a tree. Another claimed a snake dropped into the canoe, startling them into accidentally overturning the canoe. Still another said they struck a submerged object. All accounts agreed, however, that the canoe turned over close to land. The body of Michael would be found face down in deep water some fifteen feet from shore.

Ricky Hicks had been fishing in the river near the State Road 87 bridge when he heard screams for help. He turned his boat upriver and pulled Judi and James out of water. Judi told him her son Michael had fallen overboard. He thought it odd that she did not ask him to take her back upstream to try to find him. Instead, she said she wanted to be taken ashore. There she asked for a can of beer and sat on the bank drinking it while waiting for the police and an ambulance to arrive. Michael's body was recovered by a diving team roughly three hours after the accident.

Though some reports blamed Judi for negligence and bad judgment, the death of Michael was viewed officially as simply an accident. It stayed an accident until too many insurance policies and too much arsenic finally focused attention on his mother. Nearly four years went by before she was brought to the bar of justice to face the charge of murdering her own son.

The 1984 trial was held at the Santa Rosa County Courthouse in Milton. For her defense, Judi had hired an old friend, James Johnston, six-foot-two, impressive in a white linen suit and pastel shirt and tie, the image topped off by a head of thick, wavy, blond hair. By contrast, prosecutor Russell Edgar wore dark, conservative clothing.

As the trial proceeded, Detective Chamberlain was keeping the pressure on. He fitted a canoe with a metal lawn chair and packed it with roughly the same items carried on Michael's last voyage. Then he paddled up East River until he located the fishing line in the tree. When he reached the spot where Buenoano said the canoe overturned, he threw his weight to one side, dumping himself and the canoe's contents into the stream.

What he found was that everything stayed close to shore, hung up in the marshy undergrowth. There was not enough current to move coolers, ski belts or canoes downstream where they were eventually found. Chamberlain came up with what he believed had been the sequence of events. Judi and James, he concluded, had tossed the paralyzed Michael into the deep middle part of the stream. As they paddled back downstream, Judi was suddenly startled by the sound of Ricky Hicks' outboard. Judi then flipped the boat over and began calling for help. She quickly thought up the story of a snake falling from a tree and James faked a neck injury. The fishing line in the tree added one more touch to the scenario.

Russell Edgar closed with a powerful summation: "When Michael got into the canoe that day, the last thing he ever thought was that his mother would let him drown, pitch him out of that boat. He trusted her. Michael must have thought after all those years of neglect, 'Gosh, I've grown up and they do love me. They're going to take me canoeing.' And it was the last thing he ever did. . . .

"I don't know how long it took him to die. It must have been several minutes. It must have been going through his mind that any second now, she's going to reach down and pull me out of this water. But she didn't pull him out. She got that canoe and she was heading for home to get herself a cold beer. And that's what she ended up doing, sitting there drinking a cold beer. He was probably dead by then. I don't know, maybe he wasn't. . . . The right thing to do is to hold the defendant responsible for the most horrible crime, the murder of one's own child."

Just before one o'clock that night, the jury, after six harrowing hours, reached its verdict: "Guilty of murder in the first degree." They also found her guilty of a lesser crime, grand theft of the insurance companies' money.

Edgar had argued for the death penalty. He believed in it, but he knew death-sentence appeals dragged on for years. He was not all that disappointed when the sentence was life imprisonment with no parole for at least twenty-five years. Besides, he knew more trials were on the agenda for Judias Buenoano.

* * *

The night the jury began deliberations on the guilt of Buenoano for the murder of her son, Ted Chamberlain and Special ATP Agent Dewitt Fincannon served a second arrest warrant on her in her cell for the attempted murder of Gentry.

An enraged Judi lunged at Chamberlain: "I'll see you rot in hell," she screamed at the grinning policeman. Her attorney struggled to hold her back.

Later that night, Chamberlain called on her other son, James, who was being held in the juvenile detention center under half a million dollars bond.

"Gotcha," he said to a smirking James Buenoano. But he was wrong in this case. The jury found James not guilty of rigging the bomb that almost killed Gentry.

Judi would find the trial a much tougher ordeal; for that matter, so would the victim, John Gentry. A major part of attorney Johnston's defense was to attack the victim mercilessly. In attempting to raise doubts in the minds of the jurors, he charged the bombing was drug-related. Result: A headline one day in the Pensacola newspaper read: "Gentry is a Drug Dealer." Gentry lost his business, found himself unable to get a job, even to get credit. He still regarded himself as luckier than the others Judi had targeted.

When Johnston asked him why he thought Judi could conspire to kill him, Gentry said: "Greed would be the only answer. Judi tried to kill me for the five hundred thousand dollars in insurance. I didn't see it that way until the day it happened."

"What caused you to change your mind about her?"

"Six months in the hospital."

The jury that found James innocent took less than two hours to find Judi Buenoano guilty. Her sentence was twelve more years, to be served after completion of her previous term.

In leaving the courtroom, she passed by Chamberlain. "Ta ta," he said and waved goodbye.

"I'll see you in hell," she answered.

* * *

By now, the media had dubbed her the Black Widow after the deadliest, most poisonous of all spiders. On October 22, 1985, Buenoano went on trial in Orlando for the murder of her former husband, Sergeant James Goodyear. Prosecutor Belvin Perry, a small, dapper, black attorney, described the last days of the Air Force sergeant:

"On the twelfth day of August, 1971, Sergeant Goodyear felt some discomfort in his stomach. He went to the dispensary at McCoy Air Force Base. From the twenty-fifth of August to the thirteenth of September, 1971, he continued to have the stress in his stomach. He was nauseated, vomited a lot, and had some periods of hallucination. On the thirteenth day of September, Sergeant Goodyear was admitted to the Naval Hospital at the naval base here in Orlando and was treated until his death on September sixteenth, 1971."

Expert testimony established that arsenic symptoms can masquerade as natural diseases and easily be misdiagnosed unless there is some reason to suspect poisoning.

Mary Beverly Owens, who had met Buenoano through Bobby Joe Morris, had been a friend of Judi's. It was fascinating, she said, to listen to her fanciful tales. She told Owens she had grown up on an Indian reservation and had killed her stepmother with a hatchet. Later, she had burned down her house and collected forty thousand dollars in life insurance, she said.

At a time when Owens was separated from her husband, due in large part to money troubles, she said, Judi told her she had poisoned her husband and wanted to help Mary Beverly kill hers. She shrugged the suggestion off, but later her friend Bobby Joe died. All of those moments came back to her when she saw Judi on television after she was linked to Bobby's death.

"Then she said, 'If you want to do it, we can get the poison right here in the fly bait department.' She said that it has arsenic in it. . . . She said there is no way they could ever find out because an autopsy won't show up arsenic unless they are really looking for it. So that's how Judi told me she killed James Goodyear. She told me I would have to have the stomach to do it, because it was a really bad thing, and how sick it would make him. She asked me if David drank a lot of milk, which he did, and she said I would have to give it to him in milk or in a milkshake. She told me she had to give it to James several times. . . . Then she told me to take out more insurance on David."

Belvin Perry sent to the witness stand a steady stream of doctors, insurance agents and prosecutors from previous investigations. Veterans Administration officials told the jury that Judi had collected $62,642.46 after the death of Sergeant Goodyear. Insurance benefits after the death of Bobby Joe Morris totaled $80,000.

Finally, John Gentry told how Judi fed him paraformaldehyde-laced capsules that could have brought her a half-a-million dollars in death benefits — if her plot had succeeded. Then, nine days after the trial began, Prosecutor Perry delivered his closing argument: "The evidence shows that Judi Goodyear wove her web, a web that . . . contained Agent Judi who systematically eliminated Sergeant Goodyear. James Goodyear had bad luck, and there sits his bad luck, Judi Goodyear."

He would later draw still another natural-history analogy to describe her: "She brought to mind for me a Venus's flytrap — you know, the plant that gives off an odor to attract and then closes in on its prey. Well, that's what she did. Once she got men in her web, she was deadly."

Jury deliberation began just after one in the afternoon and continued on into a rainy Halloween night. Trick or treat, which would it be? After retiring to the nearby Harley Hotel, jury members resumed their duties the following morning. On the afternoon of November 1, 1985, the jury, which had deliberated ten hours, returned its verdict in the case of the Black Widow of Pensacola:

"Guilty of murder in the first degree as charged, so say we all."

For the first time, Judias Buenoano broke into tears.

"She is definitely worried about getting the electric chair," said Johnston to a group of reporters. And she was right to be worried. Before the month was over, she heard another, still more terrifying verdict from Judge Emerson Thompson: "It is the sentence of the law and the judgment of this court that you, Judi A. Buenoano, also known as Judi Ann Goodyear, for the murder of James E. Goodyear, be committed to the custody of the Department of Corrections, and at a time to be fixed by the Governor of the State of Florida, you shall be put to death by means of electrocution. . . . May God have mercy on your immortal soul."

Judi Buenoano, the first woman sentenced to Florida's Death Row in more than sixty years, was sent to the Broward County Women's Detention Center in Pembroke Pines to await execution, a slow process as appeals run their course.

As he waited for the slow wheels of justice to grind to their final chapter, Geronimo Chamberlain received a piece of good ethnic news. Knowing that the Pensacola detective had bristled with the thought that Buenoano could be a descendent of Geronimo, Bob Cousson, his ATF partner in opening up her web of evil, contacted the Bureau of Indian Affairs. Their letter reported that Judi was not a descendent of Geronimo. Furthermore, she could not be, as she claimed, a member of the Mesquite Apache tribe, because "there is no Mesquite Apache tribe."

CHERCHEZ LA FEMME

"Look for the woman in the case," the French expression goes. Sometimes a woman supplies the motive for a crime. Sometimes she is the victim, sometimes the perpetrator.

CHAPTER 20

Lilies for Mary Lily

The death of Flagler's widow, the world's
richest woman, remains a mystery.

Far from Whitehall, her opulent Palm Beach mansion, Mary Lily Kenan
Flagler Bingham, the world's richest woman, lay in her coffin in the Kenan
family plot at Oakdale Cemetery in Wilmington, North Carolina. She had
been dead less than two months, but her uneasy peace was about to be violated again.

In the soft twilight of September 17, 1917, the guards hired to protect her
grave greeted two of her brothers, a team of doctors led by Dr. Charles
Norris, director of New York's Bellevue Hospital Laboratories, and several
cemetery workers. With shovels, spades and mining picks, the workers dug
down six feet in the soft earth until they reached the coffin.

Darkness fell and still the men struggled with their task. At midnight, the
coffin was finally hoisted up from the grave and carried to the cemetery
lodge.

Immediately, physicians and pathologists began the grisly autopsy. Using
microscopes and chemical tests, they studied slices of Mary Lily's liver,
kidneys and intestines. At 3 A.M., they had seen enough to tell her brothers,
Will and Graham Kenan, the ugly truth.

Mary Lily's body had contained "enormous amounts" of morphine,
accumulated over many months, as well as traces of injected adrenaline and
heavy-metal poisons, such as arsenic, and possibly mercury. Everyone
agreed that, pending further tests, the results were to be kept secret.

It didn't happen that way. Within forty-eight hours, the *New York
American* had run a streamer across the top of its front page — MRS.
BINGHAM WAS DRUGGED! And within days, papers across the country were
filled with stories of the scandal. Had Mary Lily taken the drugs herself? Or

The Kenan family plot in the Oakdale Cemetery in Wilmington, North Carolina, where the body of Mary Lily Bingham lay until it was exhumed in 1917 (Henry Morrison Flagler Museum, Palm Beach)

had the wife of Robert Worth Bingham, of Louisville, Kentucky, been murdered?

It was her fabulous wealth that spawned the tragedy of Mary Lily, the soft-spoken widow of Henry Flagler. Ugly rumors and the damning report of one of America's leading detective agencies all added up to the over-powering suspicion that Mary Lily had not met her death on July 27, 1917, from natural causes.

The tale had begun twenty-six years earlier, in 1891, when Henry Morrison Flagler, the uncrowned "king" of Florida, who had made a vast fortune as a founding partner of Standard Oil of Ohio, met Mary Lily Kenan at the home of mutual friends in Newport, Rhode Island.

He was sixty-one; she was twenty-three. He was instantly attracted to her — and it wasn't hard to see why. Contemporaries described Mary Lily as "a strikingly beautiful young woman," the pride of a prominent North Carolina family. Her petite hourglass figure, 105 pounds on a voluptuous five-foot-one body, caught the eyes of many men, as did her thick dark hair and blue eyes. A warm, friendly, poised manner added to her charm.

When Flagler met his Southern belle, his marriage to Alice, his second wife, was falling apart. Alice was careening toward insanity, and Flagler's doctor had recently warned him that it was no longer safe to share a bed-room with a wife who was showing homicidal tendencies.

Flagler found himself growing more and more attracted to Mary Lily. He sent a special train to Wilmington, so she could visit him at his palatial Ponce de Leon Hotel in St. Augustine.

At first it was platonic. Henry still had a wife as well as a New York mistress. But along the way, the relationship heated up. Press reports titillated the public with snippets about the May-December romance between the Southern belle and the wealthy tycoon whose Florida East Coast Railway was transforming the desolate east coast of Florida into America's favorite winter resort.

The Kenan family was shocked, not so much by the affair as by the unwelcome publicity. They demanded to know Flagler's intentions. Flagler assured them that he would take care of Mary Lily, whether he obtained a divorce or not. As a token of his affections, he presented her with jewelry worth one million dollars, and another million dollars in Standard Oil stock. He also instructed his architects to design a magnificent Palm Beach mansion for her.

Next, he set about seeking a divorce. His first move came in April 1899. Since insanity was not grounds for divorce in New York State, he made Florida his legal residence. Insanity was not legal grounds for divorce in Florida either, but Flagler figured he could change the rules more easily in a state he practically owned.

Sure enough, two years later a bill was introduced into the Florida legislature making "incurable insanity" grounds for divorce. Two and one-half weeks later, it sped through the legislature and was signed into law by Governor William Jennings.

Rumors quickly spread that Flagler had "bought" the legislature. Nothing was proved at the time, but seventy years later, it was discovered that the price he had paid to members of the 1901 legislature was $125,000. The "Flagler Divorce" law, used only by the great man himself, was repealed in 1905.

Two months after the bill became law, Flagler obtained his divorce from Alice, who was now confined to a sanitorium. He gave her securities and properties worth $2.3 million, which, when she died in 1930, had grown to $15.2 million.

Ten days after the divorce, Henry married Mary Lily at the Kenan family's ancestral home, Liberty Hall, at Kenansville, near Wilmington. A special train carried some twenty wedding guests, a fifteen-piece orchestra and a team of Baltimore chefs to a nearby station. Carriages then transported them eight miles to Liberty Hall over a road Flagler had built for the occasion.

The seventy-two-year-old groom's wedding gifts to his thirty-four-year-old bride were a pearl necklace worth half a million dollars, a check for one million dollars, and two million dollars in bonds. For their honeymoon, they left the steamy August heat of North Carolina for Flagler's summer home at Mamaroneck, New York.

At Mary Lily's insistence, the tycoon scrapped his earlier plans for a mansion for her. Instead, work began on a Southern-style palace in Palm Beach, complete with columns. Mary Lily would name it "Whitehall, a house of marble."

Lavishly furnished, the four-million-dollar palace was opened on January 26, 1902. Upstairs were fourteen guest suites, each designed to represent a different epoch in world history. The modern American room boasted Florida's first twin beds.

Arthur Spalding, the organist at Whitehall, described life at the palace in letters to his sister: "The more I see of Mrs. Flagler the better I like her and she is not at all the kind of woman I was prepared to see. Of course she is not perfect any more than the rest of us are, but there is nothing snobbish about her. If you treat her well and don't appear to be using her for what you can get, you can't ask for better treatment than she will give you in return."

Mary Lily accompanied Flagler on business trips to Havana and Nassau, and it became obvious that he was finding it difficult to keep up with her swifter social pace.

Still, his love for her remained undiminished to the end. With his final anniversary gift to her in 1912, he included a particularly touching note:

"To my darling wife, in loving remembrance of the day you became my wife and the many happy days you have given to me since our marriage. May the dear Lord reward you for what you have done for me."

The "old man," as he was called around Palm Beach, stayed busy to the end of his life. Much of his energy went into what many thought was the impossible task of extending his railroad across the Florida Keys. In late 1903, he had given his famous order: "Go ahead. Go to Key West."

Built across the Keys at a cost of fifty million dollars and more than a hundred lives, the railroad reached Key West on January 22, 1912. It proved to be the last major triumph in the "old man's" life. In March 1913, he fell down the stairs at Whitehall and broke his hip. At eighty-three, he was too old to fight off complications from the injury. Two months later, on May 20, he died in one of his beachfront cottages. Mary Lily was at his side.

On that day, Mary Lily Flagler became the world's richest woman. Her

Mary Lily Kenan Flagler (Henry Morridon Flagler Museum, Palm Beach)

husband had left her cash, stock, properties and companies valued at more than one hundred million dollars, the equivalent today of about six billion dollars. In Florida alone, she now owned the Florida East Coast Railway; the Model Land Company, which held four million acres of land; eleven Florida hotels; the East Coast Steamship Company; the Miami Electric Company, which later became Florida Power & Light; two water companies; and three daily newspapers, including *The Miami Herald*.

But in that spring of 1913, two deaths many miles apart doomed Mary Lily. One at Whitehall made her a widow; one in Louisville made Robert Bingham a widower.

Only a month after Flagler's accident, Eleanor Bingham, Bob Bingham's wife, was killed in Louisville. A car in which she was riding stalled at a crossing and was hit by a trolley car.

The paths of Mary Lily and Robert Bingham were destined to cross soon afterward — and not for the first time. For him it would mean wealth, power and fame. For her it would mean a horrendous death.

Robert's ancestor, William Bingham, had come to North Carolina from Ireland in 1791. Ten years later, he accepted a post at the state university in Chapel Hill. Soon after, he was forced out because of his pro-British views. His principal foe was General James Kenan, a university trustee and Revolutionary War hero. For the next century, the Binghams and the Kenans would clash often.

Robert Worth Bingham was born in November 1871. At the age of sixteen, he became the fourth generation of his family to enroll at Chapel Hill, just twenty miles from his home.

"He was the handsomest man I ever saw," recalled a former classmate. "All the women loved him and all the men admired him. He was the social lion of our day."

At a dance in 1890 — just one year before she met Henry Flagler — Mary Lily Kenan and Bob Bingham met and began an affair. The attraction was physical: handsome Bob, voluptuous Mary Lily. And perhaps the old feud between their families may have kindled the extra excitement of the forbidden.

The two became lovers, but once again the family feud came between them. It is not clear what happened, but Bingham left school, apparently forced out by the powerful Kenan family. Against her family's wishes, Mary Lily continued to see him occasionally after he enrolled at the University of Virginia.

Then Bob's father moved the family's prestigious Bingham School, the oldest prep school in the South, two hundred miles west to Asheville, in the

North Carolina mountains. There Bob met a gorgeous and wealthy brunette vacationing from Kentucky. In May 1896, Bob married Eleanor "Babe" Miller and moved to Louisville.

Bingham plunged into the practice of law — and into the corrupt world of Kentucky politics. He was elected county attorney, and appointed mayor of Louisville and later a judge in the county circuit court. Arrogance and shady deals doomed his first efforts at politics.

Despite his political troubles, Bingham still had the advantage of marriage into a wealthy family. This benefit declined after Eleanor's death, particularly after her mother learned of his improprieties in the handling of collateral for one of the family businesses.

In the meantime, however, Bingham had run up huge debts through failed political ventures and bad investments. Louisville banks began to press him for payment. He told the bankers he had no money, but that he might obtain help through an old friend, Mary Lily Flagler, now America's wealthiest widow.

In the summer of 1915, Mary Lily was staying in Asheville at the Grove Park Inn, so Asheville was where Bingham headed. But once he was on the scene, it appears that Mary Lily may have become the huntress. Says Tom Kenan, the family historian: "The Grove Park Inn in Asheville is where she restruck her acquaintance with Bob Bingham. She was utterly lonely and she probably forced the play. She was a powerhouse."

The two years since Flagler's death had not been kind to Mary Lily. At forty-eight, graying hair topped a face marked with worry lines. It was said that she drank too much bourbon and even took laudanum, a form of opium.

Bingham brought back a sense of joy and excitement to her life. She saw him at her apartment in New York's Plaza Hotel, at her mansion in Mamaroneck, at White Sulphur Springs, West Virginia, and at Louisville. She even opened Whitehall again in February 1916, for the first time since Henry's death.

Family and Flagler business associates warned her that Bingham was a fortune hunter. But Mary Lily was a lonely woman and Bob Bingham had always been a lady-killer.

Late in 1916, Mary Lily and Bingham decided to marry. Under intense family and business pressure, they agreed to a will in which he waived his claims to her fortune.

Stories of the romance filled the nation's social columns, and Bingham found his image was improving. Instead of a sleazy politician, he was now presented, even in the staid *New York Times*, as a leading reform mayor rather than as man forced out of office by a cleanup campaign.

Shortly after marrying Robert W. Bingham, Mary Lily Kenan Flagler Bingham, with a friend in what was known as an "Afromobile" (Henry Morrison Flagler Museum, Palm Beach)

The wedding was held on November 15, 1916. Mary Lily gave Bingham a certified check for fifty thousand dollars. He gave her nothing. A few weeks later, Mary Lily's lawyers informed her that under Kentucky law, the will excluding Bob from her estate was invalid. When a new one was drawn up conforming to Kentucky law, Bingham again agreed to a waiver that excluded him. Meanwhile, Mary Lily had cleared up his enormous debts and given him seven hundred thousand dollars in Standard Oil stock, which provided him with an annual income of fifty thousand dollars.

Things soon began to go wrong. Bingham's three children, aged ten to nineteen, treated their stepmother coldly, a disheartening development for a warm and friendly woman. Bingham's daughter even spied on her and told her father that his new wife was a drug addict.

In late December, Mary Lily's health began to deteriorate. She complained of chest pains, Bingham said later. To treat a woman who could afford the best of everything, he called not a renowned heart specialist, but instead an old friend, Dr. Michael Leo Ravitch, a Russian-born, second-rate dermatologist.

That winter, when Mary Lily ordered Whitehall to be opened for the Easter holidays, Bob's children refused to go. He sided with them and a distraught Mary Lily closed Whitehall, canceled all the Palm Beach parties she had planned, and spent the holidays instead in the cold, unfriendly world of Louisville.

By late May, Dr. Ravitch had been brought in as a house guest. His job was to keep Mary Lily under twenty-four-hour sedation. She needed to be totally pacified — and Bob needed her signature on a change in her will.

He had learned he could purchase the *Louisville Courier-Journal* and *Times* for a million dollars. He figured he could raise sixty percent of that amount by selling the securities Mary Lily had given him; the rest he could borrow only if her will listed him as the beneficiary of at least part of her vast fortune.

Apparently, he had no plans to kill her, just to gain the additional leverage that a place in her will would give him. As treatment for her chest pains, Dr. Ravitch began giving Mary Lily shots of morphine. These were gradually increased until she became addicted.

To draw up a codicil to the will, Bingham needed a lawyer he could control, one who would not be suspicious of a change signed by a woman under the influence of drugs. He picked an old college friend, Dave Davies, whom he knew would trust him if he explained that his wife's dazed condition was due to a serious medical problem.

On June 19, 1917, Mary Lily agreed to meet with Davies at Dr. Ravitch's office. There she told him she did not want the Flagler trustees or her brother, Will, to know about the codicil, a secret handwritten paper she had brought with her. It stated:

". . . I give and bequeath to my husband, R.W. Bingham, $5 million to be absolutely his. . . ."

It was signed by Mary Lily Bingham and witnessed by Davies and

Ravitch. The codicil was not filed at the courthouse, and remained a closely guarded secret. For his part in the conspiracy, Ravitch was paid fifty
thousand dollars.

After the signing, Mary Lily virtually vanished from sight. Bingham, on
the other hand, was seen everywhere, busy politicking at meetings and ral-
lies. The couple spent the summer in the sweltering heat of Louisville, not
at the comfortable waterfront mansion at Mamaroneck. Then, on a day in
July when the temperature soared to 102, Mary Lily tried to relax in a cool
bath. An hour later, a worried maid found her draped over the side of the
tub, unconscious.

Ravitch, the dermatologist, was called. Suspecting a heart attack, he
called in another old friend of Bingham's, pediatrician Walter Fisk Boggess,
who brought along a young laboratory pathologist. Not one of the team was
qualified to treat or even to diagnose heart disease.

The morphine injections continued, and two nurses were fired when they
protested the dosage. Mary Lily's condition grew worse. Bob Bingham
released statements to the press, hammering away at the theme of heart disease.

On the morning of July 27, 1917, Mary Lily went into a fit. At 3:10 P.M.,
she died while experiencing convulsions. A vague death certificate listed
the cause of death as oedema, or swelling of the brain, with myocarditis, a
heart condition, as a contributing cause.

Her coffin was placed in her private railroad car and taken by train to
Wilmington. She was buried in the family plot at Oakdale Cemetery.

Mary Lily left an estate valued at roughly $150 million. Her will was
filed in the Florida courts. In August, Bingham filed the secret codicil with
the Louisville court. The Kenans and the trustees wondered if there would
be more secret thunderbolts. Would Bingham take over the Flagler system
or possibly assume a prominent role with Standard Oil?

Soon the word was out. The Kenans would contest the secret codicil.
They revealed that prominent Louisville residents had contacted them. Now
they wanted to know why Bingham had brought in a team of medical
quacks to attend Mary Lily.

The family hired one of the world's most famous detectives, William
Burns, head of the William J. Burns Detective Agency. Burns quickly
turned up detailed information on Mary Lily's drugging. The family
learned, too, that Bingham had given Ravitch a new Packard 1925 Roadster.
Burns noted that the half-million-dollar pearl necklace Flagler had given
Mary Lily had vanished, most likely stolen by Bingham.

In September, the trustees of the Flagler estate, reviewing the report in

Standard Oil's New York offices, decided to open Mary Lily's grave. They wanted to know exactly what had caused her death.

Meanwhile, Bingham hired a New York pathologist, who concluded that death had been caused by endocarditis, an inflammation of the lining of the heart.

Challenging Bingham in the Louisville courts proved to be unrewarding for the Kenans. Sympathy was strongly in Bingham's favor. The local newspapers depicted it as a battle between one lone Louisville man and the monster Standard Oil monopoly. In addition, the hometown lawyer the Kenans hired proved inadequate.

In April 1918, Bingham was informed that there would be no further contest of the will. He would receive his five million dollars on July 27, exactly one year after his wife's death.

Why did the Kenan family drop the case? No explanation was given. The report by Burns was never released. And even more startling, the official autopsy report was repressed.

David Leon Chandler, author of *The Binghams of Louisville,* concluded that one reason may have been that Mary had tertiary syphilis, probably transmitted to her by Bingham during their youthful affair.

Always a womanizer, Bingham underwent a series of confidential medical treatments that began after he quit college in 1891. He continued to receive them in later years from Dr. Ravitch, who was experienced in the treatment of syphilis.

Primary and secondary syphilis can masquerade as a fairly mild disease, sometimes involving little more than minor lesions or an unpleasant rash. Tertiary syphilis does not surface until ten to thirty years later and can be a deadly disease. It can sometimes cause endocarditis.

With syphilis, it would have been natural to call in Dr. Ravitch. The disease, so scandalous a malady that it could not even be mentioned in polite society, would also have given Bingham the opportunity for blackmail. Between the morphine and the threat of scandal, Mary Lily could have been persuaded to revise her will.

The problem was that Bingham kept the coverup going. Even after it was apparent that Mary Lily's medical condition was life-threatening, the doctors he consulted were picked because they could be trusted to keep quiet.

Why was Bingham so smugly confident in the face of the Kenans' challenge? Why did the Kenans suddenly stop contesting the will after the autopsy? Scandal is the only plausible explanation.

And what happened afterward? Did Bingham wither away, consumed by guilt? Of course not. He thoroughly enjoyed his money. He bought the

Louisville newspapers, which promptly brought him respectability.

With money and power, he became effective in Democratic circles — so effective that his staunch support for a rising young politician named Franklin Delano Roosevelt brought him a huge reward when FDR was elected president in 1932. Bingham was named ambassador to the Court of St. James in London, the highest ambassadorial position a president can bestow.

Even more important, a great communications empire developed from the five million dollars Bingham received. The empire lasted six decades, until May 1986, and then was blown apart by the "grandchildren syndrome," a condition that sometimes arises from the sheer number of third-generation owners.

A key whistleblower in forcing the sale of the Bingham newspaper empire to Gannett Publishing was granddaughter Sallie Bingham, an ardent feminist who feels the Binghams have "shortchanged" the woman whose money benefited them. Sallie has established a Mary Lily Bingham Trust Fund to provide scholarships for girls.

"He killed her, didn't he?" says Sallie, who maintains a home in Key West. "I think it's time for a Bingham to give her some credit. It's a bit of justice for Mary Lily."

CHAPTER 21

Strange Confession

---

*Adam and Eve, Cleopatra, King Herod, the Apostle Paul
and Shakespeare help free a murderess.*

The sweaty quiet of a hot August night ended suddenly. A disheveled, wild-eyed woman barged into the Orlando police station and then into the office of Chief E. D. Vestal. The chief had been around the law enforcement track a few times as a Pinkerton detective in Chicago, a deputy sheriff in nearby Hillsborough County and a railroad detective. Nothing he had heard or done before quite prepared him for the bizarre series of stories the red-haired woman began to tell that hot summer night in 1921. It was only the beginning. The stories would get stranger and stranger, involving such old friends and foes as Adam and Eve, Cleopatra, the Apostle Paul and a well-known playwright named William Shakespeare.

Agitated and incoherent, the woman — the chief judged her to be in her mid-thirties — claimed she was in Orlando on official post-office business. She was, she said, Lena Clarke, the postmistress of West Palm Beach. The chief didn't believe her, but he let her keep talking.

She told the chief a man named Fred Miltmore, a former employee, had robbed the post office of thirty-eight thousand dollars three years earlier. She had finally tracked him to Orlando, where he had bought the Arcade Restaurant on Pine Street.

Chief Vestal called West Palm Beach. Yes, he was told, red-haired Lena Clarke was the postmistress and, yes, there had been a robbery of substantial size. Now the chief listened more closely. Still, doubts lingered. Her look, her manner disturbed him.

That night, Lena said, she had lured Miltmore to her room in the San Juan Hotel. There she had drugged him with a tablet of morphine. Now all the chief had to do was send one of his men to the hotel to arrest him. The officer would have no trouble finding evidence of the robbery.

"Either a plain nut, or a very shrewd woman," thought the chief. He decided to send Detective Frank Gordon to the San Juan with orders to arrest the drugged Miltmore.

A few minutes later the detective called back. He had found Miltmore all right, but he wasn't drugged. He was dead, dead of a gunshot wound to the heart. He lay in a pool of blood. Nearby were two empty money pouches.

Turning from the phone, Chief Vestal, an imposing 240-pounder, said: "The man is dead! Miss Clarke, you killed that man, didn't you?"

"No! I didn't kill him. I only drugged him."

By now the woman was sweating heavily. With his handkerchief, he wiped the perspiration off her face, then shouted:

"Miss Clarke, you killed that man! You know you did and you might as well tell me about it!"

This time she wilted. "Yes, I shot him because he tried to implicate me and others in the postal robbery and he did it himself."

Clarke and Baxter Patterson, the chauffeur who had driven her to Orlando from West Palm Beach, were promptly arrested and indicted for murder. The trial was set for November 26, 1921.

Miltmore had worked in the post office in Chicago, where he lived with his wife and four children. Clarke, whom he met prior to World War I, helped him transfer to the West Palm Beach office to get away from the Windy City's severe winters. A romantic affair blossomed briefly at the West Palm post office. It ended when he jilted her and moved into the restaurant business in Orlando three months before his death.

* * *

Lena Marietta Thankful Clarke proved an unusual prisoner, but then she was an unusual woman. A native of Vermont, she came from a family of teachers and musicians. Her father was a Congregationalist minister, her mother a descendant of the family of Eli Whitney, inventor of the cotton gin.

Lena's sister, Maude, was the West Palm Beach city librarian and her older brother, Paul, had been postmaster. After Paul died of a snakebite on Christmas Day, 1920, Lena became postmistress of West Palm Beach.

A bright child, Lena claimed she was reading books on philosophy at five. She finished high school at thirteen, then went on to study music. In her early teens, she was delivering temperance lectures in Alabama and preaching sermons at evening church services.

James R. Knott, circuit court judge and historian who knew her in her later years in West Palm Beach, described her as "poetic, highly imaginative, affected by superstitions and vague fears, afraid to be alone, afraid of riding in boats, even cars."

With good reason, as it turned out, Maude Clarke keeps a watchful eye on her sister Lena, seated, at the annual Seminole Days Festival in West Palm Beach, shortly before World War I. (Historical Socitey of Palm Beach)

Lena Clarke seemed to enjoy jail. She even repainted and redecorated her cell, where she received friends who came up to visit from West Palm Beach.

Her strangest jail-time activity was the writing of a booklet entitled "The Life of Lena Clarke." In her narrative, in which she refers to herself as Miss Clarke, she wrote:

"Here it is that our narrative whirls into tragedy, grief and mystery, prefaced with venture and desperation; for soon after Fred A. Miltmore had gone to Miss Clarke's room, two police officials, directed to the woman's chamber by the West Palm Beach postmistress herself, found the dead body of Miltmore stretched on the floor of the room, a steel-jacketed bullet having traveled through the body in the neighborhood of the heart. On the bed, nearby, was a .32-caliber pistol with three barrels empty."

Later in the booklet, she writes that she told Chief Vestal, "Yes, I killed him," then adds, "I don't know why I did it.

"A Coroner's jury was empaneled and Miss Clarke was lodged in the jail in Orlando, on a Coroner's warrant. Then came the story of a sum of money she said she had brought with her from West Palm Beach. It was supposed to be $1,000, but later the amount recovered proved to be $745, and was found in the flush-tank of Miss Clarke's private bathroom in the hotel.

"Miss Clarke later declared that she did not remember killing Miltmore, that certainly she did not admit the crime, and that if she told Chief Vestal she had shot the man, she didn't remember making such a statement."

For her defense team, Lena Clarke hired two law firms, Davis and Gile of Orlando and Chillingworth and Chillingworth of West Palm Beach. Declared *The Orlando Morning Sentinel*: "The largest number of newspapermen ever to assemble at a trial in the Peninsular State is expected to cover the progress in detail." Four-fifths of the spectators jammed in the Orange County Courthouse were women.

Clarke's attorneys opened her defense by contending that her confession had been "extracted against the will." Judge C. O. Andrews ruled against them.

Prosecutor John H. Jones built a strong case against Lena Clarke. At the San Juan Hotel, she had registered under the name Mrs. Henry Wilson, of Atlanta. Her claim of having drugged Miltmore was quickly discredited. The autopsy report revealed that no traces of morphine were found in the victim's blood.

In jail, she had shared a cell with a woman named Rena Norman, a streetwalker who used her day in court as an open invitation to merchandise her wares. Wrote the somewhat smitten correspondent for the *Tampa Tribune*:

"She could have been a living model stepping out of the show rooms of the Maison Blanche, so stunningly was she garbed and many were the suppressed 'Ohs!' heard throughout the room as the women took in her superb ensemble, including a cockaded hat of color contrasting with her severely simple though elegant gown."

More important to the case was her testimony. On the witness stand, she said she asked Lena what she had been brought in for. The reply, she declared, was: "I killed a man."

Testimony from an Atlanta postal inspector also proved damaging. Less than a week before the killing, the Federal Reserve Bank in Atlanta received two money bags from the West Palm Beach Post Office. These were supposed to have contained thirty-eight thousand dollars in currency. Instead, bank officials found stacks of paper cut in the shape and size of paper money.

Postal Inspector W. P. Brannon rushed to West Palm to audit Clarke's books. He found large shortages dating back to 1918. These had been covered up skillfully by kiting, that is, using current receipts to cover shortages from the month just passed.

The trail took strange twists. It was learned that she had borrowed twenty thousand dollars from Joseph Elwell, a New York gambler. She never had to repay it. Shortly after loaning her the money, he was murdered in his New York apartment.

As evidence against the defendant piled up, Lena Clarke sat quietly, reading novels by Sir Walter Scott. The defense, scrambling for a break, found one when Police Chief Vestal admitted he thought she was "a plain nut."

The prosecutor objected strenuously, so strenuously the judge cautioned him he was close to impeaching his own principal witness. Carefully, the state induced Vestal to admit that he had claimed she just might also be "a very shrewd woman." Three alienists, as psychiatrists were called then, had given mixed opinions on her mental and emotional state. Still, the door was now wide open to play the insanity card, and play it the defense did.

At this point, Clarke's attorneys decided their best weapon was the defendant herself. Jury, judge, attorneys, press and spectators were about to embark on a three-and-a-half-hour fantasy voyage through time and space.

The gingham dress Lena wore was conventional enough. It was the stage prop she brought that was so nontraditional. In her hands she held a crystal ball. From time to time she paused to gaze into it, then poured forth the stuff of deranged nightmares.

Lena began with the story of how she lured Miltmore to her room at the San Juan Hotel, then seemed to drift into what the *Tribune* called a "spiritualistic seance." Spectators knew the ground had shifted when she declared: "I was a mere atom in an unformed universe when God created the solar system. . . . The stars and planets looked like a lot of soap bubbles in a big washtub and God reached in and took them out one by one, putting them where they belonged. . . .

"My next existence was in the Garden of Eden. I was there when the

Lord drove Adam and Eve out of the garden, and the same flaming sword that drove them from Paradise kept me in. I tried to go out with them, but I could not escape the sword."

In her ramblings, Lena next surfaced in Egypt in Pharaoh's time as the Goddess Isis, complete with her own temple and seven veils covering her face not because she was sacred but rather "hideous and ugly." In the Egyptian time warp she encountered Miltmore, a messenger for Pharaoh. Miltmore exposed her opposition to Pharaoh's government, ripped her seven veils off and turned her over to the chief, who had her put to death.

She bounced back quickly as Berenice, the last queen of the Jews. She was only twelve when she married King Herod. As Berenice, she "poisoned him with a grape dipped in a deadly fluid."

Next, she brought Biblical times right into the courtroom:

"In Jerusalem I heard Paul the Apostle speak when the rabble attacked him. The Apostle Paul was my brother Paul in life. . . . I next saw him after Jerusalem was burned by Titus.

"You were Titus." She pointed dramatically at the district attorney.

The Emperor Titus had her thrown into prison where Miltmore showed up again, this time as a captain of the guards. He let her talk to Paul, then reported back to Titus that she "was carrying on a big flirtation with Paul.

"So Titus dragged me out by the feet and threw me to the lions. Cleopatra was there and she laughed hilariously when the lions sprang at me and devoured me."

The next life was much better. She showed up in England, where her friend Will Shakespeare wrote for her the part of Ophelia in *Hamlet*. The part of Hamlet, she said, was written for H. F. Mohr, the assistant prosecutor.

"I finally became so saturated with the part of Ophelia that I really floated away on the current of the river Wye," she said. From there she bounced over to France in time to have her head sliced off by the guillotine during the French Revolution.

Eventually, she reached the present, then leaped into the future: "I see Eugene Debs (on the Socialist ticket) running for president in eight years. I will be vice-president and then Debs will be assassinated and I will become president."

It took the jury just two hours and twenty-two minutes to return its verdict on the self-proclaimed "president" of the United States: "Not guilty on grounds of insanity." Her chauffeur was given an unencumbered "not guilty." Some press accounts wondered why he had even been charged.

Federal officials told Judge Andrews they would charge her with post office theft unless he committed her to the Florida State Hospital in Chattahoochee. Reluctantly, since he did not believe she was insane, he sentenced her to Chattahoochee. He was not happy with the verdict and neither was Lena. She expressed a preference for the gallows over the insane asylum.

Actually, she served only a year at Chattahoochee. Then she returned to West Palm Beach to live out her life in seclusion with her sister, Maude, in their family home. There would be a difference, however. They no longer owned their house. As payment for legal services, the house had been deeded to C.C. Chillingworth, the father of Judge Curtis Chillingworth, who in 1955 would become the victim in one of Florida's most notorious murders.

According to Judge Knott, who was named to the circuit court judgeship left vacant by the murder of Curtis Chillingworth, the family showed considerable confidence in her after her release from Chattahoochee. The Chillingworths sent her to England to research their family genealogy.

So, the question persists. Was she really crazy?

Said Judge Knott: "Absolutely not."

CHAPTER 22

Ruby, Ruby

----

*A Live Oak judge kept a lid on a scandal
in a little Florida town.*

Sunday morning in August 1952: a hot, humid Sunday morning when God-fearing folk in Live Oak worshipped in the little town's Methodist and Baptist churches. Worshippers were taking Communion at White Methodist Church, just eighty yards away from the office of Suwannee County's beloved Clifford LeRoy Adams, "the poor man's doctor."

Four shots rang out, intruding suddenly on the quiet, reverent mood within the church. The first two shots came close together, then a minute later another shot and, after another pause, the fourth and final shot.

Fourteen minutes later, the Reverend E. Nash Philpot announced from the pulpit: "A member of this church, Dr. LeRoy Adams, has just been assassinated by a Negress." He dismissed the congregation.

Police were on the scene quickly. They, too, had heard the shots. The police station was just across the street from the doctor's office.

"A colored woman who paid him money, she done it," was the only statement police could get from the frightened patients who had fled the scene. The doctor, shot four times in the back, sprawled face down on the blood-drenched floor. He was a huge, pot-bellied man, six-foot-two, 270 pounds.

A powerful figure in the little north Florida town, Dr. Adams, forty-four, had just been elected a member of the Florida Senate and talk was already in the air about a run for governor. In July, he had served as a delegate to the Democratic Party Convention which had nominated Illinois Governor Adlai Stevenson to run for the presidency against General Dwight Eisenhower. Adams was also Suwannee County's busiest doctor, probably its most energetic citizen, a driven man who worked day and night, fueled always by a ravenous appetite. But now he lay dead on the bloody floor of his office, all his prodigious energy gone forever.

In his left hand he clutched a one-hundred-dollar bill. Police saw the money and knew instantly who had killed him. Only one black woman in Suwannee County would have had a one-hundred-dollar bill. It was that simple.

They drove to the two-story yellow stucco home of Sam McCollum, regarded as one of the town's finest houses. Bolita Sam, the numbers king of a three-county area, was the richest black in Live Oak. Waiting for them was Sam's wife, Ruby McCollum, thirty-seven, petite, mature, educated. With her were two small daughters, one seven years old, the other, a very light-skinned child, just ten months old. Sam had not yet come home from church with their eleven-year-old daughter. A nineteen-year-old son was attending U.C.L.A. in California.

"My, God, Ruby," asked one of the cops, "why'd you have to go and kill Dr. Adams?"

"I don't know whether I did right or not," she answered.

The officers rushed her into their police car.

"But there's nobody to stay with my children," she protested.

"They'll be all right, Ruby. Somebody'll be along in a few minutes."

The police were anxious to get her away as quickly as possible. But they didn't take her to the county jail for questioning. They drove her instead to the Florida State Penitentiary, a good fifty miles away in Starke. The police knew already that Ruby, a black woman who had murdered an idolized white doctor, wouldn't be safe in the Live Oak jail. Worse still, they feared the town's delicately balanced power structure just might come unraveled — unless somebody could find a way to keep a lid on a monstrous scandal that lurked just beneath the surface in Suwannee County.

One man tried his damndest: Hal W. Adams, the Third Judicial Court judge who presided over the trial like a banana-republic dictator. A north Florida institution, with a dark suit, string tie and a chaw of tobacco in his mouth, Judge Adams was a man who understood the workings of the segregated South in the 1950s. He was also a man with connections. He had twice been head of the Masonic Order in Florida.

Judge Adams, no relation to the doctor, might have succeeded if his high-handed tactics hadn't alarmed the only black member of the small press corps covering the trial. She was reporting on the proceedings for the Negro newspaper, the *Pittsburgh Courier*. Her name was Zora Neale Hurston.

Hurston, one of America's first important black novelists, wrote to William Bradford Huie, who had been an editor at the *American Mercury* when the Florida author was an active contributor to the magazine. She asked Huie, an Alabaman who lived fairly close to Live Oak, to visit

Suwannee County to see what he could learn about a trial she said was so unfair it could have happened in Nazi Germany or Communist Russia. Huie, author of *The Execution of Private Slovik*, called on Judge Adams and soon found himself sinking in Florida quicksand. His efforts landed him in jail for contempt of court. But somehow Huie finally pried loose the truth.

*   *   *

The little north Florida town of Live Oak, the Suwannee County seat, had slightly more than four thousand residents. The town, just twenty miles south of the Georgia border, was always at its busiest the first two weeks of August, when its six auction warehouses welcomed farmers to Florida's largest bright leaf tobacco market. But it wasn't tobacco farmers who overwhelmed the little town in early August of 1952. From all around the countryside, "poor Crackers" who loved the doctor who made house calls to their modest homes at 3 A.M., came to town to pay their respects, to see the murder scene and to mutter against "niggers." Ku Klux Klansmen without their robes walked the streets, exchanging secret signs. The county's lawmen made themselves highly visible, fearful of a riot or possibly even a lynching. One group was conspicuously absent. No blacks were to be seen anywhere.

A sketchy outline of the crime emerged, pieced together from Ruby's first faltering remarks, conversation overheard at the doctor's office and observations of neighbors. After Sam left for church, Ruby put on a neat brown dress and tan shoes and selected a matching tan leather shoulder bag. Into the bag she placed nineteen one-hundred-dollar bills and a .32-caliber Smith & Wesson used to guard Sam's safe. She had decided during a sleepless Saturday night to kill LeRoy Adams. Since she had no one to watch them, she dressed her two smallest children and put them in the back seat of her blue, two-toned Chrysler sedan. She drove to the doctor's office and parked in the alley onto which the Colored waiting room opened.

Hoping to catch the doctor alone, she walked to the waiting room and peered in, then returned to her children. The room was too crowded. Forty minutes and probably a dozen strolls to the screen door went by before she walked to the entrance for the last time, checked the contents of her bag and went in.

Dr. Adams stood alone in one of the treatment rooms, whistling. A bitter exchange followed. Ruby said she was tired of paying money she didn't owe.

"By God, I'm going to get what's coming to me, even if I have to go to the judge," said the doctor.

Novelist Zora Neale Hurston kept up the pressure to bring out the truth about Ruby McCollum. (Florida State Archives)

"Yeah, you're gonna get what's coming to you, all right."

She opened the bag, handed him a hundred-dollar bill and demanded a receipt.

"I don't write no receipts. Woman, I'm goddam tired of you."

He turned his back and walked away. Ruby fired twice. Adams fell forward into the waiting room. The patients, screaming for the police, fled from the office. Ruby walked over to the fallen giant, then fired two more shots into the doctor's back. He lay on the floor, bleeding, still clutching the one-hundred-dollar bill.

Ruby McCollum drove home, changed her dress, heated a bottle of milk for the baby and waited for the police to come.

It didn't make sense. Dr. Adams never dunned patients to pay him, never, never, never. And Ruby and Sam McCollum were admired for always paying their bills promptly. And why not? They had plenty. It was rumored that Sam kept $100,000 in cash in the safe at his home.

The story spread among the crowds milling around the streets of Live Oak. He dunned her, she lost her temper, she killed him. But the scenario dodged the basic question: Why, really, did Ruby McCollum bring a gun to commit a premeditated murder against one of the county's most esteemed citizens?

*   *   *

In the first forty-eight hours after the shooting, events moved swiftly, then slowed down as a heavy shroud of silence enveloped the murder.

At the Colored Baptist Church, Sam McCollum and the congregation were singing "Oh, Lamb of God, I come to Thee." A tap on the shoulder, a whispered message and Sam learned the awful truth.

"Lawdy, Lawdy, what'll happen to us now?" he said, quickly taking his frightened daughter to his car before the rest of the congregation learned the truth. When he neared his home, he saw the cars. He stopped short to wait for the crowd to clear. "Whichever way you figure it," he mused, "Ruby's as good as dead and so am I. They'll have to kill us and take what we've got."

Sam and Ruby both knew how vulnerable they were: rich blacks operating outside the law in partnership with whites who represented respectable society, cutting deals, making payoffs. Could the power structure allow the dirty details to surface in a murder trial?

In his forty-seven years, Sam McCollum had come a long way from the little Marion County farming community of Zuber. He and Ruby lived for a time in Nyack, New York, then came to Live Oak in 1937 with an old car and seven hundred dollars. A six-footer, Sam had one distinguishing feature which made him always stand out. His calm eyes were gray, a rarity among blacks.

Sam made his money from his cut of the bolita action in the Suwannee River Valley. By 1952, he had become rich by local standards. He owned a dozen rental houses, had one of the largest tobacco acreage allotments in Florida and was a director of the Central Life Insurance Company in Tampa. It was an impressive empire, but always it tottered precariously on the thin edge of catastrophe. Sam's world had already caught the eye of the *Tampa Tribune*, which ran a story on Live Oak in early 1952: "This land of Stephen Foster and the storied Suwannee River is in the grips of a bold and flourishing numbers racket, and the good people of the county are becoming alarmed. This is one of the 'gamblingest' counties in Florida. . . . There is a strong feeling, openly expressed in the community, that McCollum is only a lieutenant for a white gambling overlord."

As soon as the police cars left, Sam ducked into his home and immediately locked all the doors. He ignored the telephone while he packed clothes for himself and his three daughters. More important, he opened the safe and transferred eighty-five thousand dollars in cash into a suitcase. Then he loaded the car and he and the three girls drove away. He feared he would never see his home again. And he was right.

Carefully avoiding main streets and roads, Bolita Sam drove three hours south to Ruby's mother's home in the little town of Zuber, near Ocala. He went straight to bed and by the next morning it was clear that his persistent heart problems were recurring. Meanwhile, A. Keith Black, state attorney for the Third Judicial District, put out the word to the sheriff and the highway patrol: "Find Sam McCollum."

On Monday afternoon at three, Sam called Jeff Elliott, a policeman he knew was close to Dr. Adams. "I'se afraid to come back to Live Oak," he said.

"You don't have to come here," said Elliott. "Come to Lake City and meet us in the state attorney's office at ten o'clock tomorrow."

"I'll be there. I'll be there if the good Lawd lets me live."

Sam's uncle, Gurley Hill, better known as Dooley, sat that day with a subdued McCollum and listened to him.

"De good Lawd done seen fit to chastise me, Dooley. . . . I'se on my deathbed. Dis time I ain't gonna make it. . . . Dooley, a body don't always need no reason to die. Dere comes times in this wicked world when a man dies just 'cause he can't do nothing else but."

Late that afternoon, Sam's weak heart gave out on him. One who didn't believe he was dead was State Attorney Black. "Sam just switched niggers on us. He's trying to give us the slip." Black sent two policemen who knew Sam to the Ocala funeral home where his body lay.

"We want to see this nigger who's supposed to be Sam McCollum," said Jeff Elliott.

The funeral home director pulled back the sheet and the two men recognized Sam. Elliott wanted one more confirmation.

"Take the nickels off his eyes and open 'em up."

The eyes were gray.

* * *

Dr. Adams's funeral drew the largest crowd ever to attend services in Live Oak. The *Suwannee Democrat* estimated the number in the thousands "from all walks of life." Among the pallbearers were Judge Adams, State Attorney Keith Black and Jeff Elliott.

Born in 1908 in nearby Jasper, Adams came from a family that had been wealthy, but little of that wealth remained when he set out to make his fortune in the Depression years. Married at twenty to Florrie Lee Edwards, he worked for a while for the Works Progress Administration, then in 1936 ran for sheriff and was defeated. He opened a drugstore in Jasper but it failed, then burned. At thirty, he moved to Little Rock, Arkansas, where he worked in drugstores while taking pre-med at Little Rock Junior College. Two years later, he was admitted to the University of Arkansas Medical School and in 1944, after working his way through medical school, he received his degree. He finished last in his class.

At thirty-seven, he arrived at Live Oak with a wife, a child, a broken-down car and a lifetime of defeats. But he had ambition, determination and energy. His schedule would have destroyed most people. At 7:45 A.M., he would leave his home on the hospital grounds and arrive at the hospital, visiting patients and sometimes performing as many as six major operations. His office hours were from 9 A.M. to 10 P.M. At 10 P.M., he would return to the hospital. If called during the night, he would make house calls. When did he sleep? Whenever he could, wherever he could. He was a master at grabbing catnaps.

His 270 pounds were earned through an enormous intake of food, which also fueled his legendary energy. When telephoned for a house call, he would tell the patient's family, "Have a pot of coffee and a chicken leg ready for me when I get there." He would often eat first, then proceed with medical treatment. Said a former nurse: "He was always eating. His car was like a pastry wagon. You sat down at the risk of squashing a pie or a Danish pastry."

In the days after the murder, old friends and patients were pouring forth tales of how he had helped them in their time of need. One man told of how Dr. Adams had pulled him through a bad case of pneumonia. "You've got to go to the hospital," the doctor told him. The shivering man replied he had no money. Furthermore, he couldn't afford butane gas to keep his house warm. Dr. Adams gave him twenty dollars and told him to buy gas and warm up the house immediately. He would stop by that evening. He made five trips to the man's house that night, checking on his condition and giving him medication as needed. The man pulled through. When he went to see the doctor about payment, he was told, "What the hell, you ain't got no money, have you?" The doctor asked him just to pay back the twenty dollars he had advanced him to buy gas.

Another time, he drove up to the home of an elderly couple and asked why they hadn't been coming by to get their shots. They didn't have any money, they told him. "Did I say anything about money?" he said, then asked what they thought they owned him. After they said thirty or forty dollars, he wrote out a receipt, "Received today forty dollars for payment in full to date for medical services rendered." The receipt was placed in the family Bible.

"That's why the doc was loved so much," said the elderly woman. "He was good hisself, and he had the interest of poor folks at heart."

* * *

Very little time elapsed before Ruby acquired defense counsel, two fast-moving ambulance chasers from Jacksonville, a hundred miles to the east of Live Oak on U.S. 90. John Cogdill, who had a relative who was a turnkey at the penitentiary, arrived at about the same time as P. Guy "Pig Eye" Crews, tipped off by a friend about the murder. Pig Eye, figuring Ruby would be taken to Starke, drove straight to the prison. It was said of Pig Eye that if you were knocked unconscious in a fight or an automobile wreck with twenty dollars in your pocket, when you woke up your twenty dollars would be missing and Pig Eye would be representing you. Buck McCollum, Sam's brother, a numbers banker from Fort Myers, even richer than Sam, gave advances of twenty-five hundred dollars to Pig Eye and three thousand dollars to Cogdill.

At arraignment, Cogdill brought up the issue of insanity. Ruby, he announced, was undergoing psychiatric treatment in Jacksonville. Judge Adams had no choice but to appoint three doctors to examine her. They reported she was suffering from depression and hypochondria but was not psychotic.

Pig Eye joined Cogdill after arraignment. At the state prison, Ruby wrote a statement for him: "Mr. Crews, the doctor is the father of my baby. He and I have carried on for six years. I have always been afraid of him, but he has been the boss. When he'd get mad at me, he'd tear into me like a lion, and then give me a big shot of medicine to almost kill me."

She revealed, too, that she was pregnant again with the doctor's child, then added, "I don't want Mr. Cogdill working on my case. . . . He wants me to tell a lie and I'm not gonna do it. He's trying to keep all this stuff from coming out on the doctor. The doctor let my husband run numbers for my sake."

About a week after she made the statement to Pig Eye, Ruby was no longer pregnant. Said Pig Eye: "They had needled her to make her have that abortion." (In the 1950s, needles were often used to induce abortion.)

In addition to the baby, Ruby also lost both her defense attorneys.

Cogdill suddenly withdrew from the case. It was revealed he was under investigation for using the mail to defraud, a crime for which he would eventually receive a two-year prison sentence. Then, while the jury was being chosen, the Supreme Court suspended Pig Eye from practice for previous unethical practices.

By the time the trial got underway in Live Oak, Ruby McCollum had acquired two new attorneys: Odis Henderson from nearby Jasper and Frank T. Cannon, a native of Suwannee County and former county prosecutor for Duval County.

Zora Neale Hurston, living in Eau Gallie at the time, was hired by the *Pittsburgh Courier*, one of America's most powerful Negro newspapers. To the task, she brought her lively novelist's touch. Of Ruby's primary attorney, she wrote: "Frank Cannon made his entrance like a star. He was the homebred boy who had made good in the big city. He is possessed of a challenging head of thick, wavy white hair; he has a handsome profile, a becoming suntan; and tall and graceful, he wears clothes of good quality. Smiling voices called out to Cannon. Hands were extended. He was a one-man procession down the aisle."

As an anthropologist as well as a novelist, Hurston proved a perceptive observer. Her fellow blacks, she noted, were quick to distance themselves from the defendant, but they were, she thought, "play-acting in their savage denunciation of Ruby. The sprig of hyssop was in their hands, and they were sprinkling the blood of the paschal lamb around their doorways, so that the Angel of Death would pass over them. This, never you forget, was west Florida."

Judge Adams blocked her efforts to talk with the defendant, now being held in the Suwannee County jail. Denying a reporter the right to talk to a willing defendant was an almost unheard-of restriction in the American system of justice. "I was disappointed when he denied me permission to interview Ruby. But he was not curt or harsh. He said the nature of the case made it advisable to deny the press access to the defendant. He didn't want the case tried in the newspapers."

The case moved briskly along. Since Ruby had admitted she committed the murder, Hurston reasoned that the only legal function of the court was to "fix the degree of guilt. This could be done, in justice, only by hearing and weighing the defendant's own explanation of her motives."

Ruby was allowed to tell the court about how she had submitted to the doctor's advances in her own home during an extended absence of her husband. She followed with the statement that her youngest child was the doctor's.

The stage was set, Cannon thought, to move toward the next logical step — to bring out Ruby's motives for murder. Instead, the white-haired star of Jacksonville collided with a stone wall. After each of his next thirty-eight questions, the state cried out, "Objection." And thirty-eight straight times, Judge Adams ruled: "Objection sustained."

"In your long sexual relationship with Dr. Adams, was he cruel to you? Did you have any reason to fear for your life? How much of the bolita money was he extracting from you and Sam, Ruby? Why did you decide to kill him?"

"Objection!"

"Objection sustained."

The jury, of course, found Ruby McCollum guilty of murder in the first degree. Judge Adams then intoned: ". . . at the time so designated the said superintendent of state prison or one of his authorized deputies shall cause to pass through your body a current of electricity of sufficient intensity to cause your immediate death and shall continue application of such current until you are dead. And may God have mercy upon your soul."

Looking back, Hurston wrote: "My comprehensive impression of the trial was one of a smothering blanket of silence." But that was not all she wrote. Deeply disturbed by Live Oak justice, she also wrote twice to Huie. By this time, he had established himself as a fearless reporter, an author and a television personality, unafraid to tackle a controversial, even dangerous topic.

In January 1954, Huie and his wife were on their way from their Alabama home to Fort Myers for a winter vacation. Figuring Live Oak was a good halfway place to stop, Huie arrived at the town's best inn, the Blue Lodge, run by LaVergne Blue, an old friend of the doctor's. The writer, posing as a medical insurance salesman, nosed around town, generally picking up little except favorable comments about Adams. Then LaVergne Blue surprised him:

"Mr. Huie, I know who you are. I have read one of your books, I have watched you on television many nights, and I suspect why you are here. I can figure only one reason why a man in your business would spend time in Live Oak. You're looking into the McCollum case, aren't you?"

Blue told him a strange story. He said Jeff Elliott had asked if he had designated Dr. Adams as his heir. Blue said no. Elliott told him he had found Blue's will in Adams's files. It bequeathed the Blue Lodge and all his other properties to the doctor. A stunned Blue asked to see the will. Blue's name was signed to it — but not by Blue. The name was clearly in Dr. Adams's handwriting.

The innkeeper found it hard to believe. Could his best friend have conspired to cheat his heirs back in Illinois out of their inheritance? Worse yet, could Adams have been planning to kill him to get his estate? How easy it would have been for his own doctor to nudge almost any medical problem into a deadly illness.

Blue had more to tell. In 1949, Dr. Adams had been indicted by a federal grand jury. The charge: submitting fraudulent bills to the Veterans Administration. The case against him was a strong one. He rounded up some forty friends from Live Oak, among them former governor Cary Hardee, to drive to Tampa to appear in court as character witnesses. Their picture of him as a noble humanitarian swayed the jury. The verdict was not guilty.

Huie talked to attorney Frank Cannon while fishing with him in the St. Johns River. Cannon told him: "The doc is a big-shot do-gooder, and the folks think he's Jesus. He's rotten to the core . . . but nobody wants to believe it. He goes after Ruby for her money, and he catches her right at that time of life when all women are craziest. She goes for him because he's a big-shot white man and she's flattered. . . . Then her last child comes white and she's got trouble in her Negro home. She gets pregnant again, she gets neurotic, he puts her on dope and sends her to the head doctor, he neglects her and chases around with his white gal, and somebody is gonna get killed. . . . I think he hit her — he liked to hit women — and then she went for the gun."

Cannon thought Ruby was legally insane and should have been sent to the state asylum. He also warned Huie that if he kept snooping in Suwannee County, "they'll throw you in jail. Being from Alabama makes you practically a Damyankee. . . . You're gonna need a good lawyer — and maybe an undertaker. They purely don't like outside influences."

Huie talked to Releford McGriff, a successful black Jacksonville attorney engaged by Ruby to see that her children received their share of her estate.

"Ruby Jackson was a pusher," he said. "She wanted a good home, good clothes, a good life and educated children. She got them all."

Sam, however, had a few affairs and Ruby found this hard to take. She was a proud woman, even "uppity," said McGriff. "I guess most thirty-five-year-old housewives find it unpleasant to be sexually neglected. But to be rich, arrogant and also neglected is just about unbearable for a Ruby."

So Ruby McCollum, married to the most powerful black man in town, became the mistress of the most powerful white man, or as she put it, "I pick my men off the top! Black or white, I get the Big Men!"

When the baby was born white, Sam threatened to kill her. But somehow the three of them came to an agreement, a ménage à trois based on the profits the three of them were sharing from bolita.

The threesome tottered along until Adams, his eye now on the governorship, began to move away from Ruby. Neglected now by both men, she became deeply despondent. Sam and the doctor took her to three Jacksonville psychiatrists. Then Adams put her on drugs. Convinced that one or the other of the men was going to kill her, a crazed Ruby struck first.

As Huie continued to dig, he uncovered still another source of Adams's income and power — medical insurance. Blue Cross was organized in 1944 and Blue Shield in 1946. By 1947, five companies had door-to-door salesmen working north Florida, selling family health plans covering both hospital costs and doctor's bills. Dr. Adams saw health insurance as his ticket to wealth, but first he needed a hospital. The new Hill-Burton Act provided federal money for the construction of public hospitals. Adams, with the very large aid of Senator Claude Pepper, brought to Suwannee County the nation's first Hill-Burton hospital.

From the start, Blue Cross had trouble with Adams's Suwannee County Hospital. Too much glucose was used, unnecessary operations were performed and hospital stays were running up to the limit of what policies permitted. Blue Cross threatened to blacklist the hospital, but its board promised to tighten its procedures.

Dr. Adams found a new way to milk health insurance. He negotiated a contract with Blue Cross to cover his "tenants," claiming he had large farms. Blue Cross immediately began to suffer big losses. Adams had more and sicker tenants than any other landowner in Florida. The insurance company canceled his contract. Poor Crackers who thought a big-hearted doctor was treating them for nothing had no inkling that he had enrolled them as tenants and was collecting large sums for treatments they never received.

One insurance man declared: "He was the crookedest son-of-a-bitch I ever met. I ran a test on ten tonsillectomies we paid him for. Half of those kids had never been in his office."

* * *

The biggest hurdle Huie faced in his pursuit of the truth about Ruby McCollum was Judge Hal W. Adams. Huie had tried to interview Ruby, who wanted to talk to him. He was told, however, that on orders of the judge, no member of the press could speak with her. To talk to the judge, Huie drove twenty-two miles south of Live Oak, across the Hal W. Adams Bridge over the Suwannee.

A seventy-year-old Floridian, the judge looked, Huie wrote, "the way a Southern planter might have looked in 1890." A *Jacksonville Journal* reporter who signed herself "lu murphy" wrote: "And now I have met Judge Adams. . . . So I've got to write this on tiptoe. . . . I'm seven feet taller. I feel downright smug. I think I'm terrific. . . . I think the alphabet starts with A because of Adams. . . . Judge Adams looks like a Grant Wood painting of a southern judge. . . . He's an institution. He's a legend. He's a rare human being. . . . so there wasn't a thing I could do except hug him. So I did."

Huie did not hug him. Instead, he asked the judge to give him the go-ahead to talk to Ruby. He handed the judge a letter in which the condemned woman asked to talk to him. The judge still said no. He did not want the community embarrassed, a dead man smeared or the case in any way "commercialized or sensationalized."

Frank Cannon soon found himself handling two cases. He was trying to get the judge's ruling on press access to Ruby overturned and he was seeking, too, a new trial for a woman condemned to death. Huie's request was rejected on procedural grounds. With Ruby, Cannon fared better. Judge Adams had permitted the jury to visit the death scene without the defendant being present. The Florida Supreme Court voided the death sentence and ordered a new trial.

Since Ruby had deteriorated badly in the two years she had been held in the Suwannee County jail, Cannon promptly petitioned the court to determine her present mental condition. Judge Adams appointed two psychiatrists, one from Jacksonville, already familiar with the case, and a Dr. Frank A. Fernay, from the United States Veterans Hospital, Lake City. Since neither Cannon nor Huie had heard of Fernay before, they suspected he might not know much about the background of the case. Cannon thought it might be worthwhile for Huie to visit him and tell him about the heavy censorship that had been imposed around Ruby.

Huie located him late one afternoon fishing from the bank of a Lake City lake. He filled the doctor in, then left to catch a plane. A few days later, Cannon called him to tell him Fernay had informed the court he could not serve. A new psychiatrist was named and, a few days later, Cannon called again to say prospects were looking good. Huie returned to Florida and was delighted to learn at the next hearing that Ruby had been declared insane, leaving the judge no choice but to send her to the State Mental Hospital in Chattahoochee.

After the judge read his order, the sheriff suddenly appeared and served Huie with a citation for criminal contempt. His crime had been talking to Dr. Fernay. It further stated that he had compounded the offense by calling the judge "prejudiced and attempting to influence an agent of the Court."

In New York, Huie approached Arthur Garfield Hays, the noted attorney who had defended H. L. Mencken in a censorship case. Hays contended no law had been broken, but said his failing health prohibited him from defending Huie. Hays died a few weeks later, but not before he had authorized one of the firm's lawyers to represent Huie at the firm's expense.

The author assembled an impressive crew of attorneys who demolished the judge's case against Huie. Still, the judge was the boss and he found Huie guilty on a Friday afternoon and sentenced him to pay a fine of $750 or serve six months in jail. If Huie paid the fine, he couldn't appeal, so he agreed to spend sixty-three hours in jail across the weekend.

The case was appealed to the Florida Supreme Court, headed at the time by Chief Justice John E. Matthews, of Jacksonville. In 1946, Matthews had run for the state senate with the slogan, "I don't want no damned nigger votes." Six weeks after the court heard the appeal, Matthews died — but not before he had ruled against Huie.

The case next went to the Florida Cabinet. Governor LeRoy Collins advocated a pardon. The final compromise was a commuted sentence to be satisfied by the payment of the $750 fine.

At eighty, Judge Adams was finally defeated for reelection. Ruby spent twenty years at Chattahoochee. In 1974, she was released and declared innocent by reason of insanity.

By this time Zora Hurston was dead, but she had left behind a memorable account of a terrible travesty of a trial. She never contended Ruby was innocent; she simply wanted to understand this tragic woman. So she wrote: "There was one poignant moment while Ruby was on the stand. She maintained her shut-in, expressionless mask through the questioning by State and her own counsel until one felt that she was a woman without nerves. Then came the moment, as Cannon led her through the story of the actual slaying. Ruby did not break down and weep; she did not scream out in agony of memory; but there was an abrupt halt in her testimony as emotion gushed up from the deeps of her soul and inhabited her face. I saw it; the quintessence of human agony. I saw the anguish of the hours, perhaps the days and weeks which preceded the slaying. I saw the awful emotions of the resolve to slay. I saw the emotions which tightened the hand upon the gun. And I saw memories of it all, which lived down deep in barred cavities in the cellar of her soul."

CHAPTER 23

Peyton Place in Citrusland

Irene, the bookie, and the hit man brought
scandal to small-town Florida.

Johnny Sweet was about to get lucky. The odds were on his side and he was a man who knew how to figure the odds. He had been a bookie before he came to Sebring in 1964. Now, in the little town on the ridge where the oranges grew, he found himself running the poker and dice games at the Elks Club every Friday night.

The club was where he had met Irene and her husband, tall, handsome, rich Charles Von Maxcy. Dark-haired, dark-eyed Irene was easy to spot as a woman who was looking for more or maybe just different action from what her husband was giving her. Johnny had danced with her that night, holding her ample breasts against him, feeling the voluptuous warmth of her body there on the Elks Club dance floor.

Four days later, she had telephoned him and asked him to meet her and Von at the club for a drink. The odds improved when Irene suggested Johnny meet her later that night at the South Lake Wales Yacht Club, another hangout for Sebring swingers some thirty-five miles to the north on U.S. 27. It wasn't a real yacht club — no tidewater Wasps in blue blazers. In fact, it wasn't even on the water, although it was close to a small body of water bearing an apt name — Crooked Lake. Shady things went on at the yacht club, it was said. But for Johnny, it had just what he needed: a good bar, a restaurant and, in the back, rooms that could be rented by the hour.

They were made for each other. Johnny Sweet, the Boston bookie now hustling real estate in Florida's heartland, and Irene Maxcy, the former fruit packer who had snared in marriage the man who owned the packinghouse — and a good bit more.

Irene took five pictures from her purse. She spread them on the table before Johnny Sweet's startled eyes.

"What do you think?" she asked.

Sweet knew exactly what to think. They were photographs of the enticing Irene posing in the nude.

"I got up and rented a room," he said later.

In a sense, Johnny Sweet got lucky that night. But Johnny really wasn't lucky at all. And neither was Irene. Unluckiest of all was Von Maxcy.

* * *

By 1966, Sebring, the Highlands County seat, had grown into a small city with a population of roughly seven thousand. Built around the shores of Lake Jackson, it proved to be a popular winter resort, boasting fine old boom-time hotels and challenging golf courses. These days, Sebring is best known for its annual sports car race. The Twelve Hours of Sebring fills the town with racing enthusiasts for one memorable, noisy and boisterous weekend every March.

George Sebring, an Ohio pottery manufacturer who founded the town in 1912, had wanted a city of church-goers. To make it easy for them, he had given land to anyone who would agree to build a church. In 1966, the town could point to twenty-one churches — and no saloons. And one Elks Club.

A major force in the Florida citrus industry had been the Maxcy family, whose landholdings extended along the central Florida ridge from Polk County all the way south to Yeehaw Junction. Two of Florida's most powerful citrus barons were Von's uncle, Latt Maxcy, and his first cousin, Ben Hill Griffin.

In 1896, Latt and his three brothers had moved to Florida from Columbia, South Carolina, and had gone into the citrus business. Von's father, Guignard "Guy" Maxcy, married Mary Lewis VonCanon, of North Carolina — thus the unusual middle name by which the up-and-coming Von Maxcy was known in Sebring. Von, a graduate of Washington and Lee University in Virginia, owned citrus groves in Highlands and Manatee Counties as well as cattle ranches in Highlands and Hardee Counties.

"Von was a good businessman, a real entrepreneur, aggressive but friendly and outgoing," recalled his friend Bob Pollard. "He came from money, but he was not arrogant, not aristocratic in the way he dealt with people. He was at home with a fruit picker or a grove owner, with a governor or a bunch of guys out at a hunting camp."

It was inevitable that Irene's spectacular shape would sooner or later catch the roving eye of Von Maxcy. She worked as a fruit packer for his packinghouse, but not for long. She became his second wife and promptly advanced from fruit packer to secretary/treasurer of Maxcy Groves, Inc.

Irene Maxcy, the woman in the case (The *Tampa Tribune*)

Von and Irene lived just outside Sebring with their daughter, Marivon, in a big ranch house with six bedrooms, six bathrooms, a swimming pool and the Go-Go Room, equipped with a large bar and a platform for a go-go dancer. Some called it a party house. On the 324-acre ranch, Von had a landing strip for his light plane.

On October 3, 1966, Irene visited a daughter from a previous marriage who was recovering from a miscarriage at Highlands County Hospital. With her was the daughter's mother-in-law. At ten of eight that night, they left the hospital and drove to the Sparta Road ranch. When they arrived, Irene found the house dark, but strangely enough, the front door was standing wide open. Von's car was not in sight.

Irene was fearful about entering the dark, open house. Mrs. Catherine Higgins offered to go in with her and they proceeded to turn on lights as they walked through the house. In the master bedroom they found Von on a purple rug. He was lying face down in a pool of blood. A bloody sheet lay nearby. Irene went pale and began to scream. Von had been shot in the head and stabbed four times in the back and neck. He was still wearing his work clothes from the packinghouse.

Mrs. Higgins helped Irene back to her car, then drove her to the Elks Club. Irene was too upset to go in. A friend, Dutch Van Inwagen, who was standing outside the door, went in to get Sweet. Several people from the club piled into Irene's car and Inwagen followed in his own automobile.

Johnny Sweet went into the house. Like Irene, he turned pale, but instead of screaming, he went to the bathroom and threw up.

Through Inwagen's mind flashed a thought that would occur to many in the days that followed. "My God! My God! She's finally done it."

*   *   *

The task of investigating the murder of one of Sebring's most prominent citizens fell to Sheriff Broward Coker. Right from the start, the obvious suspects were Irene Maxcy and Johnny Sweet. They made no secret of their affair. Less than a week after the murder they were seen together around town. When it was learned that Von had threatened to divorce Irene, it took no genius to figure out that a fortune would slip away from her. Von's estate was valued at $1,724,847.36, the equivalent of roughly six million dollars in 1990s money.

Von's family had found Irene hard to accept. Described by a friend of the family as "a woman of common manners," she sprinkled her conversation heavily with "ain'ts" and vulgarities. Born and raised on an Alabama farm, she had carried her education only as far as the seventh grade. Von was her third husband.

Irene clearly had a motive, but she also had an alibi. She had been highly visible at the hospital. Johnny Sweet had an alibi, too. He claimed he was having dinner with his lawyer, Henry Lee, at the Circle Bar. But there was a hole in Sweet's story. The time Lee could attest to was after the murder.

The time of death had been narrowed down to late afternoon. Von had left work at five o'clock. Between five and six Vee Vee Stiles, a neighbor, had seen Von's car race away from his home at very high speed, driven by two large men. Another neighbor, Jackie Davis, had heard a single gunshot at about the same time. Irene had found the body just after eight that evening.

Lonnie Curl, Sebring chief of police, following the case closely, told Sheriff Coker: "I went to the Publix late that afternoon to pick up my wife. She was head cashier there. I ran into Johnny on the parking lot after five, but he didn't even recognize me. My wife said she waited on him. He was nervous, impatient. I think you need to call in some help from the Florida Sheriff's Bureau."

Chief Curl had another important piece of information for Coker. Irene Maxcy had told them Von's car was missing. One of Curl's policemen located it with the keys still inside. It had been abandoned on the same Publix parking lot where he had seen Johnny Sweet. It was roughly two miles from the ranch.

Funeral services for Charles Von Maxcy, forty-two, were held at the First Methodist Church, a church that enjoyed the solid support of the Maxcy family. Von had been a member and — until his marriage to Irene — a regular church-goer.

Rancher Marguerite Stewart Skipper, a friend and neighbor, was saddened by his death. "Von was a good man. He just got mixed up with the wrong people."

Johnny Sweet insisted on being a pallbearer, Irene later reported. Sweet, who was fifty, was short and balding. As is fitting for a real-estate promoter, he was a smooth talker who liked a good time. At home at the Elks Club, he was decidedly out of place in Sebring's predominantly Protestant churches.

"John Sweet was always a suave, man-about-town," said Sophy Mae Mitchell, a real-estate agent who was named one of Florida's eleven Merit Mothers in 1967. "There wasn't anybody in the world more diplomatic. He had friends all over town."

The Florida Sheriff's Bureau, now known as the Florida Department of Law Enforcement, backed up Sheriff Coker with the services of a talented and tenacious investigator, Roma Trulock. The sheriff needed all the help he could get. The Maxcy murder would prove to be an enormously complex case, requiring no less than five trials, extending over a period of eighteen years. In Florida it would reach out to Daytona Beach, Tampa and Miami. Far more ominously, it would connect the little church-going town of Sebring with the big-city crime of the Boston underworld.

For many weeks, no spectacular breakthroughs occurred in the case. The probe settled into the endless, tedious tracking down of small details. Police interviewed friends, neighbors, anyone who might have observed any part of the puzzle. The murder bore the stamp of a professional hit. Irene, born and raised on an Alabama farm, wasn't too likely to have had the contacts, but Johnny was another matter. He had come from Boston and he freely admitted he had been a bookie. Might the Boston connection hold the key?

Now interesting things began to come to light. The Boston police did indeed know Johnny Sweet. He had had one minor conviction for gambling, no time served. But he was cozy with the Winter Hill Gang, an Irish mob involved in bank and Brinks car robberies, loan sharking, marijuana smuggling, illegal gambling and contract killings. Wiretaps were placed and bank, phone and travel records were subpoenaed.

Johnny Sweet had been in touch with the Bennett brothers, Walter and Wimpy. They owned the Winter Hill Cafe, an Irish mafia hangout. And travel records placed two men from the Winter Hill Gang at Daytona Beach just before the hit. Their names were Andrew Von Etter and Billy Kelley.

Talking with Von Etter and the Bennett brothers was out of the question. In 1967, a wave of violence had swept through rival factions of the Irish Mafia. Von Etter's body was found in the trunk of his Thunderbird in Boston. He had been bludgeoned to death. The Bennetts disappeared. Kelley also was a problem. He was in jail for breaking and entering and for possession of burglary tools. Massachusetts didn't want to extradite him to testify, preferring not to surrender him to another jurisdiction unless charges were brought against him.

As information on the Winter Hill Gang began to pile up, police increased the pressure on Sweet and Irene. Ostracism by the town isolated them and weakened their defenses against the insistent questioning. Fearful that Irene might talk, Sweet, who had moved in with her, told her if she talked he would kill her and her daughter. He even drove Marivon to and from school. He took no chances. Irene had little opportunity to take her daughter and run.

Then the skills of Roma Trulock began to break down what remained of Irene's resistance. She was never noted for saying no. Some of the meetings between the buxom widow and the state's lead investigator took place in area motels.

Seven months after the murder, Irene broke. In return for total immunity, she agreed to testify against Johnny Sweet. At 6.30 P.M. on May 7, 1967, the grand jury indicted Sweet for murder in the first degree. Four days later, police, acting on information from Irene, tracked Johnny Sweet to St. Petersburg and arrested him outside a restaurant. He was carrying $2,063, including nineteen one-hundred-dollar bills. The previous week he had bought a new Cadillac to replace his 1965 Oldsmobile, which had been involved in a wreck at Winter Haven. Irene had been traveling with him at the time.

Sheriff Coker commended the "excellent cooperation from Massachusetts State Police." The investigation included lengthy surveillances, more than a thousand interviews and solid backup from the Florida Sheriff's Bureau Crime Laboratory and Investigative Section.

From the Highlands County jail, Sweet hired two red-headed defense attorneys, tall, heavy Walter Manley, from Lakeland, and James "Red"

McEwen, of Tampa, an aggressive tactician much revered in central Florida as a University of Florida football hero. In early July, his attorneys persuaded the court to release Sweet on twenty-five thousand dollars bond.

Free again, he tried to get Irene to change her story. Instead, she pressured him to try to make a deal for a lighter sentence. She wanted him to talk to Trulock. By now, she had admitted to him that she had been having an affair with Trulock during the investigation. One interview lasted all night at the Sandcastle Motel in Sarasota.

By the end of July, a distraught Sweet was ready to talk to Trulock: "I was the errand boy and she was the murderer." Once, he said, she had asked him "to put water in her husband's airplane's gasoline tank."

Looking for a deal, Sweet offered to name and to testify against the Boston assassins who stabbed and shot Maxcy to death. He said he would plead guilty to a less serious crime than first-degree murder. "He expected to do some time, but not much," Trulock said. But Sweet was too late. A deal had already been cut and that deal was with Irene.

There was a question, too, about how much Sweet knew about the Boston gang. Norman DeSilets, a state investigator working with Trulock, put Massachusetts plates on his car and posed as a member of the Winter Hill Gang. He told Sweet he was looking for Walter Bennett.

"Did you check with Wimpy?" Sweet asked.

But by this time, Wimpy and Walter were both missing and already presumed dead. Von Etter was dead.

* * *

Unable to pick a jury in Sebring, defense attorneys asked for a change of venue. The trial got underway the first week in November 1967 at the Polk County Courthouse in Bartow, about fifty miles from Sebring. It was a scruffy courtroom, with dingy green walls and a floor of scuffed brown asphalt tile. The air conditioner was so noisy it had to be turned off during testimony, a problem in November only because the courtroom was jammed with spectators and members of the press, drooling over the prospects for a scandalous trial. Adulterous murder of a millionaire, lubricated by Irene's reputation, added up to a tabloid dream. The trial would not be easy to take, however, for the extended Maxcy clan or for the wife of John Sweet, who came down from Boston to show support for her husband.

The state opened with its star witness, the widow Maxcy. The defense team made it clear they would attack her role in the crime, her credibility and her reputation. Said Red McEwen: "I promise you, we are going to be rough."

Irene Maxcy gave the jury of nine men and three women a long, rambling account of her involvement with Sweet and the plot to kill Von Maxcy. It was Sweet's idea, she said, and it surfaced early in their illicit affair. They discussed it frequently for a year and a half.

"I begged Johnny not to do it," she said, sobbing and clutching a Kleenex in her hands.

"Why didn't you warn your husband?" McEwen demanded again and again.

"I was scared," she answered. She claimed Sweet intimidated her with death threats to herself and Marivon if she ever mentioned the murder plans to anyone.

"I was at his disposal," she said. "Anything he said to do I had to do. If he said jump out a window, I would have jumped out the window."

One attempted hit by a Miami gunman failed. The next time, Johnny Sweet turned to Walter Bennett and the Winter Hill Gang. Irene testified that Sweet placed numerous calls to Boston to men she knew only as Walter and Wimpy. The prosecution contended that Bennett, Etter and Kelley were hired for the job.

"The night before Von died," Mrs. Maxcy testified, "he told me they were in town."

The next night, while she was at the hospital visiting her daughter, Sweet telephoned her, she said. "Well, it's all over," he told her.

She and Mrs. Higgins went to the Sparta Road home and found the body of Von Maxcy. Later, Sweet told her the killers wore gloves for the killing. This would explain why the sheriff's intensive search failed to produce any fingerprints.

Annette Etter, a dazzling platinum blonde from Boston, told the court her late husband, Andrew Von Etter, and Billy Kelley were in Florida near Sebring the day Maxcy was murdered. After the murder, she said, her husband sported a plentiful supply of one-hundred-dollar bills. He paid off bills and gambling debts and made advance payments on their Boston apartment. When she asked her husband where the money came from, he said, "from Walter."

Earlier that day, Irene had testified that Sweet forced her to give him thirty-six thousand dollars in one-hundred-dollar bills. Other Bostonians who testified were Barbara Bennett, who had married Walter, and Billy Kelley's wife. Both Mrs. Kelley and Mrs. Etter said their husbands were away from Daytona Beach at the time the murder was committed.

The Boston parade continued when a man guarded by a dozen policemen appeared. His name was Billy Geraway, a self-proclaimed "monument to human failure." When McEwen started to read from Geraway's six-page FBI dossier, the witness interrupted: "I think I can help you save time. There are 102 entries on my criminal record. I'm guilty of all of them."

He escaped a murder charge in the Maxcy case by turning down Walter Bennett's offer of five thousand dollars to kill the Florida citrus millionaire. He was told a man named Duke Sweet would help him with the job. Geraway told Bennett he was "a bad-check passer, not a killer."

On the stand, Johnny Sweet denied all charges and all accusations thrown at him by Irene Maxcy. His calls to Bennett, he said, were to place bets, not to hire killers. He said he did not know either Von Etter or Kelley. It was dull, routine testimony, but the courtroom was soon to hear what it came for.

McEwen figured a recital of Irene's lurid sex life would be the best way to destroy her credibility. Sweet had a long list. He said he once found Mrs. Maxcy in bed with a friend of his in Sweet's Sebring apartment just minutes after he introduced them. Johnny said that on another occasion, when a group of young people were staying at the house before the auto races, he found Irene in bed with a sixteen-year-old boy. When Sweet's twenty-five-year-old son visited his father shortly after the murder, Irene came on to him.

Then Sweet told the story that sent a gasp through the courtroom. Irene, nervous since the murder, wanted a watchdog. At the dog pound he was told females made the best watch dogs, but he bought a large male collie because she had asked him to buy "the biggest male dog" available. Once, he returned to the Sparta Road home to find Irene on the floor, trying to engage in sex relations with the dog.

"I threw the dog through the screen door," said Sweet.

Later, she often visited motels with Roma Trulock and when Sweet was in jail, she invited the investigator into her bedroom at the ranch. Sweet repeated the story of the nude pictures and pointed out that she had shown them to other men.

In his final summation to the jury, McEwen hit hard at Irene's immunity: "If the murder of Charles Von Maxcy is to be held against my client, it's got to be held against her, too. . . . Her story is from fruit packer to millionaire. She left two husbands behind, one dead and now this man Sweet. This is a dangerous woman. Who will be next?" McEwen made sure the jurors would take to their deliberations the story of Irene's affair with a large dog.

Just as McEwen and Manley had figured, the jury balked at the thought of convicting Sweet while letting Irene Maxcy go free. After four hours, the jury told the judge it was hopelessly deadlocked. Judge William Love declared a mistrial.

Free on bond, at least for the time being, Johnny Sweet headed for the Elks Club for a good steak.

A funny thing happened on the way to the retrial of Johnny Sweet. The Boston bookie and the bosomy widow got back together again. They moved to Deerfield Beach, but came back to Sebring from time to time. Irene had to settle the Von Maxcy estate.

In Deerfield, Sweet gave a magazine writer his impressions of Sebring: "This is a real close Baptist town — on the surface. But inside, it's the wildest, wideopenist [sic] place I've ever seen. Somebody sent me that book, *Peyton Place*. . . . Well, I read it, and compared to Sebring, that's nothin'. Nothin'."

Peyton Place was a popular book, movie and TV series about a small New England town, respectable on the surface but teeming underneath with scandalous secrets. In his summation, McEwen had said: "This trial makes *Peyton Place* seem like a tame book. It's hard to believe that many people live like this."

Sebring, the new Peyton Place, squirmed even more when its salacious trial became the cover story for the sensational crime magazine *True Detective*. The swinging widow and the Boston bookie had given the town what it felt was an unjustly bad image. But its travail was not about to go away.

Inevitably, the time came for Sweet to stand trial again. A first attempt to try him in May 1968 had to be postponed due to a shortage of important Boston witnesses. Von Etter's shapely blonde widow had married again and was too pregnant to travel. Billy Kelley's wife was missing. Von Etter and the Bennetts were dead. Kelley was in jail. It seemed that wicked things happened in Boston, too.

On October 28, 1968, the trial got underway, again in Bartow and again with the same attorneys on both sides. The big difference was the star witness for the prosecution. Promised immunity in return for her testimony, Irene had leveled damaging charges at Sweet in the first trial. Now reconciled with him, she was proving uncooperative with the state.

Handsome, graying Glen Darty, the prosecutor, told Judge Love he felt the widow would be a hostile witness. Then when he called for her, she failed to appear. Her attorney explained that she had gone to Lakeland General Hospital. He said she was in an "extremely agitated state, moaning, crying, mumbling 'too much pressure, too much pressure.'"

Irene Maxcy was transferred to Lakeland Manor, a psychiatric institu-

Charles Von Maxcy (The *Tampa Tribune*)

tion. By the end of the week, she was judged competent to take the witness
stand. Dressed in an orange suit, she testified reluctantly against Sweet. The
state's case was basically the same as in the first trial. Defense attorney
McEwen hit hard at the absence of the hit man Sweet had hired. "Why
haven't they indicted Kelley?" he asked. Not enough evidence to try him,
replied Darty. Kelley was still in a Massachusetts prison serving time for
possession of burglary tools.

This time it took the jury just two hours and two minutes to find Sweet
guilty of murder with a recommendation of mercy. Judge Love sentenced
him to life in prison. Red McEwen lost no time in announcing he would
appeal the verdict based principally on the judge's decision not to permit

testimony on the affair between the state's star witness and Roma Trulock, the state's lead investigator. Pending the outcome of the appeal, Sweet remained free on fifty thousand dollars bond.

Less than three months after the trial, Irene married Jerry Wells in a civil ceremony "somewhere in Georgia." She had met Wells, who ran a boat business in Pompano Beach, while she was living in Deerfield Beach.

Three weeks later, a sledgehammer blow hit the newly-wed Irene. Highlands County indicted her for perjury. She had altered her testimony on giving money to Sweet to pay for the hit. Under an archaic Florida law, a perjury conviction in a capital case could carry a penalty as severe as life imprisonment, the same sentence already given to Sweet for murder in the first degree. But then, most people in Sebring figured she was as guilty as Johnny.

Complicating her already complicated life further, Sweet sued Irene Maxcy Wells for "damages in excess of $250,000." He charged that she had testified falsely in both of his trials. In June, he dropped the suit. By that time Irene was busy divorcing Wells. She had lived with him only two weeks.

While awaiting trial for perjury, Irene returned to Deerfield Beach to live with Sweet. Two months after the murder, she had signed a Declaration of Trust which gave the ex-bookie participation in some of her business dealings. When she sold the 324-acre ranch and ranch house, complete with Go-Go Room, for $248,200, Sweet received a $60,000 cut of the proceeds. The ranch was purchased by Joe and Vee Vee Stiles, friends and neighbors of Von Maxcy.

Another year would pass before Irene's trial. In the meantime, she married Henry O'Mara, a Deerfield postal employee. As Irene O'Mara, she went on trial in October 1971 in Miami. After two previous murder trials in Bartow, it was time for a change of venue. Irene hired Frank Ragano, the famed "Mob Lawyer," who served as counselor for Santo Trafficante Jr., the Gulf Coast Godfather. Ragano wasn't enough to save her. In Sweet's second trial, she had changed her testimony about money paid to Sweet. A Miami jury found her guilty.

In mid-November, she got the bad news. Judge Alfonso Sepe sentenced her to life in prison. "Sometime justice is being done," said the judge. Hers was the toughest sentence for perjury in the state's history.

But her conviction produced a monumental irony. Since she was guilty of perjury, Sweet's attorneys could claim their client was convicted on the testimony of a perjurer. The same month Irene was sentenced to life, Johnny Sweet was turned loose. Furthermore, if there were a subsequent trial, she couldn't testify against him. Without her testimony, there was no point in another trial. Johnny Sweet, a free man, went back to Boston. Irene was behind bars, presumably for the rest of her life. Von Etter and the Bennetts were dead. Who was left? Just Billy Kelley. And there was no one who wanted to confront the six-foot-five, 250-pound, strong-arm hit man.

The case was closed. Irene went to prison the summer of 1973. Two years later, she was in the news again. She sued Ragano for one million dollars, claiming that she had given him fifty thousand dollars to buy a parole for her. By going public about her attempt to bribe her way out of the state women's prison at Lowell, she actually lengthened her stay behind bars.

The Florida Legislature repealed the perjury law under which she was sentenced, changing the maximum penalty for perjury to five years. The Florida Parole and Probation Commission released her in early January 1978 after she had served four-and-a-half years. Actually, she would have been out a year earlier if she hadn't gone public with the bribe attempt. Like Sweet, she didn't go back to Sebring. She moved instead to Orlando to live with a sister.

At last it was over. Sebring people tried to avoid talking or even thinking about it. One regret always remained. No one had been convicted of the murder.

Then a break came, not in the citrus and cattle lands of central Florida but in faraway Boston. Johnny Sweet had gone back to his hometown and had hooked up again with Billy Kelley. In 1981, the two of them got into a serious argument.

Soon Kelley and a henchmen showed up at Sweet's apartment and started beating Johnny and his latest girlfriend. Sweet was convinced Kelley meant to kill them both. Then the other thug ran out, calling to Kelley, "No killing tonight, everybody knows you're here." Kelley followed him out. Sweet wasn't seriously injured, but he was seriously scared. He went to the Massachusetts State Police and told them Kelley was out to get him. He wanted to enter the federal witness protection program and he had a big prize to offer in return.

Sweet had worked closely enough with Kelley to give Massachusetts what it needed to indict him on drug smuggling charges and on the 1980 theft of two million dollars' worth of computers. In addition, he could offer Florida an indictment for the 1966 murder of Charles Von Maxcy. Kelley was already a fugitive from North Carolina on drug charges.

On December 16, 1981, Kelley was secretly indicted by a Highlands County grand jury on a first-degree murder charge. But tracking Kelley down wasn't an easy task. For more than a year and a half, he eluded police. Then on June 16, 1983, the feds tracked him to a Tampa motel. FBI Special

Billy Kelley's police mug cut following his 1983 arrest
(The *Tampa Tribune*)

Agent Ross Davis said Billy was registered under a phony name. Kelley had three Massachusetts driving licenses listing three different names. Kelley, who gave stagehand as his occupation, had ninety-six thousand dollars on him when arrested. Informed he was wanted for murder in Highlands County, Kelley told Davis: "That must be a seventeen- or eighteen-year-old charge. I think all the witnesses in the case are dead. I don't think you can make a case against me."

The state thought it could. Still, Prosecutor Hardy Pickard knew it could be difficult. How believable would Johnny Sweet be? In return for his testimony, he had received immunity from a long lists of crimes: arson, hijacking, loan-sharking, bribery, bookmaking, prostitution and drug smuggling. Hardly a solid citizen. How good would his memory be after eighteen years? To complicate it further, transcripts of the first two trials had been destroyed and some of the evidence had been discarded. Who would have thought after all these years that the court might want the bloody sheet found beside Maxcy or the bullet that killed him?

The three previous Maxcy trials had been held in Bartow and Miami. By now the state felt the furor had quieted down enough to pick a jury and hold the trial in the county courthouse at Sebring. For his defense attorneys, Kelley had engaged a Florida lawyer, Jack Edmund, and the flamboyant, bushy-headed William Kunstler, noted for his defense of such leftist and civil-rights activists as the Chicago Seven, Angela Davis, Jerry Rubin and Abbie Hoffman. What was his interest in the nonpolitical Kelley, a straightforward, traditional thug? Kunstler was drawn to the case because the state was seeking to put Billy in the electric chair. Kunstler opposed the death

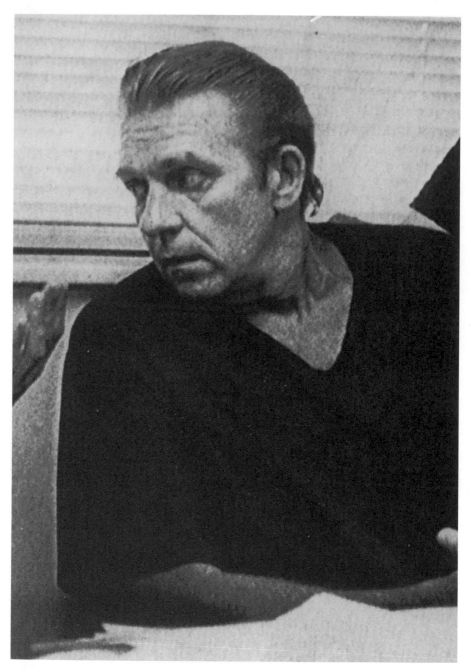

Billy Kelley in prison (The *Tampa Tribune*)

penalty. He charged Kelley no legal fees and asked him just to cover his expenses.

On January 23, 1984, the trial began. Pickard introduced records that proved that Kelley and Von Etter had checked into the Daytona Inn just prior to the murder — and checked out immediately after it. Von Etter's widow Annette, now Annette Abrams, was back again to support the motel records. Testimony and records from bankers traced a money trail from Irene to Sweet at the time of the killing. But the story on which the case would live or die would be the account a frail Johnny Sweet, looking far older than his sixty-eight years, would tell. He spoke falteringly and seemed at times to have trouble remembering events from 1966. He told the court he had dealt with Walter Bennett, missing and reported to be dead, to hire as hit men Andrew Von Etter, decidedly dead, and Billy Kelley, very much alive at forty-one, a menacing hulk of a killer.

The defense rested without calling a witness. Edmund contended that Sweet's rambling testimony was inconsistent and unconvincing. One juror agreed with him. After ten hours of deliberation, the jury announced it was unable to reach a unanimous verdict. The vote had been eleven to one to convict. The state wasted no time in calling for a retrial. "Instant replay," said Pickard.

In late March, the fifth trial in the seemingly never-ending Maxcy murder mess began. This time there seemed little interest. The courtroom, packed for the first Kelley trial, was relatively deserted. Too bad — this time the star witness delivered the performance for which he had been paid with immunity and federal protection.

Jittery and indecisive at the first trial, Johnny Sweet now seemed relaxed. His previous testimony had taken some of the edge off his fear of Kelley. Now he remembered names, places and dates and for the first time a clear, coherent account of the murder came out.

Why had he never named Kelley in the 1967 and 1968 trials? Pickard asked.

"I knew if I mentioned William Kelley's name, I wouldn't be alive today," Sweet said. "I figured I'd take my chances in court."

Sweet contended that Irene had instigated the murder. At her urging, he had arranged with Bennett for Kelley, a twenty-three-year-old giant who weighed three hundred pounds at the time, and Von Etter to come to Florida to do the hit. The afternoon of the murder, they had met Sweet in Sebring at the Publix parking lot in the Southgate Shopping Center. They parked their rental car there and Sweet drove them to the ranch just two miles away. He had a key, so he let them in to wait for Von, who would be coming home after work. Both Irene and Marivon would be away at the time of the killing.

Von Maxcy arrived shortly after five. The killers, wearing gloves, let him reach the bathroom. Later, Sweet asked Kelley to describe just how Von had died.

"He told me how he pleaded and said he would give them anything they wanted. They threw a sheet over his head and stabbed him and had to shoot him in the head to finish him because he kept coming after them. He was a big, strong man."

Asked who fired the fatal shot, Sweet said, "I assume it was Kelley because he told me what happened."

After the killing, the men took Von Maxcy's car keys and, leaving the front door open in their haste, drove away in his car to the Publix lot. They left his car there, with the keys in it, and drove back to Daytona Beach in their rental auto.

Again the defense rested without bringing forward any witnesses. This time the gambit failed. A jury of eight women and four men took a little over eight hours to find Billy Kelley guilty of first-degree murder.

"I'm glad it's over," said Marivon Maxcy Adams, who had sat through the entire trial. The twenty-three-year-old, described as a "peaches and cream" beauty in *The Sebring News*, wept openly.

"I feel like a tremendous burden has been lifted," said Guy Maxcy, Von's thirty-year-old nephew. "I just hope this thing isn't appealed forever."

An appeal was automatic, however, since Circuit Judge Randolph Bentley sentenced Kelley to die in the electric chair. The Florida Supreme Court voted unanimously to uphold the sentence. In 1986, the appeal reached the U.S. Supreme Court. The court voted, six to two, not to overturn the death penalty. Billy Kelley remains on death row at Starke.

Irene at last report was living in Orlando. Johnny Sweet is hidden somewhere in the federal witness protection program, but he may be dead by now. Said former police chief Lonnie Curl, "I've heard rumors that the mob finally got to him. They don't like snitches to get away with things."

BIBLIOGRAPHY

Anderson, Chris, and Sharon McGehee. Bodies of Evidence. Secaucus, N.J.: Lyle Stuart, 1991.

Banks, Ann. First Person America. New York: Knopf, 1980.

Bingham, Sallie. Passion and Prejudice: A Family Memoir. New York: Knopf, 1989.

Bishop, Jim. The Murder Trial of Judge Peel. New York: Simon & Schuster, 1962.

Bocca, Geoffrey. The Life and Death of Harry Oakes. London: World Distributors, 1962.

Brown, Loren G. Totch: A Life in the Everglades. Gainesville, Fla.: University Press of Florida, 1993.

Burghard, August, and Phillip Weidling. Checkered Sunshine: The History of Fort Lauderdale, 1793-1955. Gainesville, Fla.: University of Florida Press, 1966.

Burnett, Gene. Florida's Past. Three volumes. Sarasota, Fla.: Pineapple Press, 1986, 1988 and 1991.

Caudle, Hal. The Hanging at Bahia Mar. Fort Lauderdale, Fla.: Wake-Brook House, 1976.

Chandler, David Leon. The Binghams of Louisville: The Dark History Behind One of the Country's Great Fortunes. New York: Crown, 1987.

___. Henry Flagler. New York: Macmillan, 1986.

Cody, Aldus M., and Robert S. Osceola County, The First 100 Years. Osceola County Historical Society, 1987.

Curl, Donald W. Palm Beach County: An Illustrated History. Northridge, Calif.: Windsor Publications, 1986.

De Marigny, Alfred. Conspiracy of Crowns. New York: Crown, 1970.

Goddard, Donald. The Insider. New York: Pocket Books, 1992.

Hemenway, Robert. Zora Neale Hurston. Chicago: University of Illinois Press, 1977.

Huie, William Bradford. Ruby McCollum: Woman in the Suwannee Jail. New York: Signet Books, 1964.

Glassman, Steve, and Kathryn Lee Seidel, editors. Zora in Florida. Orlando, Fla.: University of Central Florida Press, 1991.

Hetherington, Alma. The River of the Long Water. Chuluota, Fla.: Mickler House Publishers, 1980.

Hutter, Ernie. The Chillingworth Murder Case. Derby, Conn.: Monarch Books, 1963.

Kearney, Bob, editor. Mostly Sunny Days. Miami: Miami Herald Publishing Company, 1986.

Kefauver, Estes. Crime in America. New York: Greenwood Press, 1968.

Kuncl, Tom. Death Row Women. New York: Pocket Books, 1994.

Kurland, Michael. A Gallery of Rogues: Portraits in True Crime. New York: Prentice Hall, 1994.

Leasor, James. Who Killed Sir Harry Oakes? Boston: Houghton Mifflin, 1983.

MacKay, D.B. Pioneer Florida. Tampa, Fla.: Southern Publishing Company, 1959.

McIver, Stuart B. Fort Lauderdale and Broward County: An Illustrated History. Northridge, Calif.: Windsor Publications, 1983.

Pacheco, Ferdie. Ybor City Chronicles. Gainesville, Fla.: University Press of Florida, 1994.

Parks, Arva Moore. Miami: The Magic City. Tulsa, Okla.: Continental Heritage Press, 1981.

Rosen, Fred. Lobster Boy. New York: Pinnacle Books, 1995.

Shirley, Glenn. Belle Starr and Her Times. Norman, Okla.: University of Oklahoma
      Press, 1982.
___. Law West of Fort Smith. Lincoln, Neb.: University of Nebraska Press, 1968.
Shofner, Jerrell H. Nor Is It Over Yet: Florida in the Era of Reconstruction. Gainesville,
      Fla.: University of Florida Press, 1974.
Smiley, Nixon. Knights of the Fourth Estate. Miami: E.A. Seemann, 1974.
Stuart, Hix C. The Notorious Ashley Gang: A Saga of the King and Queen of the
Everglades.   Stuart, Fla.: St. Lucie Printing, 1928.
Tebeau, Charlton W. The Story of Chokoloskee Bay Country. Coral Gables, Fla.:
      University of Miami Press. 1971.

Publications that have proved invaluable include:
Florida Historical Quarterly
Broward Legacy
Tequesta
South Florida History Magazine
Sunshine Magazine
Tropic Magazine
Fort Lauderdale Sun-Sentinel
The Miami Herald
The Miami News
Tampa Tribune
Sebring News
Kissimmee Valley Gazette
Key West Citizen
Solares Hill
Florida Keys Sea Heritage Journal

INDEX

Illustrations are indicated by italics

If you enjoyed reading this book, here are some other books from Pineapple Press on related topics. For a complete catalog, write to Pineapple Press, P.O. Box 3899, Sarasota, FL 34230, or call (941) 359-0955.

HISTORY/BIOGRAPHY/FOLKLORE

African Americans in Florida by Maxine D. Jones and Kevin M. McCarthy. Profiles of African American writers, politicians, educators, sportsmen, and others in brief essays covering over four centuries. Suitable for school-age readers. Teacher's manual available.

Classic Cracker by Ronald W. Haase. A study of Florida's wood-frame vernacular architecture that traces the historical development of the regional building style as well as the life and times of the people who employed it.

Everglades: River of Grass by Marjorie Stoneman Douglas. A treasured classic of nature writing in its fifth printing, this is the book that launched the fight to preserve the Florida Everglades

The Florida Chronicles, Vol. I: Dreamers, Schemers, and Scalawags by Stuart B. McIver. Engaging character sketches of unusual characters who made Florida their home: includes storytellers, tycoons, movie makers, and more.

Florida Place Names by Allen Morris. A unique reference that describes the origin and meaning of the name of every incorporated county and city in Florida as well as hundreds of others. Includes over one hundred black and white photos edited by Joan Perry Morris, curator of the Florida State Archives.

Florida Portrait by Jerrell Shofner. A beautiful volume of words and pictures that traces the history of Florida from the Paleoindians to the rampant growth of the twentieth century.

The Florida Reader edited by Maurice O'Sullivan and Jack Lane. A historical and literary anthology of visions of paradise from a diverse gathering of voices, including Ralph Waldo Emerson, Marjorie Kinnan Rawlings, and Harry Crews.

Florida's First People by Robin Brown. A fascinating account of the Paleoindians of Florida using modern archeological techniques and replications of primitive technologies.

Florida's Past (3 volumes) by Gene Burnett. A popular collection of essays about the people and events that shaped the state.

Hemingway's Key West by Stuart B. McIver. A rousing, true-to-life portrait of Hemingway the man and the writer during the 1930s when he and his family lived in Key West.

Legends of the Seminoles by Betty Mae Jumper with Peter Gallagher. Tales told around the campfires to Seminole children, now written down for the first time. Each story illustrated with an original painting by Guy LaBree.

Marjorie Stoneman Douglas: Voice of the River, an autobiography with John Rothchild. The first lady of conservation tells the story of her remarkable life and work.

Menendez by Albert Manucy. A biography of the founder of St. Augustine.

Shipwrecks of Florida by Steven D. Singer. A comprehensive reference book arranged chronologically within geographical sections of the state. For serious divers and curious readers alike.

Spanish Pathways in Florida edited by Ann L. Henderson and Gary R. Mormino. Essays, in both Spanish and English, on the influence of the Spanish in Florida, from the first explorers to the latest Hispanic migrations into Miami.

Thirty Florida Shipwrecks by Kevin M. McCarthy. The best shipwreck stories, from young Fontaneda, wrecked in 1545 and held captive by Indians for 17 years, to the Coast Guard Cutter Bibb, sunk off Key Largo in 1978. Illustrated by William Trotter.

Twenty Florida Pirates by Kevin M. McCarthy. Tales of the most notorious Florida pirates, from the 1500s to the present day. Illustrations by William Trotter.

HISTORICAL FICTION

Guns of the Palmetto Plains by Rick Tonyan. An action-packed Cracker Western that plunges the reader into the last agonizing years of the Civil War. Snake-filled swamps, Yankee raiders, and vicious outlaws block the trails between Florida and the rest of the Confederacy, leaving the untamed peninsula to the heroes and the gunslingers.

A Land Remembered by Patrick Smith. A sweeping saga of three generations of Florida settlers. Winner of the Florida Historical Society's Tebeau Prize as the Most Outstanding Florida Historical Novel.

Riders of the Suwannee by Lee Gramling. Tate Barkley returns to Florida in the 1870s after ten years on the Western frontier, only to find out that his gunfighting days are not over. When Tate pulls out his Winchester, you can count on the kind of action that will keep pages turning right on to the all-out fight at the end of this Cracker Western.

Thunder on the St. Johns by Lee Gramling. The vast unsettled lands of Florida in the 1850s are home to honest hard-working homesteaders and greedy violent power-mongers. Which kind of folk will prevail to fulfill their dreams in this gripping Cracker Western?

Trail form St. Augustine by Lee Gramling. In this Cracker Western a fur-trapper and a young woman indentured by a powerful tyrant are pursued across the Florida wilderness by murderous trackers to a showdown on the windswept sands of the Florida Gulf coast.